※涉外法律人才培养系列教材※

涉外律师实务
理念技能＊英文范例
Foreign-related Legal Practice

焦洪宝　编著

南开大学出版社
天　津

图书在版编目(CIP)数据

涉外律师实务：汉、英 / 焦洪宝编著. —天津：南开大学出版社，2021.1(2024.9重印)
涉外法律人才培养系列教材
ISBN 978-7-310-06016-0

Ⅰ.①涉… Ⅱ.①焦… Ⅲ.①涉外案件－律师业务－中国－教材－汉、英 Ⅳ.①D922.13

中国版本图书馆 CIP 数据核字(2021)第 000692 号

版权所有　侵权必究

涉外律师实务
SHEWAI LÜSHI SHIWU

南开大学出版社出版发行
出版人：刘文华
地址：天津市南开区卫津路 94 号　　邮政编码：300071
营销部电话：(022)23508339　　营销部传真：(022)23508542
https://nkup.nankai.edu.cn

天津创先河普业印刷有限公司印刷　全国各地新华书店经销
2021 年 1 月第 1 版　　2024 年 9 月第 2 次印刷
260×185 毫米　16 开本　12.75 印张　254 千字
定价:39.00 元

如遇图书印装质量问题，请与本社营销部联系调换，电话：(022)23508339

目　录

第一章　律师行业与涉外律师业务现状 ……………………………………（1）
　　第一节　律师业的过去、现在和未来 ………………………………（1）
　　第二节　外国律师制度 …………………………………………………（3）
　　第三节　我国涉外律师行业的发展现状与业务范围 ………………（6）

第二章　涉外律师的理念与素养 ……………………………………………（10）
　　第一节　西方法律公正观念与程序正义 ……………………………（10）
　　第二节　职业技能与涉外商事礼仪修养 ……………………………（12）

第三章　律师尽职调查业务 …………………………………………………（20）
　　第一节　尽职调查类别与尽职调查清单 ……………………………（20）
　　第二节　尽职调查报告与法律意见书的出具 ………………………（25）

第四章　律师规范文本格式 …………………………………………………（34）
　　第一节　传真及对外文稿格式 …………………………………………（34）
　　第二节　律师委托合同及业务函件 ……………………………………（36）

第五章　英文合同制作 ………………………………………………………（42）
　　第一节　合同结构安排 …………………………………………………（42）
　　第二节　具体条款写作及词义分析 ……………………………………（56）
　　第三节　保密协议、采购合同范例 ……………………………………（72）

第六章　英文案例阅读 ………………………………………………………（83）
　　第一节　英文案例文本解析 ……………………………………………（83）
　　第二节　案例摘要 ………………………………………………………（88）

第七章　备忘录与律师法律意见 ……………………………………………… (98)
第一节　商事谈判与备忘录制作 …………………………………… (98)
第二节　律师内部法律意见 ………………………………………… (108)

第八章　非诉涉外律师业务要略 …………………………………………… (120)
第一节　跨国投资与并购业务 ……………………………………… (120)
第二节　国际贸易与知识产权业务 ………………………………… (133)
第三节　证券与其他商事业务 ……………………………………… (138)

第九章　律师参与涉外诉讼仲裁业务 ……………………………………… (145)
第一节　涉外诉讼仲裁案件代理需知 ……………………………… (145)
第二节　诉状制作与法庭文件 ……………………………………… (153)
第三节　律师参与 WTO 相关业务 ………………………………… (165)

第十章　模拟庭审训练 ……………………………………………………… (174)
第一节　知名模拟法庭介绍 ………………………………………… (174)
第二节　模拟法庭诉状范例 ………………………………………… (182)

参考文献 ……………………………………………………………………… (198)

第一章 律师行业与涉外律师业务现状

律师是提供法律服务的执业人员，是维护社会公平和正义的专业人士。律师执业者，应对律师行业、律师制度的发展历史与现状有所认知。对于有志于从事涉外律师实务的律师而言，除对所执业法域的律师行业发展状况全面了解以外，还应对其他国家或地区的律师制度、行业状况有所掌握，以便于与客户沟通交流并提供到位的服务。

第一节 律师业的过去、现在和未来

一 中国律师制度的起源与历史发展

在中国，据考证，"律师"一语在汉代佛教传入时就作为译词开始出现。《大涅槃经》云："如是能知佛法所作，善能解说，是名律师。"其意是指通晓佛教戒律和规章制度的人，能够解释规则和戒律，可以称之为律师①。从这一词义上引申，也可以理解为现在的律师是以熟知法律为业的人，应通晓法律、善于解说法律。《不列颠百科全书》将法律职业定义为"以通晓法律和法律应用为基础的职业"。

在中国古代，熟知法律并能言善辩者，可以替打官司的人出出主意甚至代写诉状，从而参与到案件诉讼中，因此会被称为"讼师"或"大状"。虽然这些讼师也可以在所代写的状纸上署名，但在纠问式审判模式下，并没有机会作为代理人参加庭辩。有历史记载的较早有名的讼师是春秋战国时期的邓析。《吕氏春秋》记载邓析"与民之有狱者约，大狱一衣，小狱襦袴。民之献衣襦袴而学讼者，不可胜数。以非为是，以是为非，是非无度，而可与不可日变，所欲胜因胜，所欲罪因罪"，收取找他求助的案件当事人的一些长衣短裤，大致也相当于律师咨询服务费了。邓析在解释法律问题时所持的"以非为是，以是为非"的"两可说"的立场，是一种辩论的思维，同律师可能因代理诉讼原告或者被告的需要，而对同一法律问题发表不同观点的职业立场，是相通的。

我国现代意义的律师制度，始于清末。1906 年，沈家本主持起草的《大清刑事民

---

① 韩栋：《说说"律师"》，《文史知识》2007 年第 7 期。

事诉讼法草案》中明确规定了律师的地位和作用，规定律师可以写状呈堂、上堂辩护、堂询原告和证人、代被告辩护、引申案例辩论。1910年的修订草案进一步明确嫌犯可以聘请两名辩护人，规定了律师的会见权、通信权、阅卷权、验视证据权。1912年9月，当时的中华民国司法部公布了《律师暂行章程》，规定经考试合格或具备一定资格可免试的可由司法总长发给律师证书。持证律师需到高等审判厅登记方可在辖区内行使职务。

中华人民共和国成立后，1954年《宪法》规定了"被告人有权获得辩护"，从1954年到1957年，北京、天津、上海、沈阳等地推行律师事务所，全国有将近3000名律师。1980年8月26日，《中华人民共和国律师暂行条例》出台，1996年制定了《中华人民共和国律师法》，现行有效的为2008年实施的修订版。

链接

《中华人民共和国律师法》第二条：

本法所称律师，是指依法取得律师执业证书，接受委托或者指定，为当事人提供法律服务的执业人员。

律师应当维护当事人合法权益，维护法律正确实施，维护社会公平和正义。

二　西方律师起源与发展

在西方，律师职业最早出现在希腊—罗马文化之中。古希腊雅典法规定在诉讼上采取辩论式。审判时，先宣读原告人的控诉书和被告人的反驳书，然后双方当事人进行辩论。法律还允许当事人请辩护士代表自己进行辩论，诉讼程序公开进行。公元前594年，雅典的执政官还设立了具有民主特色的陪审法庭。一些刑事和民事案件，经执政官初审后，送往陪审法庭。"公民未经陪审法庭判决不得处死。"

辩论完毕，法官用秘密表决的方式作出裁判。古希腊雅典法律对以后的罗马法有着直接的影响。古罗马在制定《十二铜表法》之前就曾派十人团到雅典考察立法，归来后制定了十二铜表法。此法中就曾提到出庭辩论问题。罗马法规定在任何古罗马《十二铜表法》规定："若（当事人双方）不能和解，则（他们）应在午前到市场或会议场进行诉讼，出庭双方依次申辩。"在这种控诉式诉讼模式下，被告人与原告人处于平等地位，审判采取对质、言词、公开方式进行。诉讼程序中第一步是传唤出庭，原告首先传唤被告，如果被告拒绝出庭，原告可以强制带他出庭。但假如被告不能或不愿立即出庭，他可以提供一名被称为保护人或辩护人的人作其保证人代为出庭。被告拥有辩护权，可以提出反证，证明自己无罪，还可以请精通辩术的辩护人为自己辩护。这种公开辩论的诉讼制度实质上也是一种对执法官行使强制权的限制。可以说，诉讼中允许辩论和代理的规定是律师产生的前提条件，而随之产生的辩护士或称诉讼代理人便是现代律师的滥觞。

公元1世纪罗马进入帝国时期后，早期的刑事辩护制度发展成为律师辩护制度，即开始对受过一定法律专业教育的人通过考试制度选拔知法善辩者授予律师资格，并允许提供法律咨询和代理诉讼，允许收取报酬，从而出现了"职业律师"。15世纪前后，在伦敦先后成立了林肯、格雷、中殿、内殿四个律师学院，传授法律知识、培养法律人才。他们几乎垄断了律师业务。直到16世纪，英国律师开始划分为"出庭律师"和"事务律师"，形成了英国律师的等级制度。法国在12世纪以后，开始设立制度使一些受过法律教育者，经过律师宣誓，登记入册为职业律师。1791年的法国宪法以1789年制定的《人权宣言》作为序言，规定了被告人享有辩护权利，允许被告人接受律师的帮助等。

第二节 外国律师制度

一 美国律师制度

这项规定对美国律师制度的建立与发展起了重要作用。美国是法制最发达的国家之一，现有律师100多万名，美国历任总统中约有一半做过律师。美国的法律制度是"双轨制"，即联邦法和州法共存，再加上美国是判例法国家，所以美国没有统一的律师法。有关律师制度的法规，散见于宪法、判例法以及律师协会制定的《律师守则》中。

《美国宪法》（修正案）第6条规定，在一切刑事诉讼中，被告人应享受下列权利：由发生罪案之州或区域的公正陪审团予以迅速的公开审判，该区域当以法律先确定之；准予与对方的证人对质；有为了保护自己的利益而接受律师帮助的权利。从1870年开始，美国规定必须通过正规的律师考试后，才能做律师；从1900年开始，美国大学开始有正规的律师法学教育；从1929年到1949年，美国各州规定，律师在考试之前，必须取得正规的法学教育。各州基本都要求参与其州律师考试的学生要从美国律师协会（American Bar Association）所认可的法学院毕业（ABA-Approved Law Schools）。截至2017年3月，在ABA认可名单中的法学院一共有205所。但并不是选择了在ABA所认可的法学院就必然能参加律师资格考试了。因为法学院除了通过三年法学教育培养J. D. （Juris Doctor）之外，也有一年制的法学进阶课程LL. M（Master of Law）。大多数州都要求报考人必须取得J. D. 学位，但有少数州允许取得LL. M学位的外国学生报考，包括New York、California、New Hampshire、Alabama、Virginia等。美国的律师考试是从事律师和检察官职业的前提，而从事过一定年限的律师和检察官职业，又是从事法官职业的前提。在一个州取得律师资格，并不等于可以在其他州从事律师职业。如要在另一州从事律师工作,还需要通过另一州的律师资格考试或按程序获得许可。在通过考试后还要经过品行调查证明没有劣迹,才可给予律师资格。

根据任职情况,美国律师主要可分为三种:政府机关雇用的律师、企业/公司雇用的律师和开办律师事务所的律师。美国的政府律师主要包括美国司法部的律师和政府的法律顾问办公室律师。这些律师的数量庞大,有10万人左右。企业内部的律师被称为"in-house",即公司法务人员。开办律师事务所的律师即私人律师,在社会上执行律师职务,为社会上不特定人服务,领取营业执照,所以又称"挂牌律师"。他们可以个人执业,或联合经营事务所,或合伙经营律师事务所。美国律师的活动范围和业务是很广泛的。在社会的各个领域,都有律师活动。律师的业务从早期的刑事辩护发展到兼任法律顾问、提供咨询、代理诉讼、办理非诉讼法律事务等。

美国的律师组织是律师协会,联邦、州、县都有律师协会。其任务一是制定《律师守则》,对律师进行道德和纪律教育;二是组织律师进修和研究法律;三是对社会进行律师宣传教育。它还监督律师执行《律师守则》,受理公民对律师的控告。但律师协会没有权力对律师直接作出惩戒、停止执业或开除律师资格的处分,这些权力由法院行使。

链接

ABA-Approved Law Schools

Since 1952, the Council of the ABA Section of Legal Education and Admissions to the Bar of the American Bar Association has been recognized by the United States Department of Education as the national agency for the accreditation of programs leading to the J. D. degree in the United States.

Law schools that are ABA-approved provide a legal education that meets a minimum set of standards promulgated by the Council and Accreditation Committee of the Section of Legal Education and Admissions to the Bar. Every U. S. jurisdiction has determined that graduates of ABA-approved law schools are eligible to sit for the bar exam in their respective jurisdiction.

The ABA Standards for Approval of Law Schools assure that students who attend ABA-approved law schools will receive a sound program of legal education. Schools not approved by the ABA need not comply with these Standards and the ABA can make no representation about the quality of the program of legal education offered at non-approved law schools.

In many states, a person may not sit for the bar examination unless that person holds a J. D. degree from an ABA-approved law school. By 2017, a total of 205 institutions are ABA-approved; 204 confer the first degree in law (the J. D. degree), the other ABA approved school is the U. S. Army Judge Advocate General's School, which offers an officer's resident graduate course, a specialized program beyond the first degree in law. Three of the 205 law schools are provisionally approved.

（来源：https://www.americanbar.org/groups/legal_education/resources/aba_approved_law_schools/in_alphabetical_order.html）

二 西欧各国的律师制度

西欧多数国家的律师制度有着悠久的历史，以法国为例，在1804年和1810年，拿破仑颁发了两个法律，确立了法国的现代律师制度。200多年来，有关法律经过数十次修改，其中最重要的有：1900年向妇女开放律师职业，1971年将辩护人和法律顾问（不能出庭，只能提供法律咨询）两个职业合并为律师，1990年向欧共体成员公民开放法律服务市场。目前，法国共有律师38000多人，其中巴黎市的律师占全国总数的40%，有15000多人，律师占人口总数的万分之六点三。而德国律师总数为12万人，律师占人口总数的万分之十五。

在法国，律师是个受人尊敬的职业。在法国要成为一名律师，要在经过4年至5年的大学法律本科学习后，参加律师协会的地区律师职业教育中心的招生考试，考试通过后，在该中心接受18个月的法学理论和法务实践的培训，再通过该中心之结业考试达到合格标准后，获得《律师受训合格证书》（le certificat d'aptitude à la profession d'avocat，CAPA），可以申请律师资格，但不能申请从事法官、检察官、公证等职业。考试合格后，还须在律师事务所实习两年，才可向当地律师公会申请执业。

在德国，律师是"独立的司法机构"。只有那些依《德国法官法》有资格任法官的人才可以成为律师，德国律师作为自由职业者，其活动既不受政府的控制，也不负有公务员那种对国家效忠的义务。其意义在于使公民有机会获得不受国家影响的法律专家的服务。在德国法院诉讼，诉讼代理人必须是在德国有法官资格并取得律师执业许可的人，即执业律师。从资格获取程序来看，申请人必须具有法学本科以上的学历，且须通过两次考试。第一次国家司法考试通过后，考生须进行为期2年的实习，实习单位包括：普通法院（民事法院）、检察院或刑事法院、地方政府部门或行政法院、律师事务所等。实习期间由国家支付工资，享受准公务员待遇。实习结束后方可参加第二次国家司法考试。考试通过者即取得法官资格，成为候补文官。取得这一资格可以成为法官，也可以从事其他法律职业，如检察官、律师、公证人等法律职业。

三 日本的律师制度

在日本，律师以办理民事及刑事诉讼案件、离婚等家庭案件、对行政机关不服的申诉、和解交涉、法律咨询以及其他法律事务为其业务。在裁判当中，原则上只有律师能够成为当事人本人的代理人。不论是最高裁判所、高等裁判所、地方裁判所、家庭裁判所还是简易裁判所，律师在全国的任何裁判所都能出庭进行辩护活动。日本律师有3万多人，但有70%—80%集中在东京地区执业。除出任辩护士即执业律师外，还有相当一部分律师受雇于法务省在政府不动产登记部门从事法律工作。这一点与我国香港地区类似。在香港地区土地署的2000余名工作人员中，有1000多名为技术人员，500名左右行政管理人员，还有500名左右是负责处理土地房产等法律事务的政府律师。

在律师资格方面，日本实行法曹三者统一司法考试制度，即从事律师、法判官和检察官职业者，都必须通过司法考试，然后在最高裁判所管理下的司法研修所经过为期一年半的实务培训，并最终通过毕业考试。参加司法考试须完成法科大学院的课程，或者通过预备考试合格。日本司法考试通过率不高，在2%左右。很多取得法学学位的毕业生并不从事律师工作。

对于外国出身的律师执业问题，日本在1986年颁布了外国律师办理法律事务相关事项的特别措施法，规定外国律师得到法务大臣允许，并在日本律师联合会注册，可以在日本办理自己所持律师资格的国家的法律事务以及在一定条件下办理日本以外的第三国的法律事务。但外国法律事务律师不能代理办理日本的裁判所、检察厅及其他行政机关的各种司法或行政程序，以及原资格国以外的法律鉴定等一定的法律事务。另外日本也允许外国人参加日本的司法考试，并在获得律师资格后方可在日本的法院担任诉讼代理人或是代理对行政机关的申诉。

第三节 我国涉外律师行业的发展现状与业务范围

一 我国涉外律师行业发展现状

涉外律师应擅长处理涉外法律事务。我国《最高人民法院关于适用〈中华人民共和国民事诉讼法〉若干问题的意见》第304条规定："当事人一方或双方是外国人、无国籍人、外国企业或组织，或者当事人之间民事法律关系的设立、变更、终止的法律事实发生在外国，或者诉讼标的物在外国的民事案件，为涉外民事案件。"参照这一解释，无论是民事、行政还是刑事法律事务，只要法律关系的主体中有一方是外国自然人、法人或其他组织，或者该法律关系的设立、变更、终止的法律事实发生的外国，或者法律关系的对象或标的物在外国，或者适用于该法律关系的准据法是外国法或国际法，则该法律事务均是涉外法律事务。由此可见，涉外法律事务可以分为涉外诉讼法律事务和涉外非诉讼法律事务。其中涉外诉讼法律事务，既包括国际法庭案件、跨国诉讼、国际仲裁，也包括各类在国内进行的涉外诉讼；涉外非诉讼法律事务包括国际经济合作项目的法律事务处理、国际证券发行或涉外婚姻关系的法律咨询等各类法律事务处理。

我国执业律师数量近年来持续增长,截至 2017 年底,全国共有执业律师 36.5 万多人,共有律师事务所 2.8 万多家。据统计,2017 年,全国律师办理各类诉讼案件 465 万多件,其中刑事诉讼辩护及代理 68.4 万多件,民事诉讼代理 381.8 万多件,行政诉讼代理 15.3 万多件;办理非诉讼法律事务 89.4 万多件;为 61.7 万多家党政机关、人民团体和企事业单位担任法律顾问①。8 年间全国律师业务总收入保持了年均 12.85% 的增速,服务领域由传统的以诉讼事务为主发展到诉讼、非诉讼事务并重,由国内业务为主发展到国内、涉外业务并举。

我国涉外法律服务业起步较晚,高水平涉外法律服务人才缺乏,在国际法律服务市场上竞争力还不足,整体水平还不能完全适应我国实施更加积极主动对外开放的发展需求。截至 2017 年底,执业律师在中国境外接受过教育并获得学位的律师有 5100 多人,共有来自 23 个国家和地区的 242 家律师事务所在中国(内地)设立了 308 家代表机构。2016 年国内律师办理涉外仲裁案件 3545 件,获得业务收入 8774 万元。2012 年,司法部、全国律协制订了涉外律师领军人才培养计划,已组织四批共 150 多名律师先后赴德国、西班牙、美国、英国等国家学习交流,500 多名优秀涉外律师进入全国律协人才库。

链接

截至 2016 年 7 月,北京有律师事务所 2147 家、律师 26218 人,2015 年业务收入是 138.1 亿元;外国、中国香港律师事务所驻京代表处 108 家,律师 260 人,2015 年业务收入是 29.32 亿元,二者在涉外法律服务领域存在明显的差距。

据预测,中国的对外投资可能将在今后 3—5 年翻番,到 2020 年,中国企业将在世界各地积累 1 万亿—2 万亿美元资产。而中国公司赴外投资、贸易的最大问题就是法律问题。2013 年 3 月,主管涉外民商事法律审判的最高人民法院副院长万鄂湘指出,中国企业涉外官司输多赢少,损失很大,很多就是不懂外国当地法律。当前我们在世界贸易组织(WTO)当中大量的案件,不得不高薪聘请外国律师,中国律师只能提供低端的服务,这对我们的律师业是严峻的挑战。中国企业急需大量通晓国际经济惯例和游戏规则的法律人才,为其在海外投资、知识产权保护、反倾销等重要领域保驾护航。在我国的北京、上海、深圳等地律师虽多,但能够熟练运用外语和法律知识与国外客户洽谈业务、签订合同的从事涉外业务的律师总共不超过 300 人,熟知国际法、国际贸易法和 WTO 规则的高端律师尤其稀缺。实际上,当前涉外法律人才的需求是现有量

---

① 《律师、公证、基层法律服务最新数据出炉》,http://www.moj.gov.cn/government_public/content/2018-03/14/141_17049.html。

的五倍。大部分专家和律师都对中国涉外律师的前景非常看好。目前迫切需要加强人才培养，培养一批掌握国情、社情，熟悉国外经营发展环境和法律法规的律师。（来源：张巍：《"扬帆计划"培养国际化律师人才》，《法制日报》2017年3月2日）

二 我国涉外律师业务的范围与类型

涉外律师一般处理涉外的各类诉讼和仲裁，需要熟练掌握国际、国内相关法律法规，并通晓金融、国际贸易等知识，同时又具有优秀的外语表达能力。一般要求法学专业本科以上学历，并具有扎实的国际法、国际私法或国际经济法等相关涉外法律专业知识，通过国家统一司法考试，并获得律师执业资格证书。

涉外律师能够独立从事涉外律师工作，一般需要有相应的工作经验，例如3年以上律师事务所涉外法律工作经验，具备处理一般律师业务的扎实实践技能，例如良好的缜密的逻辑思维能力、良好的口头表达能力、富有条理的书面表达能力，既具有扎实的法学理论功底，又具有非常强的实际问题分析、处理、应变处理能力，能够独立分析和综合判断法律疑难问题，具有较强的组织协调能力和创新能力。在此基础上，涉外律师要具有相对宽阔的国际化视野，熟悉国际经贸中的一般法律规则，对业务所涉及的外国法律制度、法律文化、部分重要的法律原则、法规律师有所了解和掌握；要有流利的英文口头和书面表达能力，并具有一定的第二外语识别与运用的能力。

涉外律师开展法律服务的业务范围主要涉及三个方面。第一，为来华投资的外国企业或个人提供全方位的法律服务。这主要是基于外国企业在中国的业务拓展而相应地需要获得当地的法律服务。第二，为与华经贸往来的外国企业或个人提供跨国合作方面的法律服务。主要指外国企业的对华贸易、技术转让、融资业务以及其他与中国企业的合作项目中需要为交易双方，包括外方和中方提供法律咨询和服务。第三，为中国企业的海外投资以及其他经贸活动提供法律服务。主要指中国企业开展涉外贸易、与外方开展投资合作、向海外投资等方面需要提供法律服务。在上述业务范围中，对于涉及中国法律、中国所加入的国际条约及所适用的国际惯例的法律适用与解释，应由取得中国律师执业资格的律师提供法律服务。对于涉外法律的，中国执业律师可提供力所能及的法律咨询，必要时仍应由取得该外国法律服务资格人士提供法律服务。

具体而言，在中国执业的涉外律师可提供法律服务的业务类型包括以下情形。

（一）公司、融资、资本市场和证券业务

例如外商投资企业的设立及运营（土地、房屋、设备等）、企业重组改制、股权转让、并购、技术转让、解散清算、破产清算等相关业务；负责外商在华投资项目的法律论证；帮助外商在华设立常驻代表机构和三资企业，起草、审查外商投资企业的合同、章程等文件，并协办报批手续；为外商投资企业重组及参与国企收购等提供全面法律服务；为外商投资企业的日常经营提供包括外汇、税收、劳工、购销、进出口及

知识产权等方面的法律咨询；外商企业投资、运营纠纷仲裁诉讼；代表企业或银行参与国际银团贷款、项目融资、融资租赁及涉外债券发行等各类涉外债务性融资项目；代表境内企业参与海外股票上市、股权转让及吸收风险投资等涉外权益性融资项目；协助建立中外合作基金及外商投资基金管理公司；项目融资、资产租赁、信用担保、银团贷款等银行业务及银行业务合规性审查；进出口信贷业务、国际债务/股权重整、境外投资及收购业务、国际重组；资本证券化和结构融资、投资信托及合规性审查；境内上市、境外上市，以及国际板（外国企业在上交所发行A股）上市公司重组、收购；基金、保险业务。

（二）国际贸易与海外投资法律业务

海关进出口管理相关业务；贸易支付方式及外汇管理相关问题的处理；国际贸易、信用证、票据纠纷；海商、海事纠纷；知识产权纠纷；银行贷款、担保、融资、证券发行交易纠纷；产品责任纠纷。为境内企业的境外贸易、投资项目进行法律论证及协调；为外贸企业就国际货物买卖合同、技术转让合同、信用证及托收等国际支付、提单及国际风险防范等提供咨询，并协助外贸企业进行海外账款追收。提供世界贸易组织法律、政策咨询服务；代理国内外反倾销、反补贴、保障措施调查与应诉；就贸易政策法律的制定提供咨询；参加贸易协定谈判；协助政府相关部门参与WTO争端解决；代理参与各类涉外诉讼及仲裁，并与海外律师行合作，策划、参与国际诉讼及国际商务仲裁。

（三）其他涉外的商事运营相关法律服务

例如房地产的开发与交易业务；劳动法律业务；反垄断及反不正当竞争、反商业贿赂；企业刑事法务；代理境内外商标注册及专利申请、复议、异议；与知识产权相关的商业决策和风险防范，知识产权侵权问题的处理；知识产权许可及技术转让；版权注册、商号、域名、商业秘密的保护；知识产权纠纷的谈判、和解、提起法律诉讼；工商、海关、外汇、税务、环境保护等事宜的合规性、问题解决方法等的咨询；其他各种合同法律事务。

涉外律师的日常工作的基本方式包括：与投资、贸易、经济技术合作以及其他各种经营活动相关的一般法律咨询、论证、建议；各种合同及相关法律文件的起草、审查、修订、翻译；特定专项法律问题的研究及出具法律意见书、咨询建议文件；常见公司法务项目（公司设立、变更、终止、股权转让、合并分立、上市、融资、技术合作等）的法律服务；参与项目谈判或法律相关业务的翻译、解说、沟通；与国家行政机关、司法机关及其他有关机构的沟通、交涉，协调或办理有关报批、登记、备案手续；违约侵权的调查、调解、诉讼、仲裁代理；作为政府机关的法律顾问或者代理人参与有关国际谈判以及WTO纠纷解决程序等。

第二章 涉外律师的理念与素养

第一节 西方法律公正观念与程序正义

法治,意味着经由法律程序有秩序地实现公平和正义,既维护公民个人的权益,又实现文明的国家治理。然而对于公平正义的理解,在中西方文化中并不完全一样。开展涉外律师业务,有必要了解西方法律中的公正观念并与中国的相关法治理念形成比较认识。

一 西方法治思想中的公平与正义

莎士比亚的名剧《威尼斯商人》在第四幕将要不要执行契约处罚作为戏剧冲突,呈现出了当时的契约法文化。为资助友人巴萨尼奥追妻,安东尼奥向高利贷商人夏洛克借钱,夏洛克借此机会让安东尼奥签订了不收利息但若不能及时还款就在他胸口割一磅肉的契约。结果因种种意外,安东尼奥未能如期还款,只能在法庭上围绕是否履行契约割一磅肉与夏洛克辩论。从古罗马帝国到中世纪的欧洲,契约一直都是以等同于国法的地位而存在的,《威尼斯商人》中"一磅肉"契约具有和法律一样的强制力,可见契约在人们心中的神圣且不可动摇的地位。

从犹太教到基督教,从古罗马帝国到中世纪的欧洲,对于契约神圣的尊重,是基于对契约维护安定的社会秩序的作用的充分认识,也体现了法律至上的信仰。这种法律理念还体现在司法审判中。

正义(giustizia)。其形象为一蒙眼女性,白袍,金冠。左手提一秤,置膝上,右手举一剑,倚束棒(fasci)。束棒缠一条蛇,脚下坐一只狗,案头放权杖一根、书籍若干及骷髅一个。白袍,象征道德无瑕、刚直不阿;蒙眼,因为司法纯靠理智,不靠误人的感官印象;王冠,因为正义尊贵无比、荣耀第一;秤……比喻裁量公平,在正义面前人人皆得所值,不多不少;剑,表示制裁严厉,绝不姑息,一如插着斧子的束棒,那古罗马一切刑罚的化身;蛇与狗,分别代表仇恨与友情,两者都不许影响裁判。权杖申威,书籍载法,骷髅指人的生命脆弱,跟正义恰好相反:正义属于永恒。——利

帕（Cesare Ripa）《像章学》卷三（1593）①

司法女神蒙眼这一形象的设计，体现了西方法律审判模式的特点：法官以中立的态度听案，通过程序正义实现公正。

二 中国古代的法治思维

在中国古代，与正义女神相类似的代表司法公正的图腾形象是独角兽，又名獬豸。在中国古代法律文化中，獬豸拥有很高的智慧，懂人言知人性。它怒目圆睁，能辨是非曲直，能识善恶忠奸，发现奸邪的官员，就用角把他触倒，然后吃下肚子。它能辨曲直，又有神羊之称，它是勇猛、公正的象征，是司法"正大光明""清平公正""光明天下"的象征。

据许慎《说文解字》记载，当时"豸"被写作"廌"，即"法"的古体字。"灋，刑也，平之如水，从水；廌，所以触不直者去之，从去。""廌"，传说是一种头长独角、秉性公正的奇兽。杨孚所著《异物志》写道："北荒之中有兽，名獬豸，一角，性别曲直。见人斗，触不直者；闻人争，咬不正者。"中国的法治目标同样是追求正义，但更强调社会的运行符合天道天理，与自然的和睦相处。为实现这一目标，会使用"德、仁、义、礼、智、信"等手段，即将遵守契约的法律精神置于靠后的位置，从而将法治作为实现正义与社会和谐的一种手段。当今，中国司法坚持在党的领导下推动以实现每个案件体现公平正义为价值目标的司法改革，将中国特色社会主义法治建设作为促进国家治理体系和治理能力现代化的重要内容，全面推进依法治国。

---

① 冯象：《正义的蒙眼布》，《读书》2002年第7期，第96页。

链接：失控的电车

假设你是一辆有轨电车的司机，电车以每小时 60 英里的速度沿着轨道疾驰。在前方，你看见五个工人手持工具站在轨道上。你试着停下来，可是你不能，因为刹车失灵了。你感到无比绝望，因为你知道，如果你冲向这五个工人的话，他们将全部被撞死。突然，你注意到右边有一条岔道，那条轨道上也有一个工人，不过只有一个。你意识到，你可以将有轨电车拐向那条岔道，撞死这个工人，而挽救那五个工人。你应该怎么做呢？

第二节 职业技能与涉外商事礼仪修养

一 涉外法律职业技能的含义

法学专业是一个实践性很强的专业，合格的法律职业者，除了应具备必要的专业理论基础、良好的职业道德和思想政治素质外，还应具有较强的专业技能。但我国高校在法学教育方面通常偏重理论讲授，学生法律职业技能训练不足。

法律职业技能，指从事某项具体的法律实务时所必需的技术性能力。法律职业技能主要包括普通技能和专业技能两大类，普通技能是从事现代社会职业普遍需要的基础性技能。包括运用本国语和外语进行表达及交流的能力、计算机操作能力、社会交往、社会适应及协作的能力、自我提高及创新的能力、组织管理能力和信息处理能力等。专业技能主要包括：对法律规则和法律事实的识别、法律解释、法律推理、证据调查及运用、法律文书制作、驾驭运用法律文献资源等方面的技术、技巧和能力。这种技能不同于普通技能和其他职业技能，而且，这种技能非经法律教育和法律实践的长期训练，是无法被掌握的。

涉外法律职业技能的概念可以界定为从事涉外法律事务处理的法律职业应具备的以智力技能为主要内容的、处理各种法律事务的实践能力。有学者将之进一步操作为：①针对具体法律纠纷提炼法律争点撰写法律文书的能力；②针对具体法律或诉讼问题搜寻、整合法律和相关材料的技能；③同法律客户以及其他法律人的谈判和交往能力；④解决具体纠纷的能力；⑤在具体案件中熟练运用诉讼程序应对诉求的能力；⑥就具体案件在法庭辩论、说服法官的能力；⑦在立法中就特定法律事项游说和推动法律变革的能力①。

---

① 苏力：《中国法律技能教育的制度分析》，《法学家》2008 年第 2 期。

二　涉外法律职业技能的内容

涉外法律职业技能应当包括的能力至少有四种：法律思辨能力、沟通表达能力、职业社交能力、涉外学习能力。

（一）法律思辨能力

是指在学习一定的法律理论和积累一定的法律经验性知识的基础上，法律职业者所具有的运用法律规则思考各类与法律有关的问题的能力。具体而言，具备较高的法律思辨能力的法律职业者，能够熟练使用一些法律范畴并熟练运用法律逻辑推理对所需解决的法律问题作出明晰的判断，得出有关该问题的合法与否、权利义务内容、法律责任后果等分析结论。法律思辨能力表现为思想开放性、思维敏锐性、逻辑严密性、表达准确性[①]。法律思辨能力养成，要通过扎实的法律理论应用训练，以法律规则思考和解决各类现实问题，从而提高运用各种法律知识的思想开放性、思维敏锐性、逻辑严密性，最终表现为将有关法律结论和思考成果予以准确地表达。

（二）沟通表达能力

石油大王洛克菲勒说："假如人际沟通能力也是同糖或咖啡一样的商品的话，我愿意付出比太阳底下任何东西都珍贵的价格购买这种能力。"沃尔玛公司总裁沃尔顿说："如果你必须将沃尔玛管理体制浓缩成一种思想，那就是沟通，因为它是我们成功的真正关键之一。"可见，沟通表达能力在各行各业均被看作十分重要的职业能力，而对法律职业更是如此。沟通表达在法律职业工作中占据十分重要的地位，只有与他人保持良好的协作，才能获取自己所需要的资源，才能获得成功。所有的成功者一定都是擅长人际沟通、珍视人际沟通的人，而法律职业者以熟悉和运用法律知识为职业，特别需具备良好的口头沟通能力、较强的书面表达能力。提高沟通表达能力，能够大大提高法律职业者的工作效率。沟通表达能力的提升可以通过专门进行学习和训练，从而掌握沟通中的主导地位、提高说服力，能够快速汇报事实、观点，并获得认同，并且在对话中断断续续坚持一个观点的系统性，并形成无法动摇的立场。沟通表达能力的培养可分为八个层次，分别为：讲述、叙述、表达、讨论、汇报、陈述、解释、回应，渐次掌握以后综合和内化为法律职业者的个人素养，做到在各种场合自然、灵活的沟通和表达。

对一个成功的律师来说，良好的人际关系是其事业成功的助推剂。它会使人变得活泼，富有进取精神，充满干劲。反之，冷漠、消极的人生态度和生硬的人际关系，会把自己置于重重障碍之中，限制自己的发展。要想成就事业，就要善于沟通，建立和谐、良好的人际关系。沟通是一种技巧，是一门艺术。沟通应避免自己说得太多，

---

① 刘爱龙：《论法理学教学与法学思辨能力的培养》，《黑龙江高教研究》2006年第1期。

在与他人谈话时，可以用问问题的方式引导他人谈感兴趣的话题，多听少说，多点头、微笑。沟通高手一定首先会鼓励对方说，聆听体现良好的修养。沟通中要避免直接否定对方的观点，而要先从对方观点中先找出可以认同的地方，并加以肯定，然后提出自己的看法。沟通中还要避免自以为是，因为自己认为理所当然的事情，对方也许不这么看。不要强求别人认同你的观点和看法。沟通中的语言表达要坚定有力，富有激情和感染力，并保持平和、乐观、积极的心态，保持耐心，使人感觉与你谈话很快乐，经过多次沟通再解决期望的问题。

律师经常要与陌生人打交道。与陌生人沟通时，如有条件应尽量提前了解对方的情况，并在首次见面时调整你的形象和心态，双方刚接触的时候是最重要的，你如果给对方留下好的第一印象，那么后面的沟通就可以顺利进行。要有效突破与陌生人沟通的障碍就必须从寻找共同点着手，从而找到共同的话题，达到一见如故、相见恨晚的有效沟通效果。

链接：说服别人认同你的观点

这是一个略有名气的心理测验。L小姐和M先生是一对恋人，两人隔河而居，那条河既不宽，也不阔。有一天，M先生得了急病，L小姐知道了，心急如焚，但是那一天出现了暴风雨，河水暴涨，风急雨劲，M先生叫她不要去探他。可L小姐还是要不顾一切去看看他。于是她去找B先生，因为B先生有一条船，有能力送她过河。可是，B先生却要收过河费100万元，即使她向他解释M先生的情况，他也一样不为所动。L小姐当然没有那么多钱，于是她去找S先生，因S先生也有一条船。岂料，S先生竟是无耻之徒，他要求L小姐献上她的肉体，方才载她渡河。L小姐为了爱情，最后牺牲了自己……最后，S先生也载了她过河。M先生的急病，最后也没有恶化，化险为夷了。但当他知道L小姐居然牺牲了自己的贞节，他很生气，因为他早已告诉她不要来，何况还因此牺牲了肉体！于是，M先生和L小姐就这样分手了。L小姐很伤心，不久之后，她认识了年纪较大的F先生。当他知悉了她的过往后，不但不介意，还向她示爱。虽然L小姐并不太爱F先生，他也不太勉强……

好了，问题来了，参考故事内容，然后把故事中的五位人物L、M、B、S、F五位人物，按照你喜欢他们的程度排上一个次序。然后与同组的人讨论沟通，直到达到同样的观点。

（三）职业社交能力

德国思想家歌德说："人不能孤独地生活，他需要社会。"今天是一个扩大对外信息交流的时代，人类的交往和合作，呈更加广泛和日益复杂化，因此，社交能力更是人们必不可少的一种能力。中国工程院院士、清华大学化工科学与技术研究院院长金涌在浙江工业大学座谈时表示，社交能力、在梯队中的工作效率、信息收集能力、自学能力、信息分析能力是大学生最重要五项能力，其中，社交能力列首位①。对于法律职业者而言，培养并具备与职业有关的社交能力具有更为重要的意义，因为法律职业本身就是一项与人打交道的职业，而法律知识、法律规则是以各类社会活动经验的积累分不开的。良好的社交能力能使职业者在与社会各界人士交往中获取更多的知识与经验，良好的社交能力能帮助法律职业者积极地参加各种社会活动，并在活动中学会与人合作，妥善解决工作中的各种矛盾。

应当注意的是，法律职业社交能力的培养与一般社交能力培养有所不同，这表现为在社会交往中必须遵循法律职业道德和职业纪律的要求，按照一定的行为规范进行社交。

（四）涉外学习能力

涉外学习能力是指学习涉外法律事务所相关的新知识的能力。为成长为涉外法律应用人才，既掌握好本学科国内法的各种基础理论与技能，又学习好国际或各种外国的法律知识的难度较大，关键在于具备在将来的法律职业环境中根据工作需要学习涉外法律事务相关知识的能力，具体讲是在掌握一至二门外语的基础上，能够运用所具备的基础法律理念迅速和准确地把握某项国际或外国法律规则，并将之运用于处理涉外法律事务的实践。

链接：罗伯特议事规则的 12 条基本原则

第 1 条　动议中心原则：动议是开会议事的基本单元。"动议者，行动的提议也。"会议讨论的内容应当是一系列明确的动议，它们必须是具体、明确、可操作的行动建议。先动议后讨论，无动议不讨论。

第 2 条　主持中立原则：会议"主持人"的基本职责是遵照规则来裁判并执行程序，尽可能不发表自己的意见，也不能对别人的发言表示倾向。（主持人若要发言，必须先授权他人临时代行主持之责，直到当前动议表决结束。）

第 3 条　机会均等原则：任何人发言前须示意主持人，得到其允许后方可发言。先举手者优先，但尚未对当前动议发过言者，优先于已发过言者。同时，主持人应尽量让意见相反的双方轮流得到发言机会，以保持平衡。

第 4 条　立场明确原则：发言人应首先表明对当前待决动议的立场是赞成还是反对，然后说明理由。

第 5 条　发言完整原则：不能打断别人的发言。

第 6 条　面对主持原则：发言要面对主持人，参会者之间不得直接辩论。

---

① 《院士称社交能力位列大学生五项重要能力之首》，新华网，2008 年 12 月 24 日，http://news.163.com/08/1224/14/4TUDSTEG0001124J.html。

第7条　限时限次原则：每人每次发言的时间有限制（比如约定不得超过2分钟）；每人对同一动议的发言次数也有限制（比如约定不得超过2次）。

第8条　一时一件原则：发言不得偏离当前待决的问题。只有在一个动议处理完毕后，才能引入或讨论另外一个动议。（主持人对跑题行为应予制止）

第9条　遵守裁判原则：主持人应制止违反议事规则的行为，这类行为者应立即接受主持人的裁判。

第10条　文明表达原则：不得进行人身攻击、不得质疑他人动机、习惯或偏好，辩论应就事论事，以当前待决问题为限。

第11条　充分辩论原则：表决须在讨论充分展开之后方可进行。

第12条　多数裁决原则：（在简单多数通过的情况下）动议的通过要求"赞成方"的票数严格多于"反对方"的票数（平局即没通过）。弃权者不计入有效票。

三　涉外商事礼仪修养

礼仪是指在人际交往之中，自始至终地以一定的、约定俗成的程序、方式来表现的律己、敬人的完整行为。所谓律己，就是用一定的礼仪来规范自己的行为，表现出良好的内在修养，不仅使自己充满自信，而且获得对方的尊重。所谓敬人，就是通过一定的礼仪，更好地向对方表达尊重、友好与善意，增进彼此的信任和友谊。从事涉外律师工作，应熟练掌握涉外商事礼仪，在工作中展现良好的文化修养，特别是在跨国的交往活动中通过个人行为展现出一个国家的文明风尚。涉外商事礼仪修养主要包括仪表仪容礼仪、举止言谈礼仪、出行礼宾礼仪等。

（一）仪表仪容礼仪

在着装方面，应随时保持服装清洁、平整。在商务接洽场合男士应着西装，佩带领带，穿皮鞋，严禁卷露衣袖、裤腿等不雅行为。女士应该着套装，区分不同场合化妆。在仪容规范方面，应面带笑容，保持开朗心态，这有利于营造和谐、融洽的工作气氛。保持身体清洁卫生，头发梳理整齐、面部保持清洁。男士不留长发，女士不化浓妆。保持唇部润泽，口气清新，以便适合近距离交谈。手部干净，指甲修剪整齐，男士不留长指甲，女士不涂鲜艳指甲油。不要在人面前整理个人卫生，比如剔牙齿、掏鼻孔、挖耳屎、修指甲、搓泥垢等，宜使用清新、淡雅的香水。社交场合不宜戴墨镜（参观、旅游除外）。女员工不宜佩戴有声响的饰物。公文包（手提包）外观整洁，男士公文包以黑色为佳。

（二）举止言谈礼仪

站立时应抬头、挺胸、收腹、双肩舒展、双目平视。双臂和手在身体两侧自然下垂，女士双臂可下垂交叉放于身体前。女士站立时，双膝和脚跟要靠紧，双脚呈"V"字形。男士站立时，双脚可并拢呈"V"字形，也可分开。分开时双脚应与肩同宽。站立时，双手不可叉在腰间，不宜放入裤子口袋中，也不宜在胸前抱臂。站立时双腿不可不停地抖动。就座时，不宜将座椅或沙发坐满，也不宜仅坐在座椅边上。就座后，上身应保持正直而微前倾，头部平正，双肩放松。男士就座后，双手可自然放于膝上，或轻放于座椅扶手上，手心向下，注意手指不要不停地抖动。女士就座后双手交叉放于腿上，手心向下。行走时，上身保持正直，双肩放松，目光平视，双臂自然摆动。男士注意手不宜放在裤子口袋里。行走时应从容自然。男士步伐矫健、有力，女士步伐自然、优雅。行走时不宜左顾右盼，脚步不宜太沉重而发出较大声响。

言谈规范方面，要恰当地称呼他人。在涉外交往中，一般对男子均称某某先生，对女子均称某某夫人、女士或小姐；对已婚女子称夫人、女士，未婚女子称小姐；对不了解其婚姻情况的女子也可称作小姐或女士；对地位较高、年龄稍长的已婚女子称夫人。近年来，女士已逐渐成为对女性最常用的称呼。对于有学位、军衔、技术职称的人士，可以称呼其头衔。在社交场合，无论新朋友还是老朋友，都应称呼对方姓氏加头衔或职称，这是对他人的尊敬。使用礼貌用语。在受到对方赞扬或帮助时应表示感谢；在打扰或妨碍别人时，应表示歉意；在指称陌生的第三者时，应使用"那位先生""那位女士"等之类称呼。正式交谈前的寒暄是展开话题的重要手段，寒暄时应选取大家共同感兴趣的话题，避免涉及私人问题或某些敏感话题。与他人交谈时，不宜出现插入、打断、讽刺、模仿等不礼貌行为。在交谈过程中，不宜出现过激的言语或过分的玩笑。在交谈过程中，应合理使用行为语言以配合表达，如微笑、点头等。交谈时不可用手指点他人。

（三）出行礼宾礼仪

"女士优先"原则是国际社会公认的"第一礼俗"。在一切社交场合，每一名成年男子，都有义务主动自觉地以自己的实际行动去尊重女士、关心女士、保护女士、照顾女士，并且还要为女士排忧解难。在引导的途中，引导者应走在客人的侧前方。若被引导的是一群人，引导者应灵活处理，一般应在最前面的侧前方。指引方向时，右臂伸出，小臂与上臂略呈直角，掌心向上，拇指微向内曲，四指并拢伸直，指向所要去的方向。上楼梯时，引导者应走在客人的后面；下楼梯时，引导者应走在客人的前面。

见面时，要通过握手等礼节表达问候。握手是大多数国家见面和离别时相互致意的礼仪。握手既是人们见面相互问候的主要礼仪，也是祝贺、感谢、安慰或相互鼓励的适当表达。如对方取得某些成绩与进步时，对方赠送礼品及发放奖品、奖状、发表祝词后，均可以握手来表示祝贺、感谢、鼓励等。与日本、韩国等东方国家的外国友人见面时，可行鞠躬礼表达致意。鞠躬礼分为15°、30°和45°的不同形式，度数越高，向对方表达的敬意越深。另外还可能有拥抱礼、亲吻礼、吻手礼、合十礼等。

出行乘车应讲究礼仪，如果开的私家车的话，接送人时，一定要照顾周到。仅仅两人同车，你可以请他坐在司机旁边的位置，便于朋友之间的平等交流。你若坐车，可千万别单独坐到后面，会让别人觉得你当他是司机了。小轿车的座位，如有司机驾驶时，以后排右侧为首位，左侧次之，中间座位再次之，前座右侧殿后。如果是公家车接送你的话，可能表示你有一定的身份与地位。这时首先要等待别人帮你开关车门，上车一定要坐在后座上，特别是车上只有你与司机两人时，不要与司机平坐在前座，在车上尽量不要多说话。到达目的地时，下车后可以对司机说声"辛苦了，谢谢"。

安排西餐席次，应女士优先。在排定西餐座次时，主位请女主人就座，而男主人位居第二位。以右为尊。在排定座次时，以右为尊。面门为上：面对正门者为上座，背对正门者为下座。交叉排列：男女交叉排列，生人与熟人交叉排列。要学习正确使用西餐餐具，用餐时举止端庄、吃相文雅。嘴内有食物时，闭嘴咀嚼勿说话；喝汤忌啜，吃东西不发出声音；剔牙时，用手或餐巾遮口，嘴内的鱼刺、骨头不可直接外吐，用餐巾掩嘴取出，或轻轻吐在叉上，放在菜盘内；吃剩的菜、用过的餐具、牙签，都应放在盘内，勿放置在桌面上。忌喝酒过量、失言失态。中外饮酒习俗有差异，对外宾可以敬酒，不宜劝酒，尤其是不能劝女宾干杯。宴会进行中，如由于不慎意外情况发生，应妥善处理。

应邀出席重大的涉外政务、公务、商务活动或隆重的仪式活动，需服从礼宾次序安排。入座前，预先了解自己的桌次和座次。入座时注意桌上座位卡是否写着自己的名字，忌鲁莽或随意入座。在条件许可时应从座椅的左侧入座。入座时如遇邻座是身份高者、年长者、妇孺、残疾人士，应主动礼让或协助他们先坐下。

涉外赠送礼品要注意选择礼物。涉外交往的馈赠更多是为了表示对他人的祝贺、慰问、感谢的心意，因此在选择礼品时应挑选具有一定纪念意义、民族特色，或具有某些艺术价值，或为受礼人所喜爱的纪念品、食品、花束、书籍、画册、一般日用品等。事先了解收礼人的性格、爱好、修养，以及所在国的习俗等，因人而异。讲究礼品包装：国外非常讲究礼品包装，礼品一定要用彩色纸包装，然后用丝带系成漂亮的蝴蝶结或梅花结。要注重对等平衡。注意送礼双方身份的对等，双方身份和礼品规格要一致。送礼要讲究平衡，有多方外国友人在场的情况下尤其要注意，避免厚此薄彼。

涉外交往中应注意禁忌。各民族及不同宗教信仰的人们对数字均有一些忌讳，如信奉天主教、基督教的信徒十分忌讳"13"和"星期五"，认为这一数字和日期是厄运和灾难的象征。在涉外活动中要避开与"13""星期五"有关的一些事情，更不要在这一天安排重要的政务、公务、商务及社交活动。日本人忌讳4字，是因4字与死的读音相似，意味着倒霉和不幸，所以与日本友人互赠礼品时切记不送数字为4、谐音为4的礼品；不要安排日本人入住4号、14号、44号等房间。肢体禁忌方面，同一个手势、动作，在不同的国家里表示不同的意义，比如拇指和食指合成一个圈，其余三个手指向上立起，在美国表示Ok，但在巴西，这是不文明的手势。在中国，对某一件事、某一个人表示赞赏，会跷起大拇指，表示"真棒"。但是在伊朗，这个手势是对人的一种侮辱，不能随便使用，想赞赏伊朗人忌伸大拇指。

链接：涉外交往中的送花禁忌

不能送百合花给英国人和加拿大人，因为百合花在他们心目中象征着死亡，其他白色的花最好也不要送。

在瑞士不能送普通同事或朋友红玫瑰，因为在他们心中红玫瑰代表爱情，只能送给爱人。

不能送德国人郁金香，德国人视郁金香为"无感情之花"，如果送郁金香就代表朋友之间绝交。

不能送紫色花给巴西人，因为紫色在巴西是死亡的象征，紫色的花一般用在葬礼上。

不能送法国朋友黄色的花，因为法国人认为黄色象征着不忠诚。

在中国只有祭奠亲人的时候才用菊花，其他很多国家也是如此，在英国、法国、西班牙以及拉丁美洲等地，也不能送菊花，菊花象征着死亡。

第三章　律师尽职调查业务

"尽职调查"（Due Diligence）这一概念最早起源于英美法系的普通法，后被大陆法系采用，编入成文法中。"Due Diligence"的字面含义为"适当的或应有的谨慎"，有时还会将它翻译成审查评鉴、核查、审慎的查核、正当注意调查、相当注意义务等。伴随着中国经济的不断发展以及国际化进程的加快推进了企业并购重组、股票发行上市等交易的重大公司行为的产生，而律师在资本运作过程中发挥着重大的作用，主要是通过参与谈判、审查和起草相关合同、出具法律意见书等为委托人提供法律服务，而尽职调查是律师完成上述工作的基础和关键，且律师开展尽职调查是这一行为中必不可少的一部分。

第一节　尽职调查类别与尽职调查清单

根据尽职调查内容的不同，尽职调查在实务中通常分为法律尽职调查，财务尽职调查和管理尽职调查等。财务尽职调查一般是指调查主体对目标企业财务事项的调查，包括资产状况、负债状况、盈利状况、现金流量状况等与本次交易有关的事项，既包括既定事实的陈述，也包括基于事实的分析。法律尽职调查是调查主体对并购目标企业法律状况进行的调查，包括主体的工商登记、公司治理结构、公司的控股结构、公司的资质、公司知识产权的真实性、公司的守法状况等。管理尽职调查是调查主体对并购目标企业管理事务的尽职调查。

一　尽职调查的分类

尽职调查的概念起源于证券市场，证券市场的主要功能是连接广大投资者和上市公司，但是上市公司的信息并不为投资人所知晓，为了解决信息不对称的问题，尽职调查被引入证券市场。法律尽职调查是指就股票发行上市、收购兼并、重大资产转让等交易中的交易对象和交易事项的法律事项，委托人委托律师按照其专业准则，进行的审慎和适当的调查和分析。它包括律师对相关资料进行审查和法律评价，主要为查询目标公司的设立情况、存续状态以及其应承担的具有法律性质的责任，它由一系列持续的活动组成，不仅涉及公司信息的收集，还涉及律师如何利用其具有的专业知识去查实、分析和评价有关的信息。

（一）根据调查的执行主体分类

在经济交易活动中，交易双方都可以进行尽职调查。所以最常见的经济交易行为以并购交易为例，根据执行主体不同，可以将尽职调查分为买方尽职调查和卖方尽职调查。这两种尽职调查的区别除了执行主体不同以外，交易双方尽职调查的最终目的也不同。其目的不同之处在于：收购方主要为了了解并购的风险，借以制订防范风险的措施以及了解估计的价格；被收购方则侧重于了解自身企业的现状，由此自觉地有控制性地向收购方提交信息的进度、内容及形式，同时被收购方有时也会对自己的企业加以修饰，提高出售价格，作出对自身有利的举动，所以律师在风险应对上发挥着重大的作用。

（二）根据调查的时间分类

首先并不是所有的尽职调查都是在合同签订之前进行的。可以根据尽职调查开展的时间不同，将其分为缔约前的尽职调查和缔约后的尽职调查。这两类尽职调查的最大不同之处就是签订时间和执行时间不同。

缔约前的尽职调查主要是为了确定是否进行交易，包括交易的风险和交易的估计价格；而缔约后的尽职调查则主要是在初步确定进行交易的基础上，针对交易价格进行调整和变更。在并购实务中，有的收购方为了本公司的利益拒绝收购方进行尽职调查。但是这样做可能会使收购方担心风险过大，从而导致交易的失败或者不敢进行交易。即使想进行交易，也可能为了规避风险而尽量压低收购价格。另外，即使双方签订了保密协议，约定一方对尽职调查过程中获取的信息负有严格的保密义务，也会不经意地直接或者间接地利用它所调查到的信息，对另一方产生直接或者间接的负面影响。

缔约后的尽职调查主要体现在交易一方往往处于主动的意愿，但是又担心自己公司的信息会被披露，而最后没有交易成功。交易双方通常会事先达成约定：首先，意愿较强一方展示自身企业的情况，并对展示情况的真实性作出承诺和适当的担保，双方依此为基础签订初步收购协议。其次，合同签订后，另一方对公司的实际情况进行尽职调查，核实公司的实际情况是否与其说明与担保承诺一致，根据调查结果可以选择是否继续合作或者是调整协议的具体内容等。

（三）根据调查适用的领域分类

法律尽职调查可根据调查报告的使用目的，分为一般合同交易尽职调查、不动产购置尽职调查、应收账款转让（不良资产处置）尽职调查、企业股权并购尽职调查、债券发行尽职调查、股票上市尽职调查等。对于一些合同交易方，有时所进行的律师尽职调查是双向的，即买方对目标公司、交易对方、目标资产会进行尽职调查，而卖方也会基于充分了解买方资信的需要而对买方进行适当的尽职调查。

二 尽职调查清单

法律尽职调查主要由律师完成。律师进行尽职调查的目的主要是审核并确定被调查对象所提供相关资料的真实性、准确性和完整性，同时协助委托人充分地了解被调查对象的组织结构、资产和业务的产权状况及其法律状态；发现被调查对象的法律风险和问题，以及问题的性质和风险的程度，并给予委托方最根本利益的保护，使委托人尽可能地发现被调查对象及交易事项的全部情况，从而使委托方有效地作出判断且规避风险并作出决策。为了尽快高效地获得被调查对象的相关资料以完成尽职调查，通常在开展尽职调查工作时就要出具一份尽职调查清单，在取得被调查对象配合的基础上获得清单列明的资料。

链接：以下是一份受托为公开发行公司债券出具法律意见书而进行律师尽职调查时向发行人出具的一份律师尽职调查清单。

发行公司债券律师尽职调查清单

一、关于主体资格

1. 工商局打印的完整工商档案资料，包括公司设立文件、公司历次章程、董事会成员名单、监事会成员名单等。

2. 公司法人营业执照副本、组织机构代码证、税务登记证、房地产开发企业资质等相关资质文件、证照。

3. 公司现状与历史沿革介绍，包括公司成立背景、主营业务、员工情况、历次股份变更情况、受政府委托开展相关经营情况、中长期发展战略规划、未来三年的业务发展计划目标等相关文件。

4. 公司治理情况，组织机构图及相关部门职能的文件、三会议事规则、董事会专门委员会议事规则、总经理工作制度、内部审计制度等文件资料，公司2012—2015年工作报告（工作总结和工作计划等）。

5. 公司股东及控股、参股子公司的营业执照、公司章程、最近一年经审计的财务报告、经营情况简介等。

二、财务情况

6. 公司最近三年经审计的财务报告及最近一期的财务报表。

7. 公司已发行的公司债券、企业债券、中期票据、短期融资券等债务性融资工具的情况说明，包括但不限于发行募集情况、兑付及余额情况、是否存在延期支付本息等违约情形、是否存在改变募集资金投向之情形。

8. 公司债务明细表，包括债务类别、期限、利率、总金额、未偿还金额、担保方式等,公司负有的债务是否存在到期未清偿、延迟支付本息之情形,及其他违约行为。

9. 公司商业信用情况,包括贷款卡查询资料、企业信用报告、主要银行给予公司的授信额度、主要银行信用评级情况等。

10. 公司主营业务收入的构成及主要产品近三年的价格变动、销售情况,公司取得补贴收入、享受税收优惠政策等相关证明文件。

三、资产情况

11. 发行人所占有的全部国有资产的国有产权登记证,以及发行人取得该国有资产的有关文件,例如国有资产管理部门的批复、资产转让协议、股权转让协议、政府无偿划转的文件等。

12. 公司及控股、参股子公司在2012年至今持有土地使用权的情况,包括通过划拨、出让或受托整理储备等方式取得,需提供划拨决定文件、出让合同、整理储备的授权文件等相关文件,包括建设用地规划许可证、房地产权证等相关权利证明与现状文件。

13. 公司及控股子公司持有的房屋所有权证,或其他能够证明公司拥有该房屋所有权的相关文件(包括但不限于购房合同、竣工验收报告、法院判决书、仲裁裁决书等)及情况说明;属于公司自建房屋的,如果没有房屋所有权证书,则需要提供建设该房屋的立项批复、用地规划许可证、建设工程规划许可证、施工许可证、竣工验收报告等。

14. 与上述不动产及其相关附属设施之抵押有关的所有抵押合同、抵押登记证明和文件。

15. 商标、专利、非专利技术版权、特许经营权等无形资产的权属证明。

16. 资产是否存在被控股股东、其他关联方控制或占用情况的说明。

四、风险因素

17. 重大合同(包括已履行完毕但属于报告期内且对公司有重要影响的合同),与重大诉讼或仲裁事项相关的合同、协议,法律或仲裁机构受理的相关文件。

18. 所有对外担保(包括抵押、质押、保证等)的明细表及相关合同。

19. 公司及控股、参股子公司在2012年至今是否存在闲置土地、炒地以及捂盘惜售、哄抬房价等违法违规行为被行政主管部门调查、认定、处罚,如有请提供相关文件。

20. 是否存在其他违法或重大违规行为,是否收到过如税务、海关、环保等机构的处罚,如有请提供相应文件。

21. 是否存在金额超过公司净资产5%的现有或潜在的重大诉讼和仲裁,如有请提供相应文件,包括但不限于与重大诉讼或仲裁事项相关的合同、协议,法律或仲裁机构受理的相关文件、起诉状、答辩状、法院裁定判决、仲裁裁决等。

五、关于募集资金用途的证明文件

22. 募集资金用途的说明（可以募集说明书替代）。

23. 募集资金所投资项目的合法证明文件与实施进度，包括但不限于可行性研究报告、立项批复、环境影响报告书及批复、土地证、投资意向书、协议书、预售协议、拟投资项目存在的风险说明等。

六、信用增级资料

24. 涉及保证的，请提供担保方最新的营业执照，担保方出具的担保函、担保方经审计的最近一年审计报告及最近一期财务报告；涉及抵押的，请提供抵押人最新的营业执照、抵押物权属证明文件、抵押物评估报告、抵押协议等；涉及质押的，请提供出质人最新的营业执照、质押物权属证明文件、质押协议等；同时需担保方国资监管机构、股东大会、董事会等有权机构同意保证人出具担保函的相关文件。

25. 其他信用增级措施的相关资料。

七、税务

26. 公司目前适用的所有税种、税率说明及相关法律依据。

27. 公司所享有的所有现行有效的税收优惠及相关法律依据和批准文件。

28. 公司历史上所有有关税务争议、滞纳金缴纳、重大关税纠纷的详细情况及有关文件。

八、中介机构相关文件

29. 承销商营业执照，证券业务许可证复印件、近三年作为主承销商所承销企业债权的名录。

30. 审计机构的营业执照、证券业务许可证复印件。

31. 评级机构营业执照、相关从业资质复印件。

九、发行募集文件

32. 股东会、董事会关于发行公司债券的相关决议。

33. 国有资产监督管理部门或上级部门关于公司发行公司债券的批复文件。

34. 本次公司债券的发行公告、募集说明书及其摘要。

35. 承销协议及主承销商对本次公司债券的推荐意见。

36. 公司和本次债券信用评级报告。

十、其他

37. 公司提供资料真实、完整的承诺。

38. 公司认为对本次发行有重要影响需向律师提交的其他文件。

应当注意的是，不同的出具法律意见书的业务所进行的尽职调查的重点内容不同，相应地，尽职调查资料清单当然也不会一致。这些看似散漫的清单内容，其中每一项都应该有其充分的法律法规或行业准则作为依据。以上述《发行公司债券律师尽职调查清单》为例,第6条提及要求提供"公司最近三年经审计的财务报告及最近一期的财务报表",这是和《公司债券发行与交易管理办法》(中国证券监督管理委员会令第113号)第十七条规定的"存在下列情形之一的,不得公开发行公司债券:(一)最近三十六个月内公司财务会计文件存在虚假记载,或公司存在其他重大违法行为;……"及第十八条"资信状况符合以下标准的公司债券可以向公众投资者公开发行,也可以自主选择仅面向合格投资者公开发行:(一)发行人最近三年无债务违约或者迟延支付本息的事实;(二)发行人最近三个会计年度实现的年均可分配利润不少于债券一年利息的1.5倍;……"的规定有关,即需要核查其近三十六个月内的公司财务状况。而对于非公开发行债券的情况,按照中国证券业协会《非公开发行公司债券项目承接负面清单指引》的规定,承销机构不得承接"最近两年内财务报表曾被注册会计师出具否定意见或者无法表示意见审计报告的发行人"的非公开发行债券项目,则对于非公开发行债券项目,可以仅要求提供最近两年的财务报表。类似的情况还发生在为成为信托公司的股东出具法律意见书的情况,要求委托人提供的财务报表需涉及此前的两个会计年度,因为《中国银行业监督管理委员会非银行金融机构行政许可事项实施办法》第七条规定"境内非金融机构作为信托公司出资人,应当具备以下条件:……(五)财务状况良好,且最近2个会计年度连续盈利;……"。故,尽职调查清单的要求要严格与出具法律意见书需审核的内容相对照,做到索之有据,才能获得委托人的全力配合,便于尽职调查工作的顺利开展。

第二节 尽职调查报告与法律意见书的出具

一 尽职调查报告的准备工作

(一)审阅由被调查公司提供的资料

律师可以通过被调查公司提供的文件和资料来获取尽职调查所需要的信息,获取该部分文件的方式是向被调查公司发尽职调查问卷清单,并要求对方按照尽职调查问卷清单的要求提供相关文件和资料等。

(二)现场访谈

可以由法律尽职调查小组人员与被调查公司的相关人员进行现场谈话,尽职调查小组人员提问题,被调查公司的相关人员回答问题。现场访谈作为审阅书面文件资料的补充,有助于了解事实全貌。在企业法务看来,应该是最重要的一种尽职调查方式之一。

(三) 对尽职调查对象进行实地考察与核实

上述表达的律师开展尽职调查方法往往会存在漏洞，且书面文件只能代表被调查对象的基本情况和历史情况，所以就需要律师本着对委托方负责的心态进行实地考察和核实，这样才有助于了解被调查对象的现状和实际情况。此外，对被调查对象的实地考察还有助于核实交易对方介绍的情况以及提供的文件资料是否完整准确，是否存在隐瞒和遗漏。

(四) 网络信息和其他来源

尽职调查也可以通过互联网来开展，且互联网上的信息是公开、免费的，通过查询，可以获悉相关公司的公开信息，这部分信息能促进我们从不同角度加深对被调查对象的了解，印证尽职调查中获取的信息的真实性、准确性和完整性并进一步发现其公司可能存在的法律问题等。

二 尽职调查报告的主要内容

因不同的业务需求，形成的尽职调查报告的内容与侧重点不尽相同，以企业并购所需用于尽职调查报告为例，主要涉及的内容包括以下几个方面。

(一) 目标公司的主体资格

交易主体的合法性是我国企业并购中常见的问题，也是最基本的问题。所以对目标公司主题的合法性的调查主要有两个。一是其法人资格，即目标公司是否依法成立并合法存续，包括其成立、注册登记、股东登记、股东情况、注册资本缴纳情况、年检、公司变更、有无吊销或注销等，这些情况一方面要由委托人或目标公司配合提供，另一方面，也要通过公司登记注册机构进行进一步的核验。二是其经营资格，即是否具备从事营业执照所确立的特定行业或经营项目的特定资质，如建筑资质、房地产资质、金融牌照资格等，特别是对于有些重要的经营资质，要核实其在资质管理部门的状况，是否存在因违规被吊销或部分经营范围受限的情况。

(二) 目标企业的资产情况

物权和产权存在较为混乱的状况，有可能会导致交易完成后才发现其在法律上并不拥有某项财产的所有权，或者是其所有权还存在争议。所以需要通过调查获取相关证据确认所涉及的产权关系，确认并核实目标企业各项资产的权利状况、权利是否有瑕疵，对于有权属登记的房地产项目，要核实其不动产权属登记的情况，尚未登记仅取得土地出让合同或划拨决定书的，要向土地行政管理部门进行真实性的核实，直到对产权归属作出权属认定。在业内，曾有房地产公司收购业务中委托律师进行了尽职调查，律师经调查确认房地产项目确在合作的对方公司名下，然而最终证实该公司仅有一份失效的规划文件，项目已然转让给他人，致使委托人被骗。

(三) 目标公司的债权债务以及重大诉讼仲裁问题

律师对目标公司的债权债务调查应特别关注目标公司对外担保的风险、应收账款的诉讼时效和实现的可能性，加上目标公司的诉讼、仲裁或行政处罚是否存在尚未了结的或可预见的重大诉讼、仲裁及行政处罚案件，以及由此可能产生的赔偿责任及诉讼费用等。尤其是目标公司存在尚未了结的或可预见的重大诉讼、仲裁及行政处罚案件等，会造成因遗漏而增加的隐形收购成本。

(四) 目标公司的重要交易合同问题

公司的重要交易合同，包括长期购买或供应合同、技术许可合同、贷款合同、担保合同、代理合同、关联交易合同等。律师对这些合同进行尽职调查，目的在于确定交易完成后是否影响合同中规定的预期利益，确定这些合同中权利义务是否平衡，目标公司是否处于重大不利的情形中。

(五) 目标公司的人力资源问题

公司的人力资源状况也是律师尽职调查的主要内容之一。特别是在国有企业的并购中，能否处理好职工安置问题会对收购业务的成功与否产生重要影响。要审查本次交易对雇用人员有无影响，是否有相应的应对和激励措施，因为在当前社会保障机制不完善的情况下，对于下岗人员的安置，处理不好就会引起一系列矛盾或者是会产生额外的交易成本，甚至遭到政府的干预，所以应该多加注意是否存在对此次交易造成障碍的劳动合同，以及解除劳动合同所付出的代价。特别是如果存在企业并购导致大量工人失业的情况，往往职工安置方案需要经过职工代表大会的通过，这需要提前做好充分的沟通，在尽职调查中核实好相关处理方案的可行性，以便在尽职调查报告中准确反映。

(六) 目标公司进行本次交易行为的合法性问题

公司进行交易行为时可能会不履行特定的程序，比如主管机关的审批、公司相关机构的批准等。还有目标公司进行交易时是否有法律上的限制，这都需要律师开展尽职调查来进行风险的规避。

链接：以下是一份典型的企业并购尽职调查报告的部分构成。

Table of Contents（调查报告目录）

Ⅰ. Introductory Remarks（项目简要评论）

1　Background（背景）

2　Scope（报告范围）

3　Source of Information（信息来源）

Ⅱ. Executive Summary（行动决策小结）

1　Overview（项目概况）

2　Legal Form（并购或者投资法律形式）

3　The Plan（目标公司规划，如上市，或者扩大经营等）

4　Loans and Guarantees（贷款和担保）

5　Environmental Compliance（环保合规）

6　Employment（劳动雇工）

7　Intellectual Property Rights（知识产权）

Ⅲ．Review and Analysis（评论分析）

1　Corporate Status（目标公司）

1.1　Legal Form（目标公司设立法律形式）

1.2　Company History（目标公司历史沿革）

1.3　Registered Capital and Shareholding Structure（当前目标公司注册资本和股东结构）

1.4　Articles of Association and Promoters Agreement（目标公司章程和发起人协议）

1.5　Corporate Governance（目标公司治理结构）

2　Shareholders and Affiliates（目标公司股东）

2.1　Shareholders（股东）

2.2　The Group（集团公司）

2.3　Other Shareholders（其他股东）

3　Material Contracts（目标公司重大合同）

3.1　Overview（概况）

3.2　Supplier Contracts（供应合同）

3.3　Sales or Leases Contracts（销售或者租赁合同）

3.4　Connected Party Transactions（关联交易合同）

3.5　Loans Contracts and Guarantees（贷款合同和担保合同）

3.6　Other Material Contracts（其他重大合同）

4　Real Property（房地产）

4.1　Land Use Right（土地使用权）

4.2　Buildings（建筑）

4.3　Mortgage Status（房地产抵押）

5　Business Assets（经营资产）

5.1　Production Equipment（生产设备）

5.2　Vehicles（车辆）

5.3　Other Fixed Assets（其他固定资产）

6　Intellectual Property Rights（知识产权）

6.1　Trademarks（商标）

6.2　Technology（技术，包括专利）

6.3　Copyright（版权）

7　Human Resources and Employment（人力资源和劳动雇用）

7.1　Employees（雇员）

7.2　Labour Contract（劳动合同）

7.3　Social Contribution（社会保障）

7.4　Trade Union（工会）

8　Environmental Protection（环境保护）

8.1　Pollutant Discharge Permit（排污许可证）

8.2　Waste Water Treatment Plan（废水处理）

9　Litigation（诉讼披露）

一份普通的尽职调查报告会有几十页甚至上百页的内容，但很多内容是附件材料，这些材料是在撰写过程中根据尽职调查清单从目标公司或者相关机构收集到的资料。当然在获得这些资料并进一步要求补充的基础上，还应当带着相关文件和问题到目标公司进行实地询问和考察，进行目标公司管理人员的访谈，并形成尽职调查报告的底稿。在工作底稿的基础上，再进行尽职调查报告的撰写。各构成部分的写法可以先阐述总结目标公司提供的相关资料情况，再叙述律师开展的核查验证工作所获得的结果，再进行简短的法律评价或给出风险提示方面的律师建议。例如，对一个目标企业的劳动用工情况部分，尽职调查报告的内容可以按照如下叙述方式展开。

（七）目标公司的劳动用工

1. 目标公司的劳动用工情况。

经本所律师询证并由目标公司出具书面确认，目标公司目前签订有劳动合同或劳动合同已到期但仍在职的职工为171名；为226名职工缴纳了养老保险、失业保险和工伤保险。

经本所律师询证并由目标公司出具书面确认，目标公司未设置任何员工持股计划、期权计划或其他特殊的员工养老福利制度或计划。

2. 法律评价。

本所律师提请贵公司注意：如果本次收购为股权收购，收购完成后，贵公司将接收目标公司原有的所有签订劳动合同的职工，继续履行合同期未满的劳动合同。

三　法律意见书的出具

法律意见书是律师事务所对聘请人或咨询者的有关重大法律事务所提出的具有准

确法律依据的法律建议性的综合法律文书。律师在担任公司、法人、其他经济组织或政府的法律顾问,解答有关法律咨询时,对于重大的法律事务,或重大的经营决策行为,往往要以法律意见书的形式作出答复,为聘请人或咨询者所要从事的重要经济活动、重大的经营决策行为和重大的法律事务寻求法律依据,提出法律建议或作出法律性的解释。

律师以出具法律意见书的方式解答法律询问,应当注意为咨询者提出的法律问题作出准确、肯定、有法律依据的回答,为咨询者的决策提供具体、明确、可靠的参考意见。法律意见书可以是对诉讼案件的分析性法律意见,也可以是非诉讼事务的专项法律意见。非诉讼事务专项法律意见书通常是针对当事人委托的专项法律行为、法律事实或有法律意义的文书,依照现行法律进行审查或修改,提出综合性的法律意见。

随着法律意识的加强,各类商事行为中需要律师出具法律意见书的领域越来越多。在国有资产管理领域,国资委 2003 年 7 月 11 日发布的《关于贯彻落实〈企业国有资产监督管理暂行条例〉进一步加强企业法制建设有关问题的通知》中,明确要求:"今后,各中央企业向我委报送涉及企业改制、改组、重大投融资方案,以及要求我委出面协调有关法律问题的报告和请示,应经过本企业法律顾问专门论证,并书面提出法律建议和意见。"2004 年《企业国有产权转让管理暂行办法》规定了国有资产监督管理机构在决定或者批准企业国有产权转让行为上,应当审查律师事务所出具的法律意见书。在证券法律业务领域,按照 2007 年《律师事务所从事证券法律业务管理办法》(中国证券监督管理委员会、中华人民共和国司法部令第 41 号)的规定,律师事务所可以"首次公开发行股票及上市""上市公司发行证券及上市"等 10 类事项出具法律意见书。在很多大型公司的重大决策事项中,由律师事务所出具法律意见书几乎成为普遍要求。

(一)法律意见书出具中的事实查验

出具法律意见书,应首先对法律意见书所涉法律事务相关的事实进行尽职调查和审慎查验,然后对受托事项的合法性进行专业分析和审慎判断,之后出具法律意见,并留存工作底稿。以 2011 年实施的中国证监会会同司法部联合发布的《律师事务所证券法律业务执业规则(试行)》为例,明确要求律师在出具法律意见书业务中,对于收集证据材料等事项,应当亲自办理,不得交由委托人代为办理;使用委托人提供材料的,应当对其内容、性质和效力等进行必要的查验、分析和判断。具体查验工作程序与查验方法包括如下。

1. 查验计划的编制与落实。律师事务所及其指派的律师应当编制查验计划。查验计划应当列明需要查验的具体事项、查验工作程序、查验方法等。查验工作结束后,律师事务所及其指派的律师应当对查验计划的落实情况进行评估和总结;查验计划未完全落实的,应当说明原因或者采取其他的查验措施。律师应当合理、充分地运用查验方法。在有关查验方法不能实现验证目的时,应当对相关情况进行评判,以确定是否采取替代的查验方法。

2. 查验方式及其实施要求。这包括:①查验书面凭证。待查验事项只需书面凭证便可证明的,在无法获得凭证原件加以对照查验的情况下,律师应当采用查询、复核等方式予以确认;待查验事项没有书面凭证或者仅有书面凭证不足以证明的,律师应当采用实地调查、面谈等方式进行查验。②向有关机构查证。律师进行查验,向有关国家机关、具有管理公共事务职能的组织、会计师事务所、资信评级机构、公证机构等查证、确认有关事实的,应当将查证、确认工作情况做成书面记录,并由经办律师签名。③面谈查验。律师采用面谈方式进行查验的,应当制作面谈笔录。谈话对象和律师应当在笔录上签名。谈话对象拒绝签名的,应当在笔录中注明。④书面审查查验。律师采用书面审查方式进行查验的,应当分析相关书面信息的可靠性,对文件记载的事实内容进行审查,并对其法律性质、后果进行分析判断。⑤实地调查查验。律师采用实地调查方式进行查验的,应当将实地调查情况作成笔录,由调查律师、被调查事项相关的自然人或者单位负责人签名。该自然人或者单位负责人拒绝签名的,应当在笔录中注明。⑥查询方式的查验。律师采用查询方式进行查验的,应当核查公告、网页或者其他载体相关信息,并就查询的信息内容、时间、地点、载体等有关事项制作查询笔录。⑦函证方式的查验。律师采用函证方式进行查验的,应当以挂号信函或者特快专递的形式寄出,邮件回执、查询信函底稿和对方回函应当由经办律师签名。函证对方未签署回执、未予签收或者在函证规定的最后期限届满时未回复的,由经办律师对相关情况作出书面说明。⑧其他补充方式。除本规则规定的查验方法之外,律师可以按照《管理办法》的规定,根据需要采用其他合理手段,以获取适当的证据材料,对被查验事项作出认定和判断。

3. 重要法律事项的查验工作要求。这涉及:①律师查验法人或者其分支机构有关主体资格以及业务经营资格的,应当就相关主管机关颁发的批准文件、营业执照、业务经营许可证及其他证照的原件进行查验。对上述原件的真实性、合法性存在疑问的,应当依法向该法人的设立登记机关、其他有关许可证颁发机关及相关登记机关进行查证、确认。②对自然人有关资格或者一定期限内职业经历的查验,律师应当向其在相关期间工作过的单位人事等部门进行查询、函证。③对不动产、知识产权等依法需要登记的财产的查验,律师应当取得登记机关制作的财产权利证书原件,必要时应当采取适当方式,就该财产权利证书的真实性以及是否存在权利纠纷等,向该财产的登记机关进行查证、确认。④对生产经营设备、大宗产品或者重要原材料的查验,律师应当查验其购买合同和发票原件。购买合同和发票原件已经遗失的,应当由财产权利人或者其代表签字确认,并在工作底稿中注明;相关供应商尚存在的,应当向供应商进行查询和函证。必要时，应当进行现场查验，制作现场查验笔录，并由财产权利人或者其代表签字；财产权利人或者其代表拒绝签字的，应当在查验笔录中注明。⑤对依法需要评估才能确定财产价值的财产的查验，律师应当取得有证券、期货相关业务评估资格的资产评估机构（以下简称有资格的评估机构）出具的有效评估文书；未进行有效评估的，应当要求委托人委托有资格的评估机构出具有效评估文书予以确认。⑥对银行存款的查验，律师应当查验银行出具的存款证明原件；不能提供委托查验期银行存款证明的，应当会同委托人（存款人）向委托人的开户银行进行书面查询、函证。⑦对财产的查验，难以确定其是否存在被设定担保等权利负担的，律师应当以适当方式向有关财产抵押、质押登记部门进行查证、确认。⑧对委托人是否存在对外重大担保事项的查验，律师应当与委托人的财务负责人等相关人员及委托人聘请的会计师事务所的会计师面谈，并根据需要向该委托人的开户银行、公司登记机关、证券登记机构和委托人不动产、知识产权的登记部门等进行查证、确认。⑨向银行进行查证、确认，采取查询、函证等方式；向财产登记部门进行查证、确认，采取查询、函证或者查阅登记机关公告、网站等方式。⑩对有关自然人或者法人是否存在重大违法行为、是否受到有关部门调查、是否受到行政处罚或者刑事处罚、是否存在重大诉讼或者仲裁等事实的查验，律师应当与有关自然人、法人的主要负责人及有关法人的合规管理等部门负责人进行面谈，并根据情况选取可能涉及的有关行政机关、司法机关、仲裁机构等公共机构进行查证、确认。⑪向有关公共机构查证、确认，可以采取查询、函证或者查阅其公告、网站等方式。⑫从不同来源获取的证据材料或者通过不同查验方式获取的证据材料，对同一事项所证明的结论不一致的，律师应当追加必要的程序，作进一步查证。

（二）法律意见书的内容

办理出具法律意见书业务，应当依据法律、行政法规和有关业务领域的规定，在查验相关材料和事实的基础上，以书面形式对受托事项的合法性发表明确、审慎的结论性意见。一般而言，法律意见书应当列明以下基本内容：①标题；②收件人；③法律依据；④声明事项；⑤法律意见书正文；⑥承办律师、律师事务所负责人签名及律师事务所盖章；⑦律师事务所地址；⑧法律意见书签署日期。法律意见书正文应当载明相关事实材料、查验原则、查验方式、查验内容、查验过程、查验结果、国家有关规定、结论性意见以及所涉及的必要文件资料等。法律意见书发表的所有结论性意见，都应当对所查验事项是否合法合规、是否真实有效给予明确说明，并应当对结论性意见进行充分论证、分析。尽管要求审慎核查和分析，但法律意见不得使用"基本符合""未发现"等含糊措辞。

链接：以下为某公司公开发行公司债券之法律意见书的目录内容。

声　明

正　文

一、发行人的主体资格

二、本次发行的批准和授权

三、本次发行的实质条件

四、发行人的对外投资和其他主要资产情况

五、金融租赁业务资质及业务合规性

六、其他应收款的合规性

七、本次发行的基本情况及发行条款

八、本次发行的《募集说明书》

九、《债券持有人会议规则》和《债券受托管理协议》

十、本次发行的相关机构

十一、发行人的税务情况

十二、发行人的环境保护情况

十三、发行人诉讼、仲裁或行政处罚

十四、需要说明的其他事项

结　论

链接：以下为某国有独资公司对其所持下属公司100%的股权进行公开挂牌转让事宜出具的法律意见书的结论意见。

本律师认为：出具本法律意见书时，本次国有产权转让方及目标企业均具有法律资格；本次国有产权转让拟转让的国有资产的权属清晰；《股权转让方案》的内容客观、全面、合法、有效；本次国有产权转让方案已得到合法审议及批准。根据《企业国有产权转让管理暂行办法》、天津市《关于加强产权交易管理若干问题的通知》等相关法规及规范性文件的规定，本次国有股权转让行为符合法律规定，在报经国有资产监督管理部门批准后，可在依法设立的产权交易机构进行公开交易。

第四章　律师规范文本格式

律师在执业活动中，需要不断地制作各种业务文书，以履行律师职责，实现与当事人的沟通，解决法律问题。这些书面形式的业务文书，会成为律师所提供法律服务过程和内容的载体。一份内容严谨、结构规整、制作精良的律师业务文书，可以彰显律师良好的职业形象和勤勉的工作作风。为此，律师需要规范业务文书的制作。

第一节　传真及对外文稿格式

一　律师业务文书的种类

根据使用目的和致送对象的不同，律师制作的具有特定法律意义的文件，可以大致分为四类。

（一）沟通信函类

沟通信函是指律师与客户、潜在客户、客户的对方通过致送信函的方式进行沟通所使用的业务文书。这包括律师向其认识的潜在客户寄送的业务推销信函，律师与客户之间就委托关系的确认、委托工作进展、律师费用收取等事宜的通信，律师给客户具体法律业务出具的情况沟通函、联络函、法律文件审查建议、简单法律咨询的书面回复函件，律师受委托向对方当事人出具的主张权利、沟通法律争议处理方案等事宜的函件（这一类型文件如涉及有关纠纷的解决，通常被赋予律师函的形式），律师帮助当事人进行投诉、申诉等写给某些部门的信函。这些函件有一定的接收人，同时提出往往有一定的诉求和明确的沟通目标，并进行落款。

（二）合同文案类

合同文案是指律师受客户委托为客户交易起草的意向书、协议书、合同书等，还包括在公司治理过程中需要的公司章程、公司基本管理制度文件、股东会决议、董事会决议、业务规则、管理办法等，也包括律师受托进行立法性规范法律文件的起草。

（三）诉讼文书类

诉讼文书包括各类诉状和法律案件中的答辩、辩护等业务文件，如民事起诉状、仲裁申请书、行政上诉状、再审申请书、答辩状、代理词、辩护词、质证意见等及诉讼中的各项申请（如调取证据申请、财产保全申请等）。这些文书是参与法律争议解决程序所需，是代表当事人提出或回应某项诉求、要求，致送给公检法机关、仲裁机构、劳动仲裁部门等。

（四）综合报告类

综合报告即律师从事参与调查所得出的结果，律师要写一个类似调查报告的文件，依据委托人要求，出具的法律意见书。还有根据律师专业知识，对各种证据搜集得出的结论，形成的律师意见。

二 传真首页样式

传真不失为一种有效的快捷的法律文书送达方式，但是现在电子邮件形式逐渐要取代传真。传真可靠性不如电子邮件。电子邮件的纪实性也很强，打印出来可以作为证据使用。电子邮件附件如果用 Microsoft Word 格式，你无法知道别人是否修改了原始内容，所以正式文书的电子存档和制作，国际上都是通用 PDF 格式，PDF 作为电子邮件附件传送，对方是没有办法修改的。

（一）传真时需要注意的事项

传真一个比较正式文件的时候，事务所都会在这个文件前面加一个首页，首页除了有律师事务所标志外，还要写明该传真是给谁、信息、传真号码，甚至说明后面所发传真有多少页。在写页数的时候要写清是否包括本页。

链接：以下是两个律师事务所的传真首页样式。

天津同海律师事务所
Tianjin Tonghai Law Firm

律师、商标及专利代理人事务所、破产管理人
天津市滨海新区大港学府路 60 号 BF212　电话：(86) 022 - 63259926
传真：(86) 022 - 63259926　网址：http://www.tjfsu.edu.cn/

合伙人：
（此处列出所有合伙人的名字）

收件人：	总页数：　　（包括本页）
收件机构：	电子邮箱：
日　　期：　年 月 日	收件人文号：
发件人：	直接电话：
	直线传真：

电邮本电邮为保密档且包含法定保密内容。除收件人外，不可予以复印或用于其它任何目的或向任何人披露其内容。如阁下非电邮所指定之收件人或收件机构，谨请立即通知本律师行。

传　真

日期：＿＿年＿＿月＿＿日	案件名称：＿＿＿＿＿＿＿
date：	Ref. No.：
发往：＿＿＿＿＿＿＿	收件人：＿＿＿＿＿＿＿
To：	Attn.：
传真号码：＿＿＿＿＿＿＿	传真页数（包括此页）＿＿＿＿＿＿
Your Fax No.：	Number of page(s) sent (including this page)：
发自：<u>天津同海律师事务所</u>	发传真人：＿＿＿＿＿＿＿
From：	Biography：
国际传真/城市：＿＿＿＿＿＿＿	国家：＿＿＿＿＿＿＿
Overseas Transmission/City：	Country：

　　此传真严格保密，如您无意收到，请您立即打电话（86）022－63259926 通知我们，并不要利用或公开文件内容。

　　This fax is strictly confidential. If you are not the intended, you should notify us immediately at (86) 022 – 63259926 and should not make use of or disclose its contents in any event.

（二）传真、专递并用

　　很重要的文件，包括法庭文件，在送达的时候，我们要考虑这个文件的原件要送到对方手里，同时又要求他第一时间知道，那么我们可以在文件交给快递公司或者专递人员的时候，先把它传真过去，这样他既能接收到原始文件，又能第一时间看到文件内容。

（三）业务文稿格式

　　当今网络信息时代，法律文书制作和它的传输、保存大量是依赖计算机来应用的，开始大量运用电子邮件。编辑文件时大多数使用 Microsoft Word 软件来做，制作完成了文书，通常需要打印，有时候需要保存成 PDF 格式，这种文件格式是现在全球使用非常广泛的储存法律文件的电子格式。

第二节　律师委托合同及业务函件

　　律师开展法律服务，需以接受客户委托为前提。按照《律师法》的相关规定，律师不得私自接受委托，所以律师须以律师事务所的名义接受委托，由客户与律师事务所签署委托合同，并进一步向律师事务所出具授权委托书，明确律师的代理权限或法律服务内容，在此基础上，律师再开展各项工作。律师开展法律服务工作的主要形式是撰写出具法律文件，包括非诉讼类的法律文件和诉讼类法律文书。这些法律文件中的一个重要类型就是沟通信函类的业务函件。

一　律师委托合同

客户与律师事务所之间所签署的委托合同，一般是由律师事务所提供范本，明确双方的权利义务。实务中，律师事务所有时会与客户之间达成一份常年法律顾问合同，将一切法律事务均交给律师事务所办理，然后根据双方商定的收费标准另行确定具体工作内容所应支付的律师费用。另外有些情况是客户会将某专项法律事务交给律师事务所处理，具体委托内容非常简略，通过会明确直到将该事务处理完毕。如果是一份债务相关的委托，律师可以根据这份委托代理客户进行债权催收，发送律师函，直至提起诉讼仲裁、申请法院执行等等。很多时候客户直到去法院起诉或收到法院传票需要上法庭时才会请律师，因此，为案件代理进行律师委托从而签署聘用合同的情况亦较为常见，双方会在委托合同中明确委托事项内容、律师代理权限、律师收取费用的标准和方式、委托期限等等。律师合同中律师会明确告知要求客户就案件情况提供真实资料，有时会要求客户签署一份诉讼风险告知书，以尽量避免客户对案件处理结果不满意而对律师服务的不满意的情况。

链接：以下是一份常见的诉讼案件接受委托时由律师事务所提供给客户要求其签字确认的诉讼风险告知书的样本。

诉讼风险告知书

尊敬的委托人：

天津同海律师事务所在与委托人签订委托代理合同之时，为维护委托人的合法权益，提高对律师服务的认识，根据《律师法》以及相关法律法规的规定，特向委托人告知诉讼可能存在的风险，请委托人仔细阅读，如果委托人确认接受这些风险并继续办理委托，请签名确认！

一、诉讼并非解决社会纠纷的唯一方式，而是一种较高成本的纠纷解决方式。草率地选择发动诉讼，就会承担负担诉讼成本的风险，慎重地选择发动诉讼，可以减少风险的发生。

二、任何诉讼或仲裁均存在败诉或部分败诉的风险，这取决于双方围绕事实进行的举证、法庭或仲裁庭对证据的采信和由此查明的事实；也取决于法律规定、法庭或仲裁庭对法律的理解和运用。

三、代理人在办理委托事务或者案件过程中，提供的是法律服务；律师的代理工作是运用法律武器维护当事人的合法权益，而不是包打官司。

四、代理人在办理案件过程中，可以对法院、仲裁庭可能认定的案件事实和案件处理结果进行合理分析或推测，并告知委托人，但上述分析或推测不是代理人对案件结果的承诺。

五、当事人在办理委托前应当仔细阅读风险告知书，代理委托一旦签订后，案件经法院判决或者仲裁庭裁决后，或者在诉讼中和解、调解，或者当事人自行撤诉，代理工作即告结束，所收取的代理费不予退还。

六、法院审理案件虽有确定的审理期限，但该期限会由于难以送达、需要鉴定等情况而延长，当事人应该知道通过诉讼解决纠纷会有一段较长的时间。

七、代理人申明：

1. 代理人不通过违法、违规的方式办理法律事务。

2. 代理人承诺在委托合同签订后尽力为当事人提供法律服务，但不承诺也不保证所承办的法律事务一定成功。

3. 代理人不同意也不建议委托人采取非正当方式谋求该项法律事务的成功，委托人所采取的非正当方式由委托人承担全部后果。

4. 代理人为委托人起草的各种法律文书，委托人一经签署，视为委托人已经完全明白其中含义，所有法律后果由委托人承担。

八、本风险告知书一经委托人签署，即为委托合同的组成部分，与委托合同、委托书具有同等法律效力。

委托人确认：承办律师已经告知我方上述事项，我方已经完全了解告知书所提示的内容。

委托人签字
年　月　日

客户和律师事务所签订了委托代理合同后，客户还须向具体承办的律师出具授权委托书，作为提交给法院担任诉讼代理人的授权委托材料，在需要向第三方致送律师函的情况下，往往也随律师函会附送一份授权委托书，用以证明律师出具律师函是有有效授权的。授权委托书没有太多内容，主要是为了明确代理律师的代理权限。需要注意的是，有的授权书授予的是"一般代理"，有些授权书授予的是"全权"，这里的"全权"可以指在当事人不在场的情况下为其办理事务，其后果当事人均予以认可。但在中国法律背景下，在一般案件的诉讼仲裁代理中，仅写明"全权"是不规范的，如果拟授予律师更多的权限，应以"特别授权"的方式写明具体授权的内容，例如可以为："代为承认、变更、放弃诉讼请求，代为和解、调解，代为上诉，代为签收法律文书等特别授权。"在执行案件中，特别授权的代理权限表述可能会略不同，例如可以写为"代理权限为：特别授权代理（代为申请执行，提出、变更、放弃执行请求，进行和解，签收法律文书，收受执行款项等）"。

二　律师函

这里讲的律师函是狭义的概念，是指律师代表委托人签发的，带有警告和督促对方履行特定义务内容的函件。

律师函要具备的内容主要包括：①阐明事态。在一份律师函里头，必须让对方清楚真实的事态，不夸大也不缩小。律师函中所描述的事实，必须是经过核实的，律师要言之有据，至少是看过或者了解这样的事实，再或者有这样的资料，能够表示出律师函中叙述的事实是言之有据的。不能委托人告诉什么就写什么，如果内容没有根据，对方可能会告律师诽谤。律师在律师函中叙述的事实，要做必要的核查，如果无法核实的，可以写"据我委托人讲"等话语，避免以后因为没核实而出现的纷争。因此，一份严谨的律师函的制作，不亚于向法院提出起诉撰写的诉状，律师需要审查全部的证据材料形成事实概括，以保障言之有据。②提出主张。律师函要不露声色地告知对方你的主张。律师函中提出要求履行特定义务的时候，要求必须要很明确，不能模棱两可，也不能含糊其词。③告知后果。这个很关键，没有法律责任的法律是没有力量的，没有告知后果的律师函就像温开水。律师函要以体面、礼貌的形式来施加影响，而不是采用威胁、粗俗的语言，避免使用带有人身攻击、谩骂的语言或贬义的词语。当然这个告知的表述有很多种，有彬彬有礼型的，比如说"我方不排除采取诉讼的可能性"，有温文尔雅型的，比如说，"我方保留通过法律途径对贵方进行追索的权利"，有针锋相对型的，比如，"我方已经准备向贵方提出反诉以保障我方的权益"等。当然，各种表述各有好处，关键要达到想要的效果。

律师函起草完，得到客户确认后，承办律师签字（或盖承办律师的私章）和加盖律师事务所公章才生效。有些律师在出具律师函的时候，只签字或只盖律师私章，而不加盖律师事务所公章，这种做法是不规范的。律师须以律师事务所的名义承接业务，所以一定要加盖律师事务所公章，而且还得加盖律师事务所骑缝章，如果没有专门的骑缝章，用公章代替骑缝章也可以。律师函要由律师来寄，以显示律师函的严肃性。为了确保对方能及时收到律师函，律师函最好用邮局特快专递（EMS）来寄送，因为有的政府机关单位收发室只收中国邮政 EMS 的邮件，因此最好也不要用其他快递公司的快递寄送。律师函发出去以后，对方没有回复，或有回复但没有达到预期的效果。这时候就得跟客户沟通是否有必要采取进一步行动，实施制裁措施。一般律师函在"律师意见"部分都会要求对方在"指定的时间内，做出相应的行为，否则实施相应制裁措施"的字样。

从内容和格式上看，律师函可以分为抬头、首部、主体、尾部和脚部五部分。其中，抬头和脚部主要是使用律师事务所统一格式，没有太多技巧。

首部的格式同一般的公文写作一致或大同小异。即第一行留空，第二行写律师函件标题；第三行写发函号，一般由发函律所代字、年份和序号组成。另外还要注意送达对象一定要写全称而不能写简称。

律师函的正文一般分为四个部分：委托来源、事实概要、法条引用和律师评述、威胁性的要求或意见。

第一部分委托来源，这部分主要讲述的是委托人、受委托律师事务所、受指派的律师及委托事项。基本陈述方式如下：××律师事务所（以下简称"本所"）依法接受××（以下简称"××"）的委托，指派×××律师（以下简称"本律师"）出具本律师函。这部分常见的错误是律师往往以自己的名义向送达对象发函，这是不符合我国律师执业规范中关于由律师事务所名义统一接受委托要求和办理业务的要求的。

第二部分事实概要，这一部分不需要像法律意见书一样详细展开，只需以委托人提交的材料和委托人的陈述为基础，扼要地将事实和争议焦点总结出来即可。这是因为律师函最主要的作用是"宣示"而非"分析"，如果详加分析则显得喧宾夺主了。

第三部分法条引用和律师评述，这一部分目的是说服对方，因此要明确引用法律依据，结合事实进行评析，最后得出双方在法律上应有的权利义务。当然要根据具体情况而定，此部分写或者不写。

第四部分威胁性的要求或意见，要以专业语气告知对方，要求其在"规定期限完成规定事宜"。在提出要求的基础上进一步"威胁"，若对方不按照要求办理，将面临不利状况和后果，例如承担相关费用或损失等，强化律师函的威严性和委托人的立场。要注意这部分威胁性内容必须留有余地，用词坚定但不能过急，不应过度恶化双方关系而打消对方提出和解的积极性，更不能把本部分内容夸大，变成非法的威胁恐吓。

律师函的尾部由律所盖章、律师签名、签署日期和联系方式共四部分组成。前三部分一律右侧顶格书写，其中律师签名应该手签，下面用印刷体标注上律师姓名。签署日期为避免书写潦草，应该尽量打印事务所和签发律师的全名。最后一行注明律师的联系方式，方便对方与律师及时联系。

链接：一份简单的催款律师函

律师函　　天津同海律师事务所

地址：天津市滨海新区大港学府路60号　　邮编：300270
电话：86 - 22 - 63259926　　传真：86 - 22 - 63259926

_____公司：

　　天津同海律师事务所已接受_____的委托，并指派_____律师、_____律师全权负责处理你方拖欠_____货款一事。

　　本律师审核了_____提供的《_____合同》以及相关的材料，并经委托方确认，截止到今日，你方仍欠委托方货款_____元，本律师特发函予以催告。

此前，委托方_____多次发出通知，要求你方支付该笔货款，而你方至今仍未办理。你方无故长期拖欠货款的行为已经严重影响了我方委托人的正常经营，损害了委托人的合法权益。

鉴于以上事实，本律师特此函告：我方限你方在接函后三天内向_____交清欠款，否则我所将采取诉讼方式来保护委托方的合法权益，由此产生的一切经济损失和法律责任将全部由你方承担。

特此函告。

天津同海律师事务所
律师：　　　律师：
年　月　日

附律师联系方式：

第五章 英文合同制作

合同的草拟与审查修订是律师非诉讼业务的重要工作内容。中国执业律师开展涉外律师业务,除代理外国客户在中国诉讼外,大部分工作是处理涉外非诉讼法律业务,对中外双方开展合同交易谈判提供法律咨询服务。因此,涉外律师从业者应掌握较扎实的合同法,包括英美合同法的基础理论,并具备进行英文合同制作的能力。为此,需要对英文合同的结构安排、典型的英文合同条款、常用的英文合同文本有较好的掌握。

第一节 合同结构安排

《中华人民共和国合同法》第二条规定:"合同是平等主体的自然人、法人、其他组织之间设立、变更、终止民事权利义务关系的协议。"在涉外经贸往来中,有关各方之间在进行某种商务合作时,为了确定各自的权利和义务,通常会正式依法订立的必须共同遵守的协议条文。一般来说,合同由前言(Preamble)、正文(Main Body)和结尾(Final Clauses)三个主要部分组成。前言即合同总则,其主要内容有:具有法人资格的当事人的名称(字号)或姓名、国籍、业务范围、法定住址、合同签订日期和地点、就感兴趣问题的约因、愿意达成协议的原则等。正文是合同或协议的主体,由法律条款所组成,明确规定当事人各方的权利、义务、责任和风险等;由各类实质性的条款组成。按照合同法的一般原理,这一部分的主要内容应至少包括三部分内容,即合同货物或称合同内容、价格、数量。只有具备了货物及价格这三项要素的合同才是内容确定的。合同货物或合同内容是合同的核心。起草者应该对货物名称、质量、标准、规格、数量、交货日期和地点在合同内写得确切无误。其中,质量和数量是合同的最重要条款。合同的结尾亦称合同的最后条款,其主要内容包括合同生效、合同使用文字、补充条文及额外协议等。

链接：一份旧设备销售协议

Used Equipment Sales Agreement
旧设备销售协议

Party A（Seller）：

甲方：

Party B（Buyer）：

乙方：

Party B desires to buy, and Party A is willing to sell to Party B the materials and used equipments ("Used Equipments") listed in annex 1. The Parties therefore entered into the following agreements on 2010：

第 1 条　旧设备描述

Article 1　Description of the Used Equipments

旧设备包括原料、零部件和设备。其详情细述于附件 1

The Used Equipments include raw materials, parts and equipments. Details of the Used Equipment are described in Annex 1.

第 2 条　价款

Article 2　Sales Price

售价总金额：人民币_____元（¥_____）

Sales Price：RMB _____（rmb _____）

第 3 条　交货

Article 3　Delivery

甲方负责将旧设备运至乙方指定的地点或车船，并承担相关费用。

Party A is responsible for deliver, at its own expense, the Used Equipment to the place or vehicle/vessel designated by Party B.

第 4 条　支付条款

Article 4　Terms of Payment

乙方应于收到旧设备后的三个月内，向甲方全额支付货款。

Party A shall make full payment of the Sales Price (described in Article 2) to Party A within 3 months after receiving the Used Equipment.

第 5 条　产权与风险转移

Article 5　Title and Risk of Loss

旧设备的产权与灭失及损毁风险在甲方将旧设备运至乙方指定的地点或车船后转移至乙方。

Title to and risk of loss or damage to all Used Equipment purchased by Party B will pass to Party B upon Party delivered the Used Equipment to the place or vehicle or vessel designated by Party B.

第 6 条 声明与保证

Article 6　Representations and Warranties

各方向对方保证：（1）本公司依法成立、具有合法资格签署并履行本协议；（2）签字人为本公司的法定代表人或授权代表，有权代表本公司签署本协议，并使本公司按本协议的约定履行本协议。

Each Party represents and warrants to the other that: (1) it is a legally organized and existing entity, with the legal capacity and all necessary corporate authority to enter into and perform this Agreement; (2) the signatory is the legal representative or authorized legal representative, who has full authority to sign this Agreement so that the Party is bound by this Agreement.

另外，甲方还保证其为旧设备的合法所有者。

除上述陈述与保证外，甲方对旧设备的质量和性能不作任何保证。甲乙双方均同意本协议将出售的所有旧设备都是按其现状（不论其是否含有任何瑕疵）出售的。甲方对售出的旧设备所产生的任何直接、间接，或偶发损失不承担任何责任。

In addition, Party B also represents and warrants that it is legal owner of the Used Equipment.

Except for the above representations and warranties, Party A makes no representation or warranty, with respect to the used equipment. Both Parties agree that all Used Equipment to be sold under this Agreement is sold on an "AS IS" (no matter what kind of defect they may have) basis. Party A will have no liability with respect to the Used Equipment sold to Party B, including having no liability for indirect, incidental or consequential damages.

第 7 条 甲方的责任

Article 7　Party A's Liability

甲方对售出的旧设备的责任以退还货款为限。乙方理解并同意甲方对售出的旧设备所产生的任何直接、间接，或偶发损失不承担任何责任。

Party A's liability with respect to any Used Equipment sold to Party B will be limited to refunding payment made. Party B understands and agrees that in no event will Party A be liable for indirect, incidental or consequential damages.

第 8 条 转让

Article 8　Assignment

双方同意没有对方的同意任一方都不得将其在本协议中的权利义务转让给第三方。

Both Parties agree that neither party may assign any right or obligation in this Agreement without the written consent of the other party.

第 9 条 违约责任

Article 9 Liability for Breach

对本协议的任何条款的违背,构成违约。非违约一方有权要求损害赔偿。

Any violation of the provisions of this Agreement constitutes a breach. The Non-breaching Party is entitled to recover.

第 10 条 其他

Article 10 Miscellaneous

1. 本协议是双方达成的最终协议,取代双方先前的任何交谈、陈述、协议、安排或协议,无论是口头的还是书面的。

2. 本协议的附件是本协议的一部分,具有与本协议同样的效力。

3. 因本协议所发生或与本协议相关的争议,双方应协商解决,协商不成,应向中国国际经济贸易仲裁委员会提请仲裁,由该仲裁委员会按其现行规则仲裁。仲裁地为北京,仲裁裁决为终局裁决,对双方均有拘束力。

4. 本协议原件一式两份,每方各持一份。

(1) This Agreement is the final agreement the parties have reached. It supersedes all previous communications, representations, arrangements and agreements, either written or oral.

(2) The annex is part of this Agreement.

(3) Any dispute arising from or in connection with this Agreement shall be first resolved through consultation. If the Parties fail to find resolution through consultation, then each Party can submit the dispute to arbitration by the China International Economy and Trade Arbitration Commission ("CIETAC") in accordance with its then effective rules in Beijing. The arbitration award is final, binding on both Parties.

(4) This Agreement is made in two counterparts. Each Party holds one of them.

乙方确认理解其与甲方达成的上述协议。本协议于文首指明之日生效,对双方均有拘束力。

Party B recognizes and confirms that it understands the foregoing agreements. This Agreement becomes effective on the day first above written.

甲方代表: 乙方代表

Party A: **Party B:**

_____   _____

公章: 公章:

对于一次性交易的合同，整体的合同结构一般不会过于复杂，能解决交易流程和各方权利义务的安排即可。但是对于较为复杂的交易或长期合作的安排，除了交易方会制订可以反复适用的格式合同条款以外，往往会有一些合同结构上的安排。这主要包括：意向书+合同、订单+合同条款、专用条款+通用条款、母合同+子合同等结构安排。

一　意向书+合同

在很多情况下，双方当事人在签署正式的合同之前会先签署一份意向性文件，这份文件可以是意向书（Letter of Intent，常被简称为"LoI"），也可以是备忘录（Memorandum of Understanding，常被简称为"MoU"）还可以是框架协议（Framework Agreement），或原则协议（"Heads of Agreement"，常被简称为"HoA"，或者称为"Principle Agreement"）等。如果这类文件从内容的约束性上看，不具备完整的合同上的意义，许多内容属于留待签署正式合同时方可确定，或因内容上没有进一步明确而无法执行，则这类文件都可以称为"意向书"。但也不排除名为意向书的文件，其中某些条款被赋予了合同约束力，例如保密条款，因此成为需要遵行的合同或合同条款，违反者需承担违约责任。

如果商务谈判进行的顺利，在意向书以后双方会签署正式的合同。因为意向书本来就没有法律约束力，因此不需要考虑两者之间的效力问题。但是，既然是君子协定，之前同意的东西通常是应该遵守的（当然双方协议变更的除外），因此，在起草正式合同的时候还是需要参照意向书，看看内容上是否有冲突或者遗漏。特别应当注意的是，意向书可能是对前期沟通或谈判成果的初步概括，如果情势未发生变化而一方在后续谈判或达成正式合同时对意向书中认可的内容予以推翻，尽管不会因此而承担法律上的违约责任，但一定会给交易对方留下不诚信的印象。因此，对于不拟在合同中予以落实的内容，最好不要仅基于推进共同合作的目的在意向书中随意就涉及实体权利义务的内容作出明确表述，哪怕会在该意向书中另外写明：This LoI shall not be legally binding on the PARTIES 或者 This LoI shall have no legal binding force upon the PARTIES（本意向书对双方不具有法律约束力）。

一份正式的合同，往往会根据合同的标的进行充分的展开，相关内容会涵盖前期达成的意向书或框架协议。以下是一份中外合作经营合同的主要内容目录：

TABLE OF CONTENTS

1. Definitions

2. Parties of the Joint Venture

3. Representations and Warranties

4. Company

5. Purposes and Scope of Business

6. Total Investment and Registered Capital

7. Transfer of Equity

8. Responsibilities of the Parties

9. Board of Directors

10. Management Organization

11. Supervisors

12. Labour Management

13. Finance and Accounting

14. Costs and Fees

15. Put Option of Hbj

16. Insurance

17. Company Term

18. Termination and Dissolution

19. Confidentiality

20. Liability for Breach of Contract

21. Force Majeure

22. Applicable Law and Dispute Resolution

23. Miscellaneous

(Signature Page of Cooperative Joint Venture Contract)

SCHEDULES

1. Formula for Calculation of IRR

2. Summary of James Anti-Corruption Policy

3. Certain US Tax Provisions

4. List of Appraisers

二 订单+合同条款

订单+合同条款是另外一种非常受欢迎的合同结构，特别是在大的集团，非常喜欢预先订立一份标准合同条款，然后在日常业务中用简洁的订单说明此次具体采购或销售的需求内容，两者相结合形成一份较严谨的合同。

订单（Purchase Order，常被简称为"PO"）通常也会具有合同所必需的一些要素，比如，买卖双方的名称，货物或服务的描述，价格，交付时间等。按照中国合同法，订单如果经买卖双方签署是可以构成一份有效合同的。但是，有些订单会专门注明：This PURCHASE ORDER shall be subject to the terms and conditions of the SELLER。这样就直接引用一份标准合同，使之构成整个合同的一部分，因此，在签署这样的订单时，要预先审读背后隐藏的复杂的合同条款。

链接：一份采购合同通用条款

General Purchase Conditions
通用采购条款

General/总则

1. By accepting our order or by supplying the goods ordered, the Supplier is deemed to have accepted the present conditions.

供应商一旦接受我们的订单，或者供给我们所订购的货物，即确认接受了该通用采购条款。

2. Only orders in traceable form (in writing, by Telefax, E-mail) are binding. Verbal orders or orders by phone as well as changes and additions to our order shall be binding only if confirmed by us in traceable form. Terms at variance with our General Purchase Conditions and additional terms, including reservations regarding price or exchange rates, as well as, in particular, deviating General Conditions of Sale and Delivery of the Supplier shall be valid only if accepted by us in traceable form.

只有以可以追溯格式（书面，如传真、电子邮件）的形式发放的采购订单才具有效力。以口头或电话形式对订单进行更改或增加只在我们书面确认以后生效。与本通用采购条款和附加条款有分歧的条款，以及那些与供应商《通用销售和发货条款》相冲突的其他条款特别包括价格或者汇率的约定，只在我们以书面形式确认后才生效。

3. The Supplier is kindly asked to immediately (within 2 working days) return his order confirmation and to notify the exact delivery date.

供应商需要在最短时间（两个工作日）内确认我们的订单，并通知确切的交货日期。

4. The assignment of the order in whole to third parties shall require our prior consent in traceable form.

供应商如果要把订单整体外包给第三方，事先必须征得我公司的书面确认。

5. The Supplier shall be liable for all costs incurred by us as a consequence of his failure to observe our instructions or due to faulty or not validly agreed deliveries.

所有因为供应商失误而产生的费用都必须由供应商承担，这些失误包括供应商没有遵守我们的说明、发货不完整，或者没有按照协议发货等。

6. These General Purchase Conditions shall equally apply to future orders.

本通用采购条款同等适用于今后订单。

7. Our employees are forbidden to accept gifts, commissions or other compensations of whatever kind.

我们的员工禁止接受礼物、佣金或者其他任何形式的补偿。

Prices and Transport Costs/价格和运输成本

8. Unless otherwise agreed, the prices are considered firm.

除非另有约定,该处拟定的价格确认有效。

9. In case of orders showing no price or an indicative price only we reserve the right to approve the price following the receipt of the order confirmation.

如果采购订单中没有标明价格,或者只有指导性价格,我们保留按照所收到的确认单确定价格的权利。

10. Unless otherwise agreed, all expenses for packing, transport, customs, weighing, measuring as well as all other transport costs shall be for Supplier's account.

除非另有约定,供应商应承担所有含包装、运输、报关、计重、测量以及其他的运输费用。

Invoice and Payment/发票和付款

11. Invoices are to be submitted immediately following dispatch of the goods to the address indicated in the order.

发货后,供应商需要把发票立即送到订单指定的地址。

12. The Supplier may not claim payments being contingent on the fulfilment of his obligations, prior to the fulfilment of such obligations, unless the non-performance shall be caused by our acts or omissions.

除非由于我们的行为或疏忽所致,否则供应商不应在履行其职责的过程中或开始履行其职责之前敦促付款。

Delivery/发运

13. Deliveries arriving without the required transport documents shall be stored at Suppliers expense and risk until such documents are properly supplied.

对于没有提供相关运输单据的到货,在我公司收到所有必要单据之前所发生的所有费用和风险均由供应商承担。

14. Part shipments and advance deliveries require our prior consent.

分批发货或者提前发货必须征求我公司的同意。

15. Deliveries by messengers are only be deemed effected if evidenced by delivery notes properly countersigned by us. Deliveries are to be made to the respective departments of our works.

通过物流公司的发货只有当我公司在交货单上正式签字后才被认定有效,同时物流公司该将货物直接发给我公司相关部门。

16. The time of delivery shall be of essence. The time of delivery is met, when the goods have arrived at our works. Foreseeable delays hindering the timely delivery in whole or in part shall be notified immediately specifying the reasons for and the estimated duration of the delay. Such notice shall without prejudice to our remedies at law (e. g. partial or total termination or rescission of the order).

交货期非常重要，且交货期指货物到达我公司的时间。供应商一旦预见可能发生整体或部分延期交货的情况必须立即通知我们并阐明原因和延迟时间。该通知将不影响我方的法律补救措施（如部分或者整体终止或废除订单）。

17. In case of the delay, the Supplier shall not be excused by missing documents, hardware or components to be supplied by us unless he has timely requested their supply. In such case, the parties shall mutually agree on a reasonable extension of the delivery period.

供应商不能以需方没能提供全部文件、部件或零件为由延期交货，除非供应商曾及时向需方提出过要求；如供应商确实及时向需方提出上述要求，双方应共同协商延迟交货的期限。

18. The risk in the goods ordered shall pass on us upon their arrival at the place of fulfilment, or, if an acceptance test is agreed, upon successful completion of said test.

所购货物的风险在货物到达指定交货地点后，如果双方有约定的验收检验，检验通过后，风险才转移到我公司。

Packing/包装

19. The Supplier shall be liable if the goods are damaged on transport due to faulty packing.

供应商必须对因包装不良产生的运输过程中的货物损毁负责。

20. At our election, the Supplier shall credit us with the price charged for packaging material returned by us free of charge or shall provide for a pertinent refund.

根据我们的选择，供应商应该针对我公司退还的包装材料给予我公司相应的货款抵扣或退款。

Notification of Defects/缺陷通知

21. Without being bound by statutory inspection periods, we shall examine the goods supplied at our earliest convenience.

我们将根据自己的安排尽快检测鉴定货物/产品的质量，而不受法定的检测期限制。

22. By making payments or conducting pre-shipment tests, we are not waiving our legal remedies for faulty deliveries.

我公司的付款或交货前验收等行为并不导致我公司放弃对供应商交货过程中的缺陷采取法律补救措施的权利。

Quality Assurance/质量保证

23. The Supplier warrants that the goods comply with the order, in particular that they are free from defects impairing their value or fitness for the intended use and that they comply with the warranted characteristics and performance criteria. The Supplier further warrants that the goods are fit for the intended purpose and that in their manufacture high quality materials have been used.

供应商保证货物符合订单要求,特别是无导致货物价值或使用功能受损的缺陷发生;供应商保证其产品符合使用标准和设计目的要求并保证其产品有高质量原材料加工制造。

24. The goods must comply with all applicable laws, regulations and accident prevention rules being in force in People's Republic of China.

货物必须符合中国所有现行的法律、制度和事故预防规定。

25. In case of defects in the goods supplied we shall be entitled to avail ourselves of the pertinent remedies at law. However we General Purchase Conditions shall only be entitled to rescind the contract if the Supplier, within a reasonable period, has been unable or unwilling to repair the defect or to replace the defective product at his expense. In case of urgency or if the Supplier is defaulting in his obligation to remedy the defect, we are entitled to have the defects remedied at Supplier's cost.

如果供应商提供有缺陷产品,我们有权依据法律作出相应的补救。无论采用何种方法,如果供应商在合理的期限内无法或无意免费对缺陷产品进行修复或更换,我们有权取消合同。在紧急情况下,如果供应商未能履行对缺陷产品的补救职责时,我们有权对缺陷产品进行补救,相关费用由供应商承担。

26. The Supplier shall reimburse the costs of dismantling defective goods or products which have become defective as a result of defective goods supplied by Supplier as well as the costs of reinstalling goods or products being free from defects.

如果供应商提供的有缺陷产品导致采用(含有)该产品的产品出现质量问题,供应商应该承担更换、拆除故障产品以及重新安装无质量缺陷产品的全部费用。

27. Unless otherwise agreed, the warranty period shall be 26 months following the receipt of the goods in our works. To the extent the parties have agreed on subjecting the goods to a functional acceptance test in our works, the warranty period shall commence with the signing of the acceptance protocol.

除非另有约定,质量保证期为我方收到产品后26个月以内。如果双方约定货物必须在我方工厂通过性能测试后才可被接收,则质量保证期从我公司签署产品验收性能测试合格报告之日起计算。

28. The statute of limitations of claims for defects, which have been duly notified during the warranty period shall be 6 months from the date of notification.

对于所有发生在质保期内并且适时通知供应商的产品质量问题,索赔期限为自通知供应商之日起 6 个月之内有效。

29. Defective goods or parts thereof shall remain at our disposal up to their replacement or cancellation of the contract. Following replacement the defective goods are placed at Supplier's disposal in our works.

在得到更换之前或采购合同被撤销之前,缺陷产品或部件由我公司负责处置;缺陷产品被更换后,即使是存放在我公司也应由供应商负责处置。

30. The warranty for replacement and repairs shall be the same as agreed for the original delivery; the warranty period for replaced parts and components shall start running anew. This shall equally apply to replaced parts and components.

被更换或被修复部件的质保期应该与原始供货相同,保质期的计算应该从更换或修复之日起计算。该原则适用于所有被更换或修复的零部件。

Product Liability/产品责任

31. The Supplier shall indemnify us against any claims, damages, losses, liabilities, suits and expenses arising from the supply of defective goods or services.

供应商应该赔偿我公司任何因其提供的产品或服务缺陷而导致的索赔、财产损失、浪费、债务和费用等。

Tools, Patents, Drawings, etc/工具、专利、图纸等

32. All data, drawings, equipment, patents, tools, models, etc. placed by us at Supplier's disposal for the manufacture of the our goods shall remain our property and may not be used for other purposes, copied or disclosed to third parties. Copyrights therein shall remain vested in us. All documents shall be returned, free of charge, as soon as they are no longer needed for the execution of the order. If no deliveries are agreed, the documents shall equally be returned to us.

我公司为使供应商生产我方产品而向供应商提供的所有数据、图纸、设备、专利、工具、模据等均属我公司财产,版权归我公司所有。供应商不得用于其他用途或复印、泄露给第三方。一旦供应商在执行合同过程中不再需要上述资料,必须立即免费归还我公司。即使双方最终没能达成供货协议,所有资料也必须归还。

33. Products manufactured according to drawings, patents, confidential data, our tools or copies thereof, (our) shall not be used by the Supplier for his own use nor may they be of-

fered or delivered to third parties. This shall equally apply to printing orders.

所有按照我公司图纸、专利、保密工艺参数、工具及其副本制造的产品，供应商均不得自己使用，也不得销售或发运给第三方。以上原则同样适用于我方的订货文件。

Secrecy/保密

34. The Supplier shall treat the order and all related deliveries as confidential.

供应商必须对我公司的所有订单和相关发货承担保密义务。

Industrial Property Rights / 工业产权

35. The Supplier warrants that the goods and services supplied do not infringe third party property rights. He will indemnify us from any third party claims related thereto.

供应商保证所提供的产品和服务不侵犯第三方的知识产权并赔偿我公司因此而遭到的第三方索赔。

36. +GF+ as trademark / brand, and our company name are strictly protected by relevant laws.

+GF+作为商标/品牌和我公司名称受到相关法律严格的保护。

37. All rights to use +GF+ and our company name, which includes but is not limited to mould, print, engrave them on the product, remain with Georg Fischer AG in Switzerland.

设立于瑞士的 Georg Fischer AG 公司拥有对+GF+和我公司名称的一切相关权利，包括但不限于通过模压、印刷、雕刻等方法使用+GF+或公司名称标识产品。

38. The suppliers are strictly forbidden to apply the trademark / brand and company name without prior written consent of GFPS Shanghai and in particular strictly prohibited directly to other customers than our GF companies.

事先没有获得上海乔治费歇尔管路系统有限公司的书面授权，任何供应商都被严格禁止使用这些商标/品牌和我公司名称，特别是用来和 Georg Fischer 的各个公司以外的客户直接发生业务。

Place of Performance/执行地

39. Place of performance for the goods and the services shall be the agreed place of destination. Place of performance for the payment shall be the registered office of the business unit having placed the order.

产品和服务的执行地应在双方同意的指定地点。付款执行地应为我公司下采购订单的业务所在地。

Jurisdiction and Applicable Law / 权限及使用法律

40. Exclusive place of venue for any differences shall be our office having issued the order. We shall however be entitled to bring actions in any other competent courts.

我公司下采购订单的业务所在地将是解决纠纷的管辖地。当然我公司有权在任何能胜任的法院解决纠纷。

41. In case of disputes all supplies shall be subject to substantive laws in force at buyer's place of business, deliveries from abroad in addition to the UN Convention on the International Sale of Goods of 11. 4. 1980.

任何有关发货的纠纷必须依据采购方业务所在地的有效法律解决。对于来自国外的发货除遵照本通用采购条款外可参照1980年4月11日版《联合国国际货物销售合同公约》协定执行。

（瑞士乔治费歇尔集团网站公布的通用采购条款，来源 http：//www.gfps.com/country_CN/zh/about-GF-PipingSystems/purchasing.html）

三 专用条款+通用条款

有些合同构成的内容比较复杂，例如一份建设工程合同文件一般包括如下几项：①合同协议书；②中标通知书；③投标函及投标函附录；④专用合同条款；⑤通用合同条款；⑥技术标准和要求；⑦图纸；⑧已标价工程量清单；⑨其他合同文件。这其中，专用条款和通用条款共同构成一份完成的合同文本。把主要的合同条件分为通用条款、专用条款两部分，是有关行业主管部门或专业协会制定合同范本的普遍做法。

例如中华人民共和国住房和城乡建设部、中华人民共和国国家工商行政管理总局2017年9月制定了《建设工程施工合同（示范文本）》（GF-2017-0201），要求自2017年10月1日起执行。其指出，通用合同条款是合同当事人根据《中华人民共和国建筑法》《中华人民共和国合同法》等法律法规的规定，就工程建设的实施及相关事项，对合同当事人的权利义务作出的原则性约定。专用合同条款是对通用合同条款原则性约定的细化、完善、补充、修改或另行约定的条款。合同当事人可以根据不同建设工程的特点及具体情况，通过双方的谈判、协商对相应的专用合同条款进行修改补充。

各类范本中的通用条款是根据《合同法》《建筑法》等法律、行政法规制定的，同时，也考虑了建设工程施工中的惯例以及施工合同在签订、履行和管理中的通常做法，具有较强的普遍性和通用性，是通用于各类建设工程施工的基础性合同条款。建设工程虽然具有单件性，不同的工程在施工方案以及工期、价款等方面各不相同，但在工程施工中所依据的法律、行政法规是统一的，发包方与承包方的权利和义务是基本一致的，对于违约、索赔和争议的处理原则也是相同的。因此，可以把建设工程施工中这些共性的内容固定下来，形成合同的通用条款，实际工程可以直接原文不加修改地引用。这种做法的优点是直接使用普遍熟悉和流行的工程管理制度，提高效率，保证公平。发包方与承包方结合具体工程，经协商一致，可对通用条款进行补充或修改，在专用条款内约定。合同履行中是否执行通用条款要根据专用条款的约定。如果专用条款没有对通用条款的某一条款作出修改，则执行通用条款，否则按修改后的专用条款执行。在工程招标中,通用条款也可以作为招标文件的一部分提供给投标人。无论是否执行通用条款,通用条款都应作为合同的一个组成部分予以保留,不应只把协议书和专用条款作为全部合同内容。但鉴于通用条款是业内公知的条款内容,因此一般提供给律师审阅一份施工合同时,当事人通常不会提供通用条款,律师对此应当理解。

当然也有一些长期有同类型交易业务的单位会根据企业管理制度和业务特点,制定统一的通用合同条款,然后针对不同的具体交易标的情况制定专用合同条款。

四 母合同+子合同

有些大型的公司为了节约采购成本、加强内部控制,往往会对集团内大宗货物或服务的采购实行统一管理,制订一份总体供货的框架协议或总服务协议,然后在子公司、分支机构具体实施项目时再另外签署一份具体的合同,这种总协议加具体协议就构成了母合同+子合同的合同结构。其中的母合同通常被称为"Master Agreement",而子合同("Local Agreement"或"Subsidiary Contract")中通常会在明显的位置标出母合同同时适用于本子合同项下的交易。如果母子合同的条款发生冲突,母合同的效力并不当然优先于子合同。相反,在大多数情况下,子合同都会规定双方同意适用母合同,但是子合同中另有规定的除外。因此,这里的效力问题完全取决于双方的约定。因为子合同的一个重要作用就是修订母合同中的某些条款,使之符合当地法律的规定,或者符合当地的商务环境,因此通常子合同都会规定其效力优先于母合同。

链接:下面是一份母合同的目录,以便我们了解一下母合同的大致内容。

目录
1. Scope of Services 服务范围
2. No agency 不构成代理关系
3. Core Team and Regional Hubs 核心小组和区域性组织
4. Local Agreement 本地子合同
5. Term of Agreement 协议期限
6. Professional Fees 服务费用
7. Invoices/Billing 发票/账单
8. Taxes 税务
9. Intellectual Property 知识产权
10. Duties on Third Party Contracts 对第三方合同的义务
11. Confidential Information 保密信息
12. Service Provider and Service Recipient Personnel 服务提供商和服务接收方的人员

13. Records/Rights of Audit 记录/审计权利

14. Insurance 保险

15. Indemnification and Limitation of Liability 免责赔偿和责任限额

16. Service Standards 服务标准

17. Exclusivity 排他性

18. Conflict of Interest and Business Ethics 利益冲突和商业道德

19. Assignment and Sub-letting 转让和分包

20. Duty of Performance 义务的履行

21. Change of Control 控制权变化

22. Health, Safety and Environment 健康、安全和环境

23. Publicity 公开宣传

24. Compliance with Laws and Regulations 遵守法律和法规

25. Severability 可分割性

26. Governing Law and Jurisdiction 适用法律和管辖机构

27. Notices 通知

28. Termination 终止

29. Protection of Service Recipient's Property 服务接收方财产的保护

30. Entire Agreement 完整协议

31. Waiver 弃权

32. Force Majeure 不可抗力

33. Third Party Rights 第三方权利

34. Attorney's Fees 律师费

附件 1：Scope of Services 服务范围

附件 2：Professional Fees 服务费用

附件 3：Service Recipient's Affiliates 服务接收方关联公司

附件 4：Service Provider's Affiliates 服务提供方关联公司

附件 5：Conflict Resolution Procedures 冲突解决程序

附件 6：Confidentiality Agreement 保密协议

附件 7：Local Agreement 本地子合同

第二节 具体条款写作及词义分析

合同具体条款会根据合同的性质、用途而有所区别，但有一些一般的条款会反复

适用，具有典型意义。为此，须掌握一些可以在合同起草和修订中反复适用的典型具体条款的含义和写作技巧。

一 定义条款（Definition）

为了避免对某些重要的名词、概念出现理解上的争议，或出于行文简洁的考虑，往往订立定义条款对合同中重复出现的具有特殊意义且容易引起争议的名词概念作出专门的解释。重要的英文合同往往第一部分就是定义条款。经过定义的名词往往在合同中以首字母大写或加黑的形式出现。以下是一些定义条款的例子。

"关联方"：对于任何人士而言，指直接或通过一家或多家中介间接控制该人士、受该人士控制或与该人士处于他人共同控制之下的另一人士。"控制"一词指有能力通过拥有具有表决权的证券、合同或其他方式（包括担任该人士的普通合伙人、管理人员、董事或执行股东）直接或间接掌握该人士的重大管理和政策制定的决策权（该决策权在针对涉及相关人士的某些重大决定时可能受制于其他人士的审批权）。

"**Affiliate**": means, with reference to a Person, any other Person that, directly or indirectly through one or more intermediaries, Controls, is Controlled by or is under common Control with the first Person. With respect to any Person, Control and Controlled by means the ability, directly or indirectly, whether through the ownership of voting securities, by contract, or otherwise (including by being a general partner, officer, director or managing member of the Person in question), to possess decision-making authority over the major management and policy decisions of the Person in question (which may be subject to the approval rights of other Persons with respect to certain major decisions regarding the Person in question).

"登记机关"：指有权向公司签发营业执照的国家工商行政管理总局或其获得授权的地方分支机构。

"**Registration Authority**": shall mean the State Administration for Industry and Commerce or its authorised local counterpart, which is authorized to issue a business license to the Company.

二 陈述与保证条款（Representations and Warranties）

陈述与保证条款往往是对与双方合作项目能够顺利进行有关的合作各方的法律地位、财务状况、获得签署授权、履约能力等情况作出的承诺和声明。这一条款的主要目的是保障合同签署与生效的基本条件得到确认，并可与违约责任条款相勾连，对于在陈述与保证条款中做不实陈述的情况直接认定构成违约而要求承担违约责任。以下是一份中外合作经营合同中所使用的陈述与保证条款文本。

陈述与保证

Representations and Warranties

每一方在此向另一方作出如下陈述与保证：

Each Party hereby represents and warrants to the other Party that:

（a）该方是一家依据其设立地法律合法设立、有效存续而且经营状况良好的（对甲方而言）有限责任公司和（对乙方而言）有限公司；

It is a limited liability company in the case of Party A and a limited company in the case of Party B duly organized and existing in good standing under the laws of the jurisdiction where it is incorporated;

（b）该方已经采取所有适当的和必要的公司行为，以（i）授权其法定代表人或在本合同上签字的经适当授权的其他代表签署本合同，并（ii）批准该方签署、交付并履行本合同；

It has undertaken any and all appropriate and necessary corporate action to (i) authorize its legal representative or such other duly authorized representative whose signature is affixed hereto to execute this Contract, and (ii) approve its execution, delivery and performance of this Contract;

（c）该方已经取得其有效签署、履行和交付本合同所需的所有同意、批准和授权，并且拥有履行其在本合同项下的各项义务所需的所有同意、权力、批准和授权，但是，本合同须得到主管审批机关批准之后方可生效；

It has obtained any and all consents, approvals and authorizations necessary for the valid execution, performance and delivery of this Contract, and is in possession of any and all consents, powers, approvals and authorizations necessary for the performance of its obligations hereunder, provided that this Contract shall not become effective until approval of this Contract is obtained from the competent Approval Authority;

（d）一经主管审批机关批准，本合同即应立即构成对该方合法、有效和具有约束力的义务，并可对该方强制执行；

This Contract shall, immediately upon approval of the competent Approval Authority, constitute its legal, valid, binding and enforceable obligation;

（e）不存在已提起的清算该方的申请，亦未曾就该方任命任何破产管理人或接管人，在任何其他法域未曾发生与该方相关的任何类似事件；且

No petition has been presented to wind it up and no administrator or receiver has been appointed in respect of it and no similar or analogous event has occurred in any other jurisdiction in respect of it; and

（f）该方签署、交付、履行和终止本合同或本合同中所提及的并且其为一方的任

何其他合同，均不会违反该方的章程、任何组织性文件，或对该方或其任何资产具有约束力的其他协议或义务，亦不会违反在任何方面可能适用于该方或本合同项下拟议交易的任何法律法规。

Its execution, delivery, performance of and termination of this Contract or any of the other contracts referred to herein to which it is a party will neither breach any of its articles of association, constitutional documents, or other agreements or obligations which are binding upon it or any of its assets, nor violate any law or regulation that may be applicable to it or the transactions contemplated herein in any respect.

三 合同方的权利义务（Rights and Obligations of Contract Parties）

合同方的权利义务条款往往明确合同方开展交易中各自的权利和义务，从而对合同交易的实质内容进行明确。因为合同性质、标的指向不同，合同方的权利义务可能完全不一样。比如在常见的买卖合同中，通常需要对买卖的标的物进行具体描述，明确交易的价格、数量、付款时间、交货时间、验收标准等。这些实质性的交易内容本身是合同方必须遵守落实的权利义务事项。而在一份借款合同中，贷款人要按照足额发放贷款，借款人要按照合同要求还本付息，这就是他们双方的主要权利义务内容。围绕合同方的权利义务内容，可进一步展开就细节问题和特殊要求作出更为细致的规定。

例如在一份精密仪器的买卖合同中，对货物的验收作了较为详细的规定：

"7. 验收内容包括设备外包装验收和设备开箱验收。

7.1 设备外包装验收

7.1.1 所有产品的外包装印有运输标识、厂商标识、机器序列号等有关标记；包装箱不相邻的两面各有一个倾斜指示标识；包装箱上有震动指示标识；若外包装箱没有破损，运输标识均指示正常（正常时包装箱两侧倾斜指示下小球应在20以内，震动标志不变红），则表示外包装正常。

7.1.2 若发现外包装破损或倾斜标志超出正常范围、震动标志变红，则表明运输不当，甲方可以拒绝接收该设备（并负责拍照），否则被认定为所交付的设备外包装是完好的。

7.2 设备开箱验收

7.2.1 开箱方式为甲乙双方现场，开箱参加者为甲乙双方人员，开箱必须在有关技术人员的指导下进行。

7.2.2 检查包装箱两侧倾斜指示标识是否完好无损并拍照；照片必须能清楚显示包装箱两侧倾斜指示标识中的小球位置及设备编号。检查包装箱上震动指示标识是否完好（正常应为白色）并拍照；照片必须能清楚显示包装箱上震动指示标识及设备编号。检查包装箱是否完好并拍照；照片应能准确反映包装箱及运输底盘的实际情况。

7.2.3 开箱后如发现异常情况，须针对具体情况拍照。开箱后应对设备进行加电运行测试。"

四 不可抗力条款（Force Majeure Clause）

Force Majeure 条款是一种免责条款，对于发生不可抗力事件导致合同一方不能履行合同义务，则在所证明的不可抗力事件影响的范围内，该方可免除部分或全部合同责任。一般应规定的内容包括：不可抗力事件的定义（Definition of Force Majeure）以及不可抗力事件的后果（Consequences of Force Majeure）。

我国《合同法》对于 Force Majeure 的定义如下。

本法所称不可抗力，是指不能预见、不能避免并不能克服的客观情况。

For purposes of this Law, force majeure means any objective circumstance, which is unforeseeable, unavoidable and insurmountable.

以下是 Force Majeure 条款的举例：

Force Majeure

(1) No party to this Contract shall be liable to the other party for any failure of or delay in performance of its obligations hereof nor be deemed to be in breach of this Contract, if such failure or delay has arisen from "force majeure".

(2) "Force Majeure" means circumstances and conditions beyond the control of either parties, that would render it impossible for either the Owner or the Contractor to fulfill their obligations under this Contract, or delay such fulfillment. Any of the following matters are considered "force majeure":

a. war, hostilities, act of foreign enemy, invasion, warlike operations (whether war to be declared or not) or civil war;

b. mutiny, civil commotion assuming the proportions of or amounting to a popular rising, military rising, insurrection, rebellion, revolution, military or usurped power, or any act of any person acting on behalf of or in connection with any organization with activities directed towards the overthrow by force of the Government de jure or de facto, or to the influencing of it by terrorism or violence;

c. earthquake, flood, fire or other natural physical disaster;

d. denial of the use of all ports, airports, shipping services or other means of public transport;

e. strike or lock out or other industrial concerted action by workers, affecting the fulfillment of Contractor's and subcontractors' obligations;

f. and other unforeseen circumstances beyond the control of the parties so affected rendering the fulfillment of their obligations impossible.

(3) If either party to this Contract is prevented or delayed from or in performing any of his obligations under this Contract by force majeure, then he may notify the other party of the circumstances constituting the force majeure and of the obligation performance of which is thereby delayed or prevented and the party giving the notice shall thereupon be excused from the performance or punctual performance, as the case may be, of such obligation for so long as the circumstances of prevention or delay may continue.

(4) If by virtue of the preceding sub-clause dither party shall be excused from the performance or punctual performance of any obligation for a continuous period of _____ months, then either party may at any time thereafter terminate this Contract by giving a written notice to the other party.

不可抗力

(1) 如果任何一方因不可抗力而不能履行或推迟履行其义务，则不对另一方负责，也不应视作违反合同。

(2) "不可抗力"指业主或承包商无法控制的情况，使当事人未能按本合同履行其义务，或者不得不延迟履行其义务。下列情况均被视作"不可抗力"：

a. 战争、敌对事件、外敌行动、入侵、类似战争的军事行动（不管是否宣战）、内战；

b. 士兵哗变、民众暴乱、军事叛乱、起义、造反、革命、篡权，或者任何个人代表某个组织或与某个组织有联系、旨在以暴力推翻合法或现存政府，或以恐怖主义或暴力对政府施加影响的行为；

c. 地震、洪水、火灾或其他自然灾害；

d. 所有港口、机场、船运或其他公共交通工具的使用均遭拒绝；

e. 工人罢工、工厂停工，或其他的劳工联合行动，影响了承包商和分包商履行其义务；

f. 当事人无法控制从而使其不能履行义务的其他任何意外情况。

(3) 如果本合同任何一方因不可抗力不能或延迟履行本合同规定的任何义务，他可将不可抗力和由此造成的延迟或妨碍情况通知另一方。发出通知的一方允许根据具体情况及妨碍或延迟持续的时间免于履行或推迟履行合同。

(4) 根据本条款第3分条规定，如果任何一方免于履行或推迟履行其义务的时间持续了_____个月，那么任何一方都可随时向另一方发出书面通知，终止本合同。

五 违约条款（Default Clauses）

英文合同中通常会载明违约条款（Default Clauses/Breach of Contract），其主要内容在于约定构成违约的条件、明确违约责任承担的方式、约定免责事项及/或责任限制等。通常在合同法中会对当事人一方不履行合同义务或者履行合同义务不符合约定所应当承担的法律责任作出规定，但是在具体合同中，仍有必要对违约条款加以约定，以补充法律规定的不足。

（一）违约事件（Event of Default）

违约事件有两类：一类是实际违约事件，就是对合同本身约定的不履行；另一类预期违约事件，又称先兆性的违约事件，即借款人不履行合同的义务只是个时间问题，未来的某个时期肯定是要违约的，例如在借款合同约定的还款期限截止前，借款人失去了偿付能力。无论是实际违约还是预期违约，如果能够在合同中明确作出约定，则在事件发生时守约方可以较无争议地依据该合同条款对违约事实的存在加以认定，并继而可以启动违约救济措施。以下是一份国际商业贷款合同中的违约事件条款。

第八条 违约事件

Article 8 Events of Default

8.1 如果发生下列一种或更多种违约事件，或该违约事件正在继续（不管该违约事件的原因是什么，或者是自愿的或非自愿的，或者受法律实施的影响或根据任何法院的判决、命令，或者任何行政或政府机关的命令、规则、法规和法令）：

Section 8.1 If any one or more of the following "Events of Default" shall have occurred and be continuing (whatever the reason for such Event of Default and whether it shall be voluntary or involuntary or be effected by operation of law or pursuant to any judgment, decree or order of any court or any order, rule, regulation or decree of any administrative or governmental body):

（a）借款方未能根据本协议条款和票据支付贷款本金和应计的利息或票据，或其他任何应付款项，当根据协议条款规定的相同贷款到期和应支付时（不管是否到期，都应根据动议通知提前偿还或其他）；或者

(a) Failure by the Borrower to pay, in accordance with the terms or this Agreement or the Note, the principal of or interest accrued on the Loan or the Note, or any other amounts payable hereunder, when the same becomes due and payable in accordance with the terms hereof (whether at maturity, by notice of internation to prepay or otherwise); or

（b）借款方没有履行和遵守协议或票据中的任何其他条款，约定事项或双方达成的一致；或者

(b) Failure by the Borrower to perform or observe any other term, covenant or agreement contained herein or in the note; or

（c）借款方所作的任何声明和保证及其在根据协议交付的任何证明、报告或意见中的声明和保证被证明是不正确的或者在一些重大方面有误解；或者

（c）Any representation or warranty made by the Borrower herein or any statement or representation made in any certificate, report or opinion delivered pursuant hereto shall prover to have been incorrect or misleading in any material respect when made; or

（d）任何登记、政府的同意或批准或与本合同有关的要求事项、票据和担保等满期或终止、废除或以任何方式修改或归于无效；或者

（d）Any registration or governmental consent or approval granted or required in connection with this Agreement, the Note or the Guaranty expires or is terminated or revoked or is modified in any manner or fails to remain in full force and effect; or

（e）借款方或担保人非法履行它在票据和担保书中设定的任何义务和其他预定文件中的既定事项；或者

（e）It becomes unlawful for the Borrower or the Guarantor to perform any of its obligations hereunder or under the Note or the Guaranty, as the case may be, or any other document contemplated hereby or referred to herein; or

（f）担保人拒绝履行或者修改它在担保书中的义务；或者

（f）The Guarantor shall renounce or modify its obligations under the Guaranty; or

（g）借款方或担保人没有到期或在适当的限期内偿还债务；没有遵守或履行能证明债务存在和为债务作保的任何协议中规定的条款约定事项或达成的一致；如果不履行的结果是加速偿还，或允许持有人加速履行部分义务，到期支付和其他义务，不管是否加速偿还发生或这些违约被放弃；或者

（g）The Borrower the Guarantor shall fail to pay at maturity, or within any applicable period of grace, any Indebtedness; or fail to observe or perform any term, covenant or agreement contained in any agreement by which it is bound evidencing or securing Indebtedness; if the effect of such failure is to accelerate, or to permit (assuming the giving of notice or lapse of time or both, if required) the bolder or holders thereof or of any obligations issued thereunder to accelerate, the maturity thereof or of any such obligations, whether or not such acceleration occur or such default shall be waived; or

（h）借款方或担保人被裁定破产或无偿债能力，或在贷款到期时书面宣告无偿债能力，或为债权人的利益进行了转让，借款方或担保人为了全部或者部分财产申请或同意接收者、受托人或类似的官员的选定；这样的接收者、受托人或类似的官员没有借款方或担保人的申请和同意而选定并且这种选定将连续存在14天并不可撤销；借款方或提保人（根据请求、申请、答辩、同意和其他）已开始无力偿还贷款、破产、破

产整顿、整理财产、再调整、解除债务、清算并依照法律和管辖权进行有关的类似程度，或者开始一些针对借款方和担保人的程序（依据请求、申请或其他），并且这种程序 14 天期限内不开始进行；签发判决书、令状、拘留证或执行文书及办理其他手续，或者没收借款人或担保人的部分财产，并且判决书、令状及类似手续在签发或没收财产后 14 天内不能被解除或撤销；或者

(h) The Borrower or the Guarantor shall be adjudicated a bankrupt or insolvent, or admit in writing its inability to pay its debts as they mature, or make an assignment for the benefit of creditors; or the Borrower or the Guarantor shall apply for or consent to the appointment of a receiver, trustee, or similar officer for or for all or any substantial part of its property; or such receiver, trustee or similar office shall be appointed without the application or consent of the Borrower or the Guarantor and such appointment shall continue undischarged for a period or fourteen (14) days; or the Borrower or the Guarantor shall institute (by petition, application, answer, consent or otherwise) any suspension of payments, bankruptcy, insolvency reorganization, arrangement, readjustment or debt, dissolution, liquidation or similar proceeding relating to it under the laws of any jurisdiction, or any such proceeding shall be instituted (by petition, application or otherwise) against the Borrower or the Guarantor and shall remain undismissed for a period of fourteen (14) days; or any judgment, writ, warrant of attachment or execution or similar process shall be issued or levied against a substantial part of the property of the Borrower or the Guarantor and such judgment, writ, or similar process shall not be released, vacated or fully bonded within fourteen (14) days after its issue or levy; or

(i) 借款人在终局裁决日或在其后将会获得一份被要求给付金钱的终局裁决，该裁决金额超过_____美元或数量上相当，且在该裁决做出后的 14 天内，因该裁决处于上诉期而没有被撤销、履行或执行，或在 14 天的上诉期满后，该裁决仍没有被撤销或履行；或者

(i) A final judgment for money, in excess of _____ or its equivalent on the date of final judgment or at any time thereafter shall be rendered against the Borrower and if, within fourteen (14) days after entry thereof, such judgment shall not have been discharged, satisfied or execution thereof stayed pending appeal, or if, within fourteen (14) days after the expiration of any such stay, such judgment shall not have been discharged or satisfied; or

(j) 借款方或担保人的全部或部分基本财产被宣告没收、押收或被拨用、或经政府授权（依照法律或事实上）这些财产的保管和控制被其他人或实体承担或意欲承担，借款方和担保人不能再通过任何人或任何实体对它的全部或部分财产实施管理控制；

(j) All or any substantial part of the property of the Borrower or the Guarantor shall be condemned, seized or otherwise appropriated, or custody or control of such property shall be assumed, by any person or entity acting or purporting to act under authority of government (de jure or de facto) or the Borrower or the Guarantor shall have been prevented from exercising managerial control over all or said substantial part of its property by any such person or entity;

则前述任何违约事件的发生和继续，将导致贷款银行发放贷款的立即终止，银行可以宣布贷款本金和应计利息及票据立即到期，并且应该支付，由此，贷款本金和应计利息和其他应支付的款项立即到期和应支付，不需要提示，要求付款，做成拒绝承兑证书或任何种类的通知，所有这些都已经借款方明示放弃。只要8条1款h项中说明的任何违约事件发生，贷款和票据将立即到期并应支付，不需要对借款方再行宣布或通知。

Then, upon the happening of any of the foregoing Events of Default which shall be continuing, the obligation of the Bank to make the Loan hereunder shall immediately ceas, and the Bank may declare the principal of and accrued interest in respect of the Loan and the Note to be immediately due and payable whereupon the principal and accrued interest and any and all other amounts payable hereunder shall become immediately due and payable without presentment, demand, protest or other notice of any kind, all of which are hereby expressly waived by the Borrower, provided that upon the happening of any event specified in Section 8.1 (h) hereof, the Loan and Note shall be immediately due and payable without any declaration or other notice to the Borrower.

(二) 违约金 (Default Penalty)

违约金，顾名思义，是违反约定带来的金额支付。对于违约金的性质有三种观点。第一种观点认为，违约金仅具有惩罚性。第二种观点认为，违约金的性质只能是补偿性。第三种观点认为，违约金既具有惩罚性，也具有补偿性。所谓违约金的惩罚性是指对债务人过错违约的惩罚，除了支付违约金外，违约方仍须赔偿损失和继续履行合同义务。所谓违约金的赔偿性是指当事人预先估计的损害赔偿总额，其功能是为了补偿另一方因违约所遭受的损失，违约金与实际损失应大体相当，且不能与赔偿损失、继续履行并用。从两大法系的立法来看，英美法系国家一般不承认惩罚性违约金，而是承认第二种观点。一般认为违约金是"约定的预期损害赔偿额，违约金之目的，在保证契约之必能履行，且减轻债权人就债务不履行或不为适当履行所受损害之举证责任。双方当事人在契约中所约定之数额过高，超过实际上所受之损害，借此手段促使对方履行契约，此项约定属惩罚性之损害赔偿（penalty），不为法律及法庭所允许"。① 而大陆法系国家承认违约金兼有赔偿性和惩罚性双重属性。例如，《德国民法典》第339条规定："债务人与债权人约定，在其不能履行或不能依适当方式履行时，应支付

---

① 杨桢：《英美契约法论》，北京大学出版社2000年版，第345页。

一定金额作为违约金者,在其迟延时,罚其支付违约金;以不作为为支付者,于违反行为时,罚付之。"此即体现违约金的惩罚性。但大陆法系仍以赔偿性违约金为主。如《德国民法典》第343条规定:"约定违约金过巨者,法院应依债务人的申请以判决至相当数额。"又如《法国民法典》第1229条规定:"违约金为债权人因主债务不履行所受损害的赔偿。"

我国《合同法》第114条第2款的规定:"约定的违约金低于造成的损失的,当事人可以请求人民法院或者仲裁机构予以增加;约定的违约金过分高于造成的损失的,当事人可以请求人民法院或者仲裁机构予以适当减少。"最高人民法院《关于适用〈中华人民共和国合同法〉若干问题的解释(二)》认为:"当事人依照合同法第一百一十四条第二款的规定,请求人民法院增加违约金的,增加后的违约金数额以不超过实际损失额为限。增加违约金以后,当事人又请求对方赔偿损失的,人民法院不予支持。""当事人主张约定的违约金过高请求予以适当减少的,人民法院应当以实际损失为基础,兼顾合同的履行情况、当事人的过错程度以及预期利益等综合因素,根据公平原则和诚实信用原则予以衡量,并作出裁决。当事人约定的违约金超过造成损失的百分之三十的,一般可以认定为合同法第一百一十四条第二款规定的'过分高于造成的损失。"从我国相关法律规定来分析,违约金是建立在预先约定基础上的赔偿性的违约赔偿金额,由约定不当带来的对违约当事人的惩罚性只有在当事人存在误解的基础上才可以诉请法院减损,且此时申请人承担举证责任。违约金不足以弥补当事人的损失时,由该当事人举证可对不足部分加以赔偿。支付违约金后,原则上当事人不再承担继续实际履行的责任,除非约定表明该违约金是专门针对当事人有过错的不适当履行。由此可见,在合同中约定违约金条款,能够起到在对方违约时转移有关损失数额的举证责任的作用。对于守约方可径行以违约金数额向对方主张,违约方如欲抗辩该违约金高于实际损失应当减损,则违约方应承担举证责任。

在违约金约定中还应注意,要区分不同的违约形式确定不同的违约金,尽量避免笼统地不分违约形态地约定违约金。至少可以分为两种:第一种是不履行合同的违约金,对于明确约定一方不履行合同应支付违约金的,在具体适用时通常不可以再要求实际履行;第二种是针对不完全履行、履行不当行为约定的违约金。例如就迟延履行,可以约定相应的违约金。通常对于当事人就不完全履行、履行不当约定违约金,支付违约金后仍不妨碍要求继续实际履行合同,如违约金不足以弥补损失,亦可以另行以实际损失为依据要求增加赔偿额。

(三)违约责任限制条款(Limitation of Liability)

因违约而给守约方造成损害予以赔偿,一般的法律原则是要赔偿因违约而使受害人受的全部损失,即适用完全赔偿的原则,赔偿的范围包括两个方面,即积极损失的赔偿和可得利益的赔偿。完全赔偿是对守约方的利益实行全面、充分保护的有效措施。

从公平和等价交换原则来看，由于违约当事人的违约而使受害人遭受损害，违约当事人也应以自己的财产赔偿全部损害。但基于合同意思自治的原则，双方可以在合同中就因违约而产生的责任范围予以限制，特别是在某些特殊行业的合同交易中，也经常会看到对违约责任限制作出规定的条款。

例如在《建设工程设计合同示范文本（房屋建筑工程）》（GF-2015-0209）中，通用条款第14条（2）款3项约定："设计人对工程设计文件出现的遗漏或错误负责修改或补充。由于设计人原因产生的设计问题造成工程质量事故或其他事故时，设计人除负责采取补救措施外，应当通过所投建设工程设计责任保险向发包人承担赔偿责任或者根据直接经济损失程度按专用合同条款约定向发包人支付赔偿金。"然而一般在签署专用合同条款时，通常会把设计人设计文件不合格的损失赔偿金的上限设定为设计费总额或实际损失的一定比例。在某些医用设备、通信设备的购销合同中，也经常会有这样的条款"任何一方在本合同下承担的责任都不超过引起该责任的产品的价格，不管该责任是基于违反合同还是侵权"。

这种免责条款或责任限制条款并不当然有效，仍然要受法律调整。特别是双方签署的是格式合同，格式合同中的免责条款或责任限制条款需要在签署合同时给对方以充分的提示说明，以避免因对方忽略或不了解而影响其真实意思的表达，进而在出现纠纷时被法院或仲裁机构否认该责任限制条款的法律约束力。具体对格式条款进行提示和说明的形式与程度，应考虑对象和条款内容的特殊性，对不同的免责或限制责任条款、针对不同的交易对象，进行不同程度的提示和说明。英国21世纪最负盛名的大法官丹宁勋爵就曾明确指出：免责条款越不合理，提请对方当事人注意的程度就越高。"依我看来，某些免责条款必须用红色字体印在文件的正面，并以红色手指为标志予以指示，其提醒注意才能被认为是充分合理的。"

这种免责条款有时还会设置最低的索赔金额、最高的索赔金额以及索赔时限。例如在一份股权转让协议中，其在违约责任条款方面约定了如下内容。

"12.5 买方有权就其因符合本第12.3条规定的卖方违约而遭受的实际损失向卖方提出索赔，但买方权利的行使应始终受制于下述限制：

"（a）买方向卖方提出的任何一笔单一索赔的金额须超过人民币壹拾万元，且累计索赔的金额须超过人民币贰拾万元；

"（b）卖方对买方提起的任何及所有索赔的累计赔偿额不得超过买方已向卖方实际支付的转让价格；及

"（c）自成交后十二个月届满之日起，买方不得再向卖方提起有关任何卖方违约的索赔。"

六 争议解决条款（Dispute Resolution Clause）

英文合同中关于争议解决，程序上一般先约定友好协商，协商不成，则根据仲裁条款或补充的仲裁协议进行仲裁，如果没有仲裁条款，争议发生后又没有补充的仲裁协议，才选择诉讼解决，双方可能会约定管辖法院，实体上也可能约定适用的法律。

合同中争议解决条款关系到双方在发生争议时，选择仲裁还是诉讼解决争议的问题。当事人应当根据具体交易情况及各种争议解决方式的特点，谨慎选择争议解决方式。在商事活动中，仲裁这一解决争议的方式，具有一裁终局的特点，且由于联合国《承认及执行外国仲裁裁决公约》（The New York Convention on the Recognition and Enforcement of Foreign Arbitral Awards）有140多个成员，仲裁裁决要比司法判决更广泛便捷地得到外国的承认和执行，因此在商事交易合同约定的合同争议解决方式中经常被普遍采用。根据《中华人民共和国仲裁法》的规定，当事人在合同中约定了有效的仲裁协议，就排除了法院的管辖，人民法院不再予以受理。因此，当事人选择仲裁解决争议应当在合同中予以明确。如果在合同中没有约定仲裁条款，当事人可以补充协议，达不成补充仲裁协议的，双方发生争议只能到法院去诉讼。

依照《中华人民共和国仲裁法》的规定，仲裁协议应当具备下列内容：请求仲裁的意思表示；仲裁事项；选定的仲裁委员会。例如，中国国际经济贸易仲裁委员会向当事人推荐的合同中约定的示范仲裁条款为：

"凡因本合同引起的或与本合同有关的任何争议，均应提交中国国际经济贸易仲裁委员会，按照申请仲裁时该会现行有效的仲裁规则进行仲裁。仲裁裁决是终局的，对双方均有约束力。"

"Any dispute arising from or in connection with this Contract shall be submitted to China International Economic and Trade Arbitration Commission (CIETAC) for arbitration which shall be conducted in accordance with the CIETAC's arbitration rules in effect at the time of applying for arbitration. The arbitral award is final and binding upon both parties."

在合同中约定完整的仲裁条款，对当事人及时解决争议是十分有利的。一旦出现纠纷，要及时利用仲裁等法律手段，保护自身合法的经济利益。

七 其他规定条款（Miscellaneous）

除了以上介绍的各种一般条款外，往往在英文合同的最后还有一个其他规定条款或称杂项条款（Miscellaneous），其他规定条款会把一些较为简单的条款会合在一起。常见的有语言（Language）、协议的完整性（Entire Agreement）、可分割性（Severability）、标题效力（Headings/Captions）、通知（Notice）、修订（Amendment）、弃权（Waiver/Disclaimer）、免责（Exculpation）等。具体条款内容可见本章节其他部分给出的完整合同范例。

应当注意的是，使用英文起草合同，法律本身的特质决定了法律英语本身结构严谨，用词考究，逻辑严密，文体较其他体裁更为正式、刻板，因此英文合同在单词选择上也有意选择一些非常正式的单词或词组进行表达，这些词在日常用语中很少使用，但在法律英语中出现频率非常高，且不能被普通英语中意思相同的词或词组代替。下面对我们在英文合同中经常遇到或使用的一些正式表达进行分析和比较。

Determine/decide

分析：在作为"决定、确认"理解时，determine 较 decide 更为正式，因此，英文合同中选用 determine 而不是 decide 来表达该含义。如：

Where the price of the goods is not speicified in the contract, it shall be determined with reference to the fair market value of the similar commodity.

合同中没有明确货物价格的，应当根据类似商品的公平市场价格进行确定。

但同时，decide 也是法律英语中的一个单词，但一般不是表示决定或确定，而是判决、裁决。如：

The tribunal decided against awarding any damages.

仲裁庭裁定不给予任何损害赔偿。

Due to/because of

分析：due to 和 because of 无论是在含义、词组结构还是在用法上都是相同的，但 due to 比 because of 更为正式，因此，在英文合同中经常使用，且不能用 because of 替换。如：

The contract was terminated due to changes in such unforeseeable circumstances as production and management conditions.

合同因生产经营条件变化等不可预见的情况而解除。

Exclusive of/excluding

分析：两个词组/单词都是由动词 exclude 演变过来的，都是"不包括"的意思，作为法律英语中的常用语，我们通常选用 exclusive of，而不是 excluding。如：

All Rates quoted herein are exclusive of tax and service charge.

本报价中的所有费用均不包括税收和服务费。

In accordance with/according to

分析：两个词组都是由动词 accord（如何）变化而来，意思也完全一样。但由于 in accordance with 比 according to 用法更为正式，因此，在法律英语中用 in accordance with，而不是 according to，但可以用其他用法同样正式的词组（如 pursuant to, in pursuance with 或 as per）替换。如：

A contract made in PRC may not be performed in accordance/pursuance with its related laws and regulations.

在中华人民共和国订立的合同不一定根据中华人民共和国的相关法律法规进行履行。

Comply with/abide by/observe

分析：用来表示遵守的词和词组很多，我们大致列举出像 follow、observe、abide by、comply with 等。在前面这些词和词语中，comply with 是最正式的一个表达，因此，也常常在法律英语中使用。从语法上来说，comply with 的主语通常是物，而其他几个单词或词组的主语通常为人。如：

Both parties Shall abide by/All the activities of both parties shall comply with the contractual stipulations.

双方都应遵守/双方的一切活动都应遵守合同规定。

Deem/believe

分析：deem 和 believe 都是"相信、视为"的意思，其中，deem 是法律英语中常用的单词，且经常用作被动形式，即 be deemed to do。如：

Silence or failure to give prompt notice of Party A within a reasonable period of time shall be deemed to be the consent of Party A to the extension of the contract.

甲方在合理期间内保持沉默或没有及时发出通知，视为甲方同意对本合同的延续。

Intend to/wish to

分析：intend to 和 wish to 都可以表示希望或打算做什么事情，其中，wish to 经常用在口语中，如 I wish to see you next year。而且，wish 还通常表示不太可能实现的愿望，因此，英文合同中一般不用 wish 来表示要做某事，而使用 intend to do。如：

Where the parties do not intend to be bound until a formal contract is prepared and signed, there is no contract, and the circumstance that the parties do intend a formal contract to be drawn up is strong evidence to show that-they did not intend the previous negotiations to amount to an agreement.

如果在准备和签署正式合同以前，各方不愿意受到约束，则双方之间不存在合同关系。双方希望订立正式合同的情况是表明他们不希望把之前的磋商当做协议的有力证据。

In case/the event that/if

分析：in case/the event that 和 if 都表示假设——"如果"，但前者在法律法规、合同中经常使用，if 则更多的是出现在法学论著等非正式的法律文件中。如：

In the event Party A breaches any of the Anti-Corruption Policy Provisions, the Party B shall be entitled, at its sole option, to terminate this Agreement, whereupon Party A shall forfeit any claim to future payments hereunder.

如果甲方违反任何反腐败政策条款，乙方有权自行决定终止本合同，甲方将无权针对本合同项下之未来付款提出任何权利主张。

Interim/temporary

分析：两个词的含义都表示临时的、暂时的，但法律英语中一般用前者，即 interim 表示，而不用后者。如：

Shareholders' Meetings shall consist of regular meetings and interim meetings. Regular Shareholders' Meetings shall be convened once a year.

股东大会包括定期会议和临时会议，定期会议应当每年召开一次。

Notwithstanding/though/although/even if

分析：Notwithstanding 与 though、although、even if 在使用中并没有太大区别，但前者在法律法规和英文合同中更多地被使用，特别要注意其后面紧接的内容应放在次要位置考虑。如：

Notwithstanding any other provision of the contract, if the contractor intends to claim any additional payment pursuant to any clause of these conditions or otherwise, he shall give notice to his intention to the engineer, with a copy to the employer, within 28 days after the event giving rise to the claim has first arisen.

尽管本合同有其他规定，如果承包商根据本合同的条款或其他有关规定打算索取任何追加付款，他都应在引起索赔的事件第一次发生后 28 天内，将其索赔意向通知工程师，并将一份副本呈交业主。

在上面这句话中，notwithstanding 后面紧跟 any other provision of the contract，则这一其他规定应放在次要位置考虑，而在此之后的后面内容应予以优先考虑，即该其他规定条款不得与后面内容抵触。

Without prejudice to/subject to

分析：这两个词后面都是紧跟合同条款或法律条文，如 without prejudice to/subject to section 3 of this contact，且大多时候出现在句首。但 without prejudice to 对有关条款的限制程度没有 subject to 强硬，前者是"在不影响……的情况下"就可以，而后者是"受……限制""按照"或"根据"。如：

Without prejudice to the Article mentioned above, the Security Agent may allow any bank providing safe custody services or any professional adviser to the Security Agent to retain any of those documents in its possession.

在不影响上述条款规定的情形下，担保代理行可以允许任何银行或专业顾问为其提供安全保管服务，来保管其所掌握的相关文件。

Subject to the requirements of this Agreement, the Company may be a party to a merger, an exchange, or acquisition.

按照本章程的要求，本公司可成为兼并、交换或收购的一方。

第三节 保密协议、采购合同范例

一 保密协议范例

保密协议,是指协议当事人之间就一方告知另一方的书面或口头信息,约定不得向任何第三方披露该信息的协议。负有保密义务的当事人违反协议约定,将保密信息披露给第三方,将要承担民事责任甚至刑事责任。保密协议一般包括保密内容、责任主体、保密期限、保密义务及违约责任等条款。保密协议可以分为单方保密协议和双方保密协议。单方保密协议是指一方对另一方单方面负有保密义务的协议。

在一项重要的商事交易中,由于需要相互进行资信调查,就项目合作的情况相互提供有关资料,所以,往往在开始洽谈合作之前就会先行签署一份保密协议,或者在备忘录、合作协议及正式的合同中订立保密条款。因此,起草或审查保密协议、保密条款是从事法律服务所经常进行的工作,严谨的保密协议条款对保护公司的商业秘密,或者判断公司对外所承担的保密义务均有很大作用。另外,在公司内部即用人单位和员工之间,往往基于企业经营的性质及员工岗位,也会由单位与接触、知悉、掌握商业秘密的员工签订保密协议,要求员工对技术信息、经营管理信息及其他有必要采取保密措施的特殊秘密内容进行保密。

以下是一份商业合作项目的保密协议范例。

Confidentiality Agreement

This Confidentiality Agreement (this "Agreement") is entered into and made effective as of this August 24th, 2016 (the "Effective Date"), by and between Tonghai Co., Ltd., a company organized and existing under the laws of Japan, with its principal place of business at Tokyo, Japan ("THC"), Hongbao (Tianjin) Co., Ltd., a company organized and existing under the laws of Peoples Republic of China with its principal place of business at TEDA Tianjin, Republic of China (HBC") and Tonglin Company Limited, a company organized and existing under the laws of Japan, with its principal place of business at Tokyo, Japan ("TLC") (each, a "Party" and all of them, the "Parties"), as follows:

Recitals

THC is a development and marketing company engaging in household business and have specialized and extensive knowledge in development of moth proofer products and their formulation and application technologies.

HBC is a marketing and sales company engaging in household business and have extensive knowledge and experiences in marketing and sales of moth proofer products in China.

TLC is a research, development and marketing company engaging in moth proofer and household insecticides and have specialized and extensive knowledge and experience in research and development on insecticidal active ingredients, their formulation and application technologies.

THC, HBC and TLC are interested in evaluating the possibility of joint product development, manufacturing and marketing for moth proofer and household insecticide products in the Republic of Chinese market.

1. Purpose

In order for the Parties to discuss possible product development, manufacturing and marketing in the field of moth proofer and household insecticide products in the Republic of Chinese market (the "Purpose"), each Party (the "Disclosing Party") shall, at its sole discretion disclose to the other Party (the "Receiving Party") certain information which the Disclosing Party deems necessary and the Receiving Party agrees to receive for the Purpose.

2. Confidential Information

Confidential Information means any information, orally or in writing, exchanged by the Parties relating to the Purpose.

3. Protection of Confidential Information

3.1 The Receiving Party agrees, unless it has received the express written consent of Disclosing Party to the contrary, which consent shall be limited to the particular instance and restricted to such of the Confidential Information as may be expressly designated by the Disclosing Party, (i) to hold the Confidential Information in strict confidence and to take all reasonable precautions to protect such Confidential Information (including, without limitation, all precautions the Receiving Party customarily employs with respect to its confidential information), (ii) not to divulge any of the Confidential Information or any information derived therefrom, or the existence of this Agreement to any third party, and (iii) not to make any use whatsoever at any time of the Confidential Information except for the Purpose.

3.2 The Receiving Party further agrees only to disclose Confidential Information to the Receiving Party's or Approved Affiliates' directors, officers, employees and attorneys (collectively "Representatives") who need to know such information for the Purpose and provided that all such Representatives shall be bound by written agreements or fiduciary obligations securing their compliance with this Agreement. "Approved Affiliate" means an affiliate of a Party (i) as approved hereto by the other Parties, which names are as set forth in Schedule 1 or (ii) approved by the other Party's duly authorized representative in writing before disclosure of Confidential Information.

3.3 Without granting any right or license, the Disclosing Party agrees that the obligations in Sections 3.1 and 3.2 shall not apply with respect to any information that the Receiving Party proves (i) is or through no improper action or inaction or breach by the Receiving Party or any Representative of the Receiving Party of any provisions of this Agreement or any other similar agreement to which the Receiving Party is a party, has been made generally available or known to the public, or (ii) was already in the possession of the Receiving Party prior to receipt from the Disclosing Party, (iii) was lawfully disclosed to the Receiving Party by a third party (provided that the Receiving Party was in compliance with any restrictions imposed by the third party with respect to such disclosure), or (iv) was independently developed by or on behalf of the Receiving Party without reference to any disclosure by the Disclosing Party, as documented by written records.

3.4 In the event that the Receiving Party or any of its Representatives are requested or required (by deposition, interrogatories, requests for information or documents in legal proceedings, subpoena, civil investigative demand or other similar process) to disclose any of the Confidential Information, the Receiving Party shall provide the Disclosing Party with prompt written notice of any such request or requirement so that the Disclosing Party may seek a protective order or other appropriate remedy and/or waive compliance with the provisions of this Agreement. If, in the absence of a protective order or other remedy or the receipt of a waiver by the Disclosing Party, the Receiving Party or any of its Representatives are nonetheless, in the written opinion of the Receiving Party's counsel, legally compelled to disclose Confidential Information to any tribunal or else stand liable for contempt or suffer other censure or penalty, the Receiving Party or its Representative may, without liability hereunder, disclose to such tribunal only that portion of the Confidential Information which such counsel advises the Receiving Party is legally required to be disclosed; provided, that the Receiving Party exercises its best efforts to preserve the confidentiality of the Confidential Information, including, without limitation, by cooperating with the Disclosing Party to obtain an appropriate protective order or other reliable assurance that confidential treatment will be accorded the Confidential Information by such tribunal.

4. Return of Proprietary Information

Immediately upon a request by the Disclosing Party at any time, the Receiving Party shall turn over to Disclosing Party all Confidential Information of the Disclosing Party and all copies thereof, and shall destroy all extracts, studies, analyses, notes or other writings that contain or refer to information contained in the Confidential Information and will ensure that none of its Representatives make any further use of any of the Confidential Information of the Disclosing

Party. Notwithstanding the return or destruction of the Confidential Information, the Receiving Party and its Representatives shall continue to be bound by their obligation of confidentiality and other obligations hereunder.

5. No obligation

The Receiving Party understands and agrees that nothing herein (i) requires the disclosure of any Confidential Information of the Disclosing Party, which shall be disclosed if at all solely at the option of the Disclosing Party, or (ii) requires the Disclosing Party to proceed with any proposed transaction or relationship in connection with which any Confidential Information may be disclosed.

6. Ownership

The Confidential Information including any material support containing Confidential Information shall remain the exclusive property of the Disclosing Party and the Receiving Party shall not acquire any right, title, license or interest on or to the Confidential Information, the supports containing Confidential Information, or any patent covering Confidential Information.

7. Damages

Any Party who discloses Confidential Information in a manner contrary to this Agreement shall be liable for damages incurred by another Party or Parties, arising out of or resulting from any breach of this Agreement or the use of Confidential Information for a purpose other than the Purpose.

8. No warranties

The Disclosing Party makes no representation or warranty as to the accuracy or completeness of any Confidential Information. The Receiving Party agrees that neither the Disclosing Party nor any of its Representatives shall have any liability to the Receiving Party or to any of its Representatives relating to or resulting from the use of Confidential Information.

9. Term

This Agreement shall be effective on the Effective Date and shall continue for one (1) year thereafter. Notwithstanding the foregoing, Articles 3 and 4 shall remain in full force for ten (10) years after any termination or expiration of this Agreement; and Articles 6 and 8 through 14 shall remain in full force thereafter indefinitely.

10. Notices

Any notice or request delivered pursuant to this Agreement shall be deemed given when actually received by means of first class postage prepaid or courier service to the Receiving Party's address set forth hereinafter:

If to THC:

Tonghai Co. , Ltd.

Aderss and postcode:

Telephone Number:

Facsimile Number:

Attention: President

If to SMDC:

If to SCC:

or at such address as shall be designated in writing by such Party to the other Parties upon at least ten (10) days prior notice thereof.

11. Severability

In the event that any of the provisions of this Agreement shall be held by a court or other tribunal of competent jurisdiction to be illegal, invalid or unenforceable, such provisions shall be limited or eliminated to the minimum extent necessary so that this Agreement shall otherwise remain in full force and effect.

12. Governing Law; Resolution of Disputes

12.1 This Agreement is governed by and shall be construed in accordance with the laws of England without regard to the conflicts of law provisions thereof. The Parties agree that remedies at law would be inadequate to protect each Party's respective interests in the event of any actual or threatened breach of the provisions of this Agreement and that each Party shall be entitled to equitable relief, including the form of injunctions and orders for specific performance, in addition to all other remedies available to each Party at law or in equity as a remedy for any such breach or threatened breach.

12.2 All disputes arising under, out of or in connection with this Agreement, if unresolved by amicable discussions among the Parties, shall be submitted to an arbitration procedure, under the rules of the London Court of International Arbitration in effect at the time of applying for arbitration. The arbitral award is final and binding upon both parties. The arbitration proceeding shall be held in the city of London, the United Kingdom. The Parties agree that service of any notices in the course of such arbitration at their addresses as given in this Agreement shall be valid and sufficient. Judgment upon the award rendered in the arbitration may be entered in any court having jurisdiction, or application may be made to such court for a judicial acceptance of the award and an order of enforcement, as the case may be. Each Party to the dispute shall pay the expenses of its own arbitrator and equally share the remaining expenses of the arbitration proceedings.

13. Entire Agreement

This Agreement supersedes all prior discussions and writing and constitutes the entire agreement between the Parties with respect to the subject matter hereof.

14 Waiver; Modification

Waiver or modification of this Agreement will not be binding upon either Party unless made in writing and signed by a duly authorized representative of such Party and no failure or delay in enforcing any right will be deemed a waiver of such right.

In witness whereof, the Parties have executed this Agreement in triplicate by their respective duly authorized representatives, with each Party retaining on original.

Signature.

二 采购合同范例

买卖合同是最常见的商业合同，制作相对简单。其他涉外法律领域，中外合资合作、企业并购交易的合同也非常常见，但由于篇幅关系，本章仅提供一份简要的采购合同范例如下，以供学习借鉴。更为复杂的涉外法律事务合同，往往大型的律师事务所会有较为精良的合同模板可以参考。当然，对于国际工程承包领域常见的诸如国际咨询工程师联合会（FIDIC）合同条款等业内常用的合同，涉外律师执业者也应该非常熟悉。以下是一份简单的采购合同。

采购合同
Purchase Contract

买方 Buyer：	地址 Address：	
邮编 Postal Code：	电话 Tel.：	传真 Fax：
开户行 Bank：	账号 A/C No.：	联系人 Contact Person：
卖方 Sellers：	地址 Address：	
邮编 Postal Code：	电话 Tel.：	传真 Fax：
开户行 Bank：	账号 A/C No.：	联系人 Contact Person：

1. 总则 General Conditions

本合同是建立在买卖双方同意的基础上，依据以下条款对下述货物进行买卖：

This contract is made by and between the Buyer and the Seller, whereby the Buyer agrees to buy and the Seller agrees to sell the under-mentioned commodity according to the terms and conditions stipulated below.

2. 商品种类及总价 Commodity and Total Value

详见所附报价。See enclosed the offers as attachment to this contract

3. 原产地和制造商 Country of Origin and Manufacturers

4. 包装 Packing

4.1 用结实的木箱或纸箱，包装要适合长距离运输，并应防潮、防震。

To be packed in strong wooden case(s) or in carton(s), suitable for long distance transportation and well protected against moisture and shocks.

4.2 因包装不当和包装防护措施不当造成货物的损失和由此而产生的费用应由卖方负责。

The sellers shall be liable for any damage of the commodity and expenses incurred on account of improper packing or improper protective measures taken in regards to the packing.

5. 唛头 Shipping Mark

卖方应在每一个包装上用不褪色漆刷上编号、毛重、净重、尺寸和发货人公司名称、设备名称、以及如下标示"KEEP AWAY FROM MOISTURE"、"HANDLE WITH CARE"、"THIS SIDE UP"及货物的唛头。

The Sellers shall mark on each package with fadeless paint the package, gross weight, net weight, measurement and shipper's company name and equipment description, also the wordings: "KEEP AWAY FROM MOISTURE", "HANDLE WITH CARE", "THIS SIDE UP" etc. and the shipping mark.

6. 交货期限 Time of delivery

收到预付款后6个月交货。

Upon the receipt of down payment within 6 months.

7. 装运口岸 Port of shipment

8. 目的口岸 Port of Destination

9. 保险 Insurance

由卖方按发票金额110%投保。保险种类为一切险。

To be covered by the Sellers before shipment for 110% of total invoice value. The insurance is for all risk.

10. 付款 Payment

合同签订后预付合同总价的30% T/T 电汇。

装运前支付合同余款70% L/C 电汇。

30% by T/T down payment after signing contract.

70% balanced by L/C prior to the shipping

11. 装运条件 Terms of Shipment FOB

12. 质量保证

12.1 卖方保证本合同下的货物用一流的工艺和最好的材料制造，不是旧货物。

本合同规定货物质量和性能均与技术指标和技术说明书一致。货物的质保期为从签署验收合格证明之日起 12 个月或 2000 个工作小时,以两者之先为准。

The Sellers guarantee that the commodity hereof is made of the best materials with first class workmanship and unused, and complies in all respects with the quality and specification stipulated in this Contract and conforms to the data sheets or technical manuals of the commodities contracted. The guarantee period for all equipment shall be 12 months or 2000 working hours after the signature of the acceptance certification, whichever comes first.

12.2 若设备发生故障,设备自身原因造成的故障,卖方将提供免费维修服务;买方操作人员使用不当导致的设备故障,卖方应安排维修人员到买方现场进行维修,相关费用另行协商。

If the system broken down due to the machine manufacture reason, the Seller shall offer the repair service at the Seller expenses. If the system broken down due to the negligence of the operator by the Buyer, the Sellers should send service to repair the system on user site, related fee will be discussed.

13. 安装调试培训及服务 Erection & Commission & Training & Service

13.1 安装调试应由生产商完成,应在安装现场条件完成,收到买方书面通知后 30 日内完成。安装调试期间所需备件应免费提供。

Erection & commissioning shall be done by the Seller. And the activity shall be executed within 30 days upon the receipt of notice in writing which the installation place is completed by the buyer. All spares shall be provided free during erection & commissioning.

13.2 卖方提供技术服务时,买方应提供相应的支持,并对工作环境的安全负责。

Buyer shall provide necessary support and is responsible for the safety of the working environment while the Seller providing service at Buyer's site.

14. 不可抗力 Force Majeure

因不可抗力,卖方无法在合同规定期限内交货或不能交货,诸如制造期间或发货期间或运输期间发生战争、严重火灾、洪水、台风和地震,或其他买卖双方同意的情况,卖方不负责任。卖方应以任何可能的方式立即通知卖方,陈述不可抗力情况,并应以挂号函向买方提供行政当局提供的买方可接受的发生不可抗力的证明文件。

The sellers shall not be held responsible for the delay in shipment or non-delivery of the commodities due to the Force Majeure, such as war, serious fire, flood, typhoon and earthquake, or other events agreed upon between both parties, which might occur during the process of manufacturing or in course of loading or transit. The Sellers shall advise the Buyer immediately of the occurrence mentioned above in any possible manner and within fourteen days thereafter, the Sellers shall send by registered airmail to the Buyers for their acceptance a certificate of the accident issued by the Competent Government Authorities where the accident occurs as evidence thereof.

15. 延迟交货和罚金 Late delivery and penalty

除本合同第 14 款规定的不可抗力外若卖方未能在合同约定时间内交货，买方在卖方同意交罚金的情况下应同意延期交货。罚金应由付款银行从货款中扣除，延期交货的罚金不超过货物总价的 5%。罚金应按每延期 7 日为货值的 0.5% 计算，不满 7 日按 7 日计算。若卖方比合同约定交货期晚 8 周以上交货，买方有权取消本合同。同时，卖方应立即支付上述罚金给买方。

Should the Sellers fail to make delivery on time as stipulated in the Contract, with exception of Force Majeure causes specified in Clause 14 of this Contract, the Buyers shall agree to postpone the delivery on condition that the Sellers agree to pay a penalty which shall be deducted by the paying bank from the payment. The penalty, however, shall not exceed 5% of the total value of the commodities involved in the late delivery. The rate of penalty is charged at 0.5% for every 7 days, less than 7 days treat as 7 days. In case the Sellers fail to make delivery eight weeks later than the time of shipment stipulated in the Contract, the Buyers shall have the right to cancel the Contract and the Sellers, in spite of the cancellation, shall still pay the aforesaid penalty to the Buyers without delay.

16. 索赔 Claims

货物到达 90 天内，买方如发现货物的规格质量或数量不符合合同约定，除属于保险公司或船公司的责任外，买方可凭中国商品检验局出具的检验证明要求卖方更换货物，或赔偿或修理，由此产生的全部费用，如检验费、修理费、因退货、发新货和修复货物而产生的运费、保险费、存储、装货和卸货费等等由卖方承担。卖方应保证在本合同第 12 条款规定的质量保证期内因产品质量缺陷、制造工艺落后或使用不合格的原材料等造成使用时的损坏由卖方负责。买方应以书面形式立即通知卖方，并以中国商品检验局的证明提出索赔。

中国商品检验局的证明应作为索赔的依据。卖方应根据买方索赔的要求立即销毁次品，全部或部分更换货物，或根据次品情况减价。如果卖方在收到上述索赔后一个月内未答复，视为接受上述索赔。

Within 90 days after the arrival of the commodities at destination, should the specification or quantity be found not in conformity with the stipulations of the Contract except those claims for which the insurance company or the owners of the vessel are liable, the Buyers shall on the strength of the Inspection Certification issued by China Commodity Inspection Bureau, have the right to claim for replacement with new commodities, or for compensation or repair and all the expenses (such as inspection charge, repairing fee, freight for returning the commodities and for sending the replacement, or the repaired commodities, insurance premium, storage and loading and unloading charges etc.) shall be borne by the Sellers. As regards quality, the Sellers shall guarantee that if, within the guarantee period stipulated in Clause 12 of this Contract, damages occur in the course of operation by reason of inferior quality, bad workmanship or the use of inferior materials, the Buyers shall immediately notify the Sellers in writing and put forward a claim supported by Inspection Certification issued by China Commodity Inspection Bureau.

The Certificate so issued shall be accepted as the base of a claim. The Sellers, in accordance with the Buyers' claim shall be responsible for the immediate elimination of the defect (s), complete or partial replacement of the commodity or shall devaluate the commodity according to the state of defect (s). If the Sellers fail to answer the Buyers within one month after receipt of the aforesaid claim, the claim shall be reckoned as having been accepted by the Sellers.

17. 保密条款 Confidential Clause

卖方及卖方的代理、代表或卖方的雇用人、与卖方有合同关系的任何人在与买方发生合同关系时，或者履行合同过程中，应该遵守买方的有关公司人力资源、生产、财务、销售、采购等公司信息保密的管理规定，未经买方书面同意，卖方不得复制或传播上述信息。对任何卖方及上述人员的原因泄露买方信息从而导致影响买方的正常生产、销售活动或侵害买方的商标、专利、著作相关权利或买方的名称、名誉等无形资产的行为，卖方都应赔偿买方由此引起的一切损失。

Seller, the proxy or representative for Seller, employees of Seller shall observe the rules of management of confidential information on human resources, production, finance, purchase laid down by Buyer. Seller is not allowed to copy or spread the information of Buyer without the prior written consent issued by Buyer.

Seller shall take the liability to compensate all the losses incurred by Buyer about Trade mark, IP, Copyright and Name, Reputation etc. of Buyer due to Seller's violation of rules set in this confidentiality article.

18. 违约责任 Liability for Breach of Contract

如果任何一方单方面终止合同，应向另一方支付相录于合同总价百分之五十（50%）的违约金。

In case one party terminates the Contract unilaterally, the other party shall be entitled to be paid by the former at 50% of the total Contract value as liquidated damages.

19. 税费承担 Taxes bear

19.1 所有本合同项下按照税法由中国政府向买方征收的税费由买方承担。

All taxes in connection with the execution of this contract levied by the Chinese Government on Buyer in accordance with the tax laws in effect shall be borne by Buyer.

19.2 所有本合同项下中国境外发生的税费由卖方承担。

All taxes arising outside of China in connection with the execution of this contract shall be borne by the Seller.

20. 语言 Language

本合同以中、英两种文字各签订，两种文本具有同等效力，如中英文本存在不一致，应以根据英文正确解释并执行。

This Contract is written and executed in Chinese and English, and both language versions shall be equally valid. If there is any discrepancy, this Articles of Association shall be interpreted and executed according to English.

21. 仲裁 Arbitration

凡因执行本合同或与本合同有关事项而发生的一切争议，应通过双方友好协商解决。如果不能取得一致，应由中国国际经济贸易仲裁委员会北京总会仲裁。仲裁结果为最终结果，对双方具有同等效力。任何一方均不得寻求诉诸法律和其他机构来要求改变仲裁结果。仲裁费用由败诉方承担。除仲裁进行期间外，双方应继续执行本合同。

All disputes in connection with this Contract or the execution thereof shall be settled friendly through negotiations. In case no settlement can be reached, the case may then be submitted for arbitration to the China International Economic and Trade Arbitration Commission Beijing Commission (CIETAC) in accordance with its Rules of Arbitration promulgated by the said Arbitration Commission. The decision of the Arbitration Commission shall be final and binding upon both parties; neither party shall seek recourse to a law court, nor other authorities to appeal for revision of the decision. Arbitration fee shall be borne by the losing party. In the course of arbitration, both parties shall continue to execute the present Contract except those under arbitration.

本合同自签字之日起生效，一式两份，双方各执一份。

This contract comes into force upon the date of signing and stamping. It is worked out with two copies, each company has one copy.

买方 The Buyer：　　　　　　代表 Representative：

日期 Date：

卖方 The Seller：　　　　　　代表 Representative：

日期 Date：

第六章 英文案例阅读

从事涉外律师工作，需要对国外的法律理念、法律传统、法律制度有充分的了解，除需要尽可能地遍览世界各国法律相关知识之外，更要对世界主要法系国家的法律有较为深入的了解。我国是成文法国家，重要的法律制度和原则都体现在成文法中。而在英美法系国家，其部分法律精华是深藏在法院判决中的，因为英美法系国家有着遵循判例的传统，先前的法院判决阐明的法律原则或理论对此后案件的判决具有一定的约束力。这样一来，要充分了解英美法系国家的重要法律精神与法律规定，就不得不学会研读案例。

第一节 英文案例文本解析

受先例约束原则的影响，英美法系国家的法官在作出案件判决时，经常需要引用先前的判例来支持自己观点。基于频繁引用判例的需要，法律学习者、律师和法官均不得不经常地阅读和分析法院的判决书。这也推动了英美国家法院需要充分公开判决书，使有需求者能够便利地获得。法院的官方网站通常会公布其作出的判决书，但要求使用者对单个法院作出的判决进行一一检索显然是低效率的，因此就有一些组织和机构开展了判例汇编工作，专门收集和汇编既有案例的判决，便于人们使用。这些案例汇编在早期通常都是通过公开发行出版来实现，随着互联网技术的发展，大量的案例汇编是通过在线数据库的形式实现的。

目前经常使用的在线判例检索网站很多，对英格兰及威尔士法域的案例而言，可以推荐尝试英国和爱尔兰法律信息研究所网站，其网址为http://www.bailii.org。这一网站是公益性的，可以让公众免费看到很多英国和爱尔兰的法院判决书。对于美国的判决书，除在各法院官方网站查看外，推荐在找法网（http://lp.findlaw.com）进行免费的查找。另外就是商业机构提供的数据库检索服务，常用的就是LexisNexis和westlaw，这两个数据库都需要使用账号才可登录使用。在这两个专业的数据库网站上，除可以检索到判例外，还可以看到很多法律研究文章及英国、美国之外的其他一些国家的法律信息。

当然，英美法系国家只是以判例法为主，即除了判例法以外，也有成文法。对于成文法的检索，推荐使用的可免费查询的网站包括英国国家档案局的政府立法查询网站，网址为 http：//www.legislation.gov.uk/browse，美国联邦法典的免费查询网站推荐使用美国国会众议院下属的法律修订顾问办公室（the Office of the Law Revision Counsel of the United States House of Representatives）的网站 http：//uscode.house.gov 和康奈尔大学法学院法律信息研究所（Cornell Law School's Legal Information Institute）网站 https：//www.law.cornell.edu/uscode/text。

由于英美法系国家的法院判决以说理充分、分析透彻的特点见长，往往篇幅较长，我们在阅读时，要善于抓住要点，并事先要对这种判决书的文体结构特点有概括地了解。通常我们获得判决书，是通过互联网从数据服务商那里查询获得，这些判决书资料都是经过了数据服务商整理的，其在体例上一般由下列几个部分构成。

一　标题部分

这一部分主要包括案件名称、判决法院、索引出处、判决时间。例如 New York Times Co. v. Sullivan 一案下载到的判决原文标题部分如下。

New York Times Co. v. Sullivan
No. 39
Supreme Court of the United States
376 U. S. 254；84 S. Ct. 710；11 L. Ed. 2d 686；1964 U. S. LEXIS 1655；
95 A. L. R. 2d 1412；1 Media L. Rep. 1527
January 6，1964，Argued
March 9，1964，Decided

（一）案件名称

列出诉讼双方当事人的名称，有时会注明当事人在诉讼中的法律地位，例如，Helen Palsgraf, Respondent, v. The Long Island Railroad Company, Appellant。刑事案件的一方通常是政府，在上诉或申诉程序中，上诉或申诉方的名称往往位于左边，"v."是 versus 的缩写。

（二）判决法院

判决法院是出具本判决的法院全称。案例名称与判决法院之间的编号为法院内部对案例的编号，也可能并没有该编号。

（三）索引出处

索引出处对该判决文件原始文献出处的缩写。例如 376 U. S. 254，是指本判决文件出自《美国案例汇编》第 376 卷第 254 页；有时一个案件会注明多个出处，例如 84 S. Ct. 710，是指《最高法院案例汇编》第 84 卷第 710 页；1964 U. S. LEXIS 1655 是

Lexis 数据库内部的编码；95 A. L. R. 2d 1412 指《美国法律报告》第二辑第 95 卷第 1412 页。这些缩写代表的汇编主要包括以下几种。

1. 官方汇编，包括 United States Reports（简写为 U. S.）《美国案例汇编》，收录美国最高法院判例；另外美国的各个州法院也有自己的官方正式判例汇编。例如 Boomer v. Atlantic Cement Co. 一案注明的索引出处为：26 N. Y. 2d 219；257 N. E. 2d 870；309 N. Y. S. 2d 312；1970 N. Y. LEXIS 1478；1 ERC（BNA）1175；40 A. L. R. 3d 590，其中 26 N. Y. 2d 219 是指纽约州法院自己的官方判例汇编。

2. 非官方的汇编，以西方出版公司（West Publishing Corporation）的美国全国判例汇编系统（National Reporter System）为例，包括：

S. Ct. 即 Supreme Court Reporter《最高法院案例汇编》

F. 即 Federal Reporter《联邦判例汇编》

F. 2d. 即 Federal Reporter, 2d Series《联邦判例汇编第二辑》

F. 3d. 即 Federal Reporter, 3d Series《联邦判例汇编第三辑》

F. Supp. 即 Federal Supplement《联邦判例补编》

F. Supp. 2d. 即 Federal Supplement, 2d Series《联邦判例补编第二辑》

F. R. D. 即 Federal Rules Decisions《联邦诉讼规则判例汇编》

F. Cas. 即 Federal Cases《联邦判例汇编》

Fed. Appx 即 Federal Appendix《联邦判例附录汇编》

A. 即 Atlantic Reporter《大西洋地区判例汇编》

A. 2d. 即 Atlantic Reporter, 2d Series《大西洋地区判例汇编第二辑》

A. 3d. 即 Atlantic Reporter, 3d Series《大西洋地区判例汇编第三辑》

N. E. 即 Northeastern Reporter《东北地区判例汇编》

N. E. 2d. 即 Northeastern Reporter, 2d Series《东北地区判例汇编第二辑》

N. W. 即 Northwestern Reporter《西北地区判例汇编》

N. W. 2d. 即 Northwestern Reporter, 2d Series《西北地区判例汇编第二辑》

S. E. 即 Southeastern Reporter《东南地区判例汇编》

S. E. 2d. 即 Southeastern Reporter, 2d Series《东南地区判例汇编第二辑》

S. W. 即 Southwestern Reporter《西南地区判例汇编》

S. W. 2d. 即 Southwestern Reporter, 2d Series《西南地区判例汇编第二辑》

S. W. 3d. 即 Southwestern Reporter, 3d Series《西南地区判例汇编第三辑》

So. 即 Southern Reporter《南方地区判例汇编》

So. 2d. 即 Southern Reporter, 2d Series《南方地区判例汇编第二辑》

So. 3d. 即 Southern Reporter, 3d Series《南方地区判例汇编第三辑》

P. 即 Pacific Reporter《太平洋地区判例汇编》

P. 2d. 即 Pacific Reporter, 2d Series《太平洋地区判例汇编第二辑》

P. 3d. 即 Pacific Reporter, 3d Series《太平洋地区判例汇编第三辑》

N. Y. S. 即 New York Supplement《纽约判例补编》

N. Y. S. 2d. 即 New York Supplement, 2d Series《纽约判例补编第二辑》

Cal. Rep. 即 California Reporter《加利福尼亚州判例汇编》

Cal. 2d. Rep. 即 California Reporter, 2d Series《加利福尼亚州判例汇编第二辑》

Cal. 3d. Rep. 即 California Reporter, 3d Series《加利福尼亚州判例汇编第三辑》

3. 美国律师合作出版公司出版的相关判例汇编主要有：

A. L. R. 即 American Law Reports《美国法律报告》

A. L. R. Fed. 即 American Law Reports, Federal《美国联邦法律报告》

L. Ed. 即 U. S. Supreme Court Reports, Lawyers' Edition《美国最高法院判例汇编律师版》

L. Ed. 2d. 即 U. S. Supreme Court Reports, Lawyers' Edition, 2d Series《美国最高法院案例汇编律师版第二辑》

（四）判决时间

判决时间即判决作出的时间，有时还会注明辩论时间，如果判决作出时间与判决成文时间不一致，有时会另行注明判决书提交时间。

二　首部信息

除在标题中提供的判决信息外，在判决意见正文之前，判决书还会在首部对判决书的一些相关信息加以注明，这些首部信息通常并不是判决文件的原有组成部分，而是由出版公司委托专业人士精心整理的，通常包括以下项目。

（一）Prior History（案件历史）及 Procedural Posture（程序状况）

案例历史主要介绍这一判例在此前经历过的审理程序，大多时候会注明原审判例的索引出处；程序状况主要介绍本次审判程序的启动依据。从这两部分材料里通常能够简要看清楚这一案件的来龙去脉及各级法院的先前裁判结果。在数据库中有时还能够进一步链接到与本案有关的所有程序的文件数据。

（二）Disposition（处置情况）和 Outcome（判决结果）

案例的处置情况主要是说明对本案之前的程序是如何在本判决中作出处置的，例如对上诉的案件通常会有维持（maintain）、推翻（reversed）、推翻并要求继续审理（reversed and remanded）三种情况。判决结果主要是说明本判决自身所得出的最终结论。

（三）Case Summary（案例总结）、Overview（案情概览）和 Syllabus（判决要旨）

案例总结对本案判决涉及的事实与法律问题要点作出整理；案情概览较多阐述事

实与处理程序；判决要旨主要概括案件适用的法律原则。

（四）Judges（法官）和 Counsels（律师）

主要说明参与案件审理的法官以及代理各方当事人的律师信息。

（五）Core Terms（关键词）和 Headnotes（批注）

关键词是对本案涉及的重要法律术语的概括整理；批注是对案件精彩之处作的引述，有时会注明该段表述在某一法律领域受关注或被引用的情况，这也是数据服务商在判决书原文中对重要段落作出的标记。如果一个案例篇幅过长，除阅读首部的案例总结内容以外，可以通过跳读判决中的批注内容，基本可以把握这篇判决书所作出的重要论述的要点。

三　判决意见

这是判决书的正文部分，通常由主审法官或受法庭委托的法官或法官助理起草，有时还会注明是法官的口头意见或由谁宣读。判决书开头通常会注明该判决意见是由哪个法官作出的，如果是由合议法官全体一致意见作出的，会注明为 Per Curiam。由法庭经投票作出的多数意见（即法庭意见）是具有法律拘束力的意见，但同时根据案件情况也允许载明同案法官的附和意见和反对意见。附和意见在判决结论上与法庭意见相同，但可能具体理由和表述有所不同。反对意见通常是对法庭意见表示异议的意见。

通常我们看到的多数是上诉判决，因此会在叙述意见的过程中重述案件事实。也有对案件事实问题或法律适用问题专门作出一审结论的判决。通常判决意见写作开始都会归纳出本案需要解决的法律问题，再极具条理地阐明本案适用的规则并进行严密的推理和反复的说理，最终形成判决决定。判决结果（Decision）是在法庭意见的最后部分加以明确的。

除法庭意见外，有部分判决会有法官附注自己的附和意见或不同意见。附和意见（Concur）也译为协同意见，是指同意法庭决定，但对法庭推理有不同看法的意见。这充分体现了英美国家法官的独立性。协同意见不具有法律拘束力，但里面体现的思想往往会与法庭意见互为映照，甚至进一步解释了法庭规则。反对意见（Dissent）是不同意法庭意见的意见。反对意见亦无法律拘束力。如同附和意见一样，反对意见往往也会孕育新思想、新规则。在一个案件中的反对意见，有时会在后来的案件中作为正面意见在判决中被引述作为论据。

四　附录

除判决意见正文中会大量出现文献引用和注释外，判决书最后有时还会出现 Reference（附录），以注明与判决有关的信息或案情资料。

第二节 案例摘要

从案例研读的角度来看，为全面准确地把握一个英文案例的内容，通常要对案例进行摘要。对案例进行摘要的过程，也是对案例内容进行深入概括和提炼的过程，同时，形成的案例摘要，可以作为进行相关主题法律专题研究的素材，为将来在法律实务中引用这些案例作为引证使用提供基础。的确，我们在一份英美法院判决中随处可见到对其他案例的引用，因此，通过案例摘要的方式充分熟悉一些重要的判例，本身也是学习英美法的重要环节。对于中国法学专业学生而言，学会用英文作英文案例的摘要并形成习惯，也可以提高法律英语水平。

一 案例摘要的格式要素

案例摘要可以基于使用目的的差异选择不同的重点进行，有时可以格式周全内容齐备一些，有时可以仅做简略的摘要。通常而言，一份较为正式全面的案例摘要，可以参考下面的格式。

（一）编号索引（Citation）

这是该案例在判例汇编中的编号或在数据库中的索引号。如前所述，这一编号能够清楚地表明该案例可以在哪份判例汇编文本中的哪卷、哪页找到，将来在提及这个案例时，完全可以以该编号指代，这实际上是为这个案例提供了一个参考文献的出处。我们在英文法律文献及判决书中，经常只需要提及以当事方名字命名的某个案件名称，然后配合该案例的编号索引，即可清晰地指向该案例。

（二）当事方（Parties）

包括本案的所有当事方和他们在诉讼中地位的变化。比如，某个公司在一审中是以被告身份出现的，但在二审上诉中却可能成为上诉人，而且自始至终否认他们是侵权人。那么该公司的身份就应该被确认为被告－上诉人－侵权人（Defendant-appellant-tortfeasor），而另一方就应该被确认为原告－被上诉人－受害人（plaintiff-respondent-victim）。当然，也有可能出现原告上诉的情况，此时原告一方的身份就是原告——上诉人（plaintiff-appellant），被告即为被告——被上诉人（defendant-respondent）。

（三）诉讼历史（Prior Proceedings）

这里包括该案件以前所进行的诉讼程序和历史。比如 Trial court found against the defendant（初审法院判决被告败诉）；Defendant appealed（被告上诉），court of appeals reversed the trial court's decision（上诉法院推翻了初审法院判决）；and now this appeal is before the supreme court（改判判决后另一方不服再上诉到最高法院）。也可能是上级法

院对下级法院原审案例要求调卷复审（on writ of certiorari）。

（四）当事人的诉由（Theories of the Parties）

当事人的诉由主要是指原告起诉的理由或上诉人上诉的理由。类似于案由，例如 breach of contract（合同违约），sexual harassments（性骚扰），false imprisonment（非法拘押）等。

（五）寻求的法律救济（Objectives）

指当事方通过诉讼希望实现的目标。例如：getting specific performance（要求实际履行），absolute divorce（完全离婚），getting damages in the amount of ＄5,000（要求得到5000美元的损害赔偿），getting acquitted（要求被宣布无罪或释放）。

（六）案件事实（Facts）

案件事实即要对案例相关法律事实进行概括。特别是对于理解本案判决意见所必需的相关法律事实（legally significant facts）和与本案审理有关的背景资料（background facts）。有时在一份判决意见中难以获得全面的案件事实资料，因英美法系案件的审理经常会针对双方当事方在案例审理进行到不同的阶段所提出的动议给出单独的判决意见，因此有时一个案例，即便只有一个审判程序，也会有几份法院判决文件。这几份法院文件之中经常会出现对不再重复阐述已知案件事实的情况，这时就需要扩展阅读其他的案例判决以获得全面的案例事实资料。

（七）争议焦点（Issue）

所谓争议焦点，就是法院判决所必须预先解决的关于事实和法律的争议。能否把握案例的争议焦点，是能否准确理解这一案件判决意见的关键，也是写好案例摘要的关键要素。对案例争议焦点的陈述要尽量具体清楚，能够构成一个需要由法院回答的具体问题，从而针对这一争议焦点，能够进一步整理出争议各方对同一问题的不同看法，最后才能进一步理解法院的抉择。例如，Whether Plaintiff's loss and inconvenience constituted sufficient consideration to make Defendant's promise a binding contract?（原告所遭受的损失和不便是否构成充分的对价，从而使被告的允诺成为一个有约束力的合同?）

（八）法院观点（Holding）

法院观点即法院对本案争议焦点给出的看法。这些观点有时非常简洁，因为这些观点通常是充分总结和阐述了争议各方的立场和态度之后形成的，而在阐述过程中，法官通过叙述的措辞、语气基本上已经夹叙夹议，对当事方的看法作了评述，因此法官对该问题的看法有时是不言而明的，有时还会引用相关的判决观点、成文法的条款或法学研究文献来证明法官的看法，真正阐明的理由可能并不长，往往是通过最后的判决结果来给出答案。因此，对于法院的观点要在把握全文意见的基础上准确概括。

(九) 分析推理 (Reasoning)

分析推理即要由案例摘要者运用自己的言语阐明本案的法律推理过程,通常涉及这个案例所适用的法律规则,这些规则在本案中是如何适用的以及法院通过适用这些规则对本案给出的判决结果。

(十) 法官的附带意见 (Dictum)

在有的判决之中,有时法官会附带提出一些和该案件无关的法律意见 (obiter dictum)。这些附带意见未必和本案的争议焦点有直接关系,但至少会和本案涉及的某个问题有关联性。这些附带意见也是法官有感而发,其所阐明的法律规则或主张,可能也会对后来的案例审理具有启发和佐证的意义。

(十一) 心得体会 (Comments)

可以在阅读和分析案例后给出一些综合性的评述意见,阐明通过学习本案例所获得的启发。

尽管有上述 11 项要素可以在做案例摘要时一一提及,但在此较为完备的案例摘要格式基础上,也可以进一步调整适用。只要能够简要地阐明所研读的案例的内容、达到案例摘要的目标即可。

二 案例摘要范例

(一) 案例摘要范例一

以下是一份案例判决意见全文,在研读案例的基础上可形成一份课堂阅读案例摘要。

Charles RUFF, Plaintiff-Appellant, v. St. Paul Mercury Ins. Co., Defendant-Appellee

No. 431, Docket No. 31929

UNITED STATES COURT OF APPEALS FOR THE SECOND CIRCUIT

393 F. 2d 500; 1968 U. S. App. LEXIS 7192

April 9, 1968, Argued

April 25, 1968, Decided

DISPOSITION: Affirmed.

JUDGES: Lumbard, Chief Judge and Waterman and Kaufman, Circuit Judges.

OPINION BY: Per curiam

OPINION: The sole issue on appeal is whether a work-connected disability which appellant sustained in Liberia due to contracting poliomyelitis, which conceded is an endemic disease in Liberia, entitles him to benefits under the terms of an insurance policy which his employer had taken out for the benefit of appellant and its other employees serving in foreign countries.

Charles Ruff, a Pennsylvania citizen, commenced this action in the Southern District against the St. Paul Mercury Insurance Company, a Minnesota corporation, for specific performance of an employer's liability insurance policy issued to Ruff's employer, the Institute of International Education, Inc. Admitting that Ruff, who was teaching law at the Arthur Grimes School of Law of the University of Liberia, was covered by the policy, the insurer pleaded as an affirmative defense that Ruff's injury, resulting from endemic disease, was excluded from coverage under the terms of the policy. Judge Wyatt sustained the defense and dismissed the complaint.

Ruff contends that the district court erred in adopting this construction of the policy and he argues that the insurer agreed to pay benefits to the insured's foreign employees as if they were injured in New York State and covered by New York Workmen's Compensation Law, McKinney's Consol. Laws, c. 67. We do not agree with this contention.

The insurance contract is on a form designated as "Standard Workmen's Compensation and Employers' Liability Policy." Endorsement No. 1, entitled "Foreign Workmen's Compensation Endorsement" provides in Section 2 that the "Coverage A" of the policy is deleted in its entirety and the following is substituted therefor: "A. The company agrees to pay voluntarily on behalf of the insured to the employees... The compensation, medical and other benefits specified in the Workmen's Compensation Law and Occupational Disease Law of the state designated... In the same manner as if such employees were covered under the provisions of said law or laws." Section 4 of the same endorsement states "The provisions of this policy shall not apply to injury or death due to or arising out of endemic disease." Condition 8 of the policy states "All of the provisions of the Workmen's compensation law shall be and remain a part of this policy as fully and completely as if written herein, so far as they apply to compensation and other benefits provided by this policy... ." The "Foreign Workmen's Compensation Endorsement" provided that condition 8 is deleted and it substituted "All of the provisions of the Workmen's Compensation and Occupational Disease Law applicable in accordance with Section 2 of this endorsement shall remain a part of this policy as fully and completely as if written herein, so far as they apply to compensation and other benefits provided by this policy... ."

We agree with Judge Wyatt that Section 2 provides for voluntary payment of benefits of the kind and amount and in the same manner as provided by New York law to employees of the insured working outside the United States who were not entitled to insurance by New York law, on such terms and conditions as the parties contracted for in the policy. It is clear that the parties were not compelled to provide coverage coextensive with that required under New York law and that it was specifically agreed to exclude from the policy any coverage for disabilities due to endemic disease. This specific provision of Section 4 must prevail over any other more general language in the endorsement. While the result is not one which we like to reach, we can not rewrite the policy because of our sympathy for Ruff.

Ruff's other contention, that this court should take judicial notice of the Liberian Workmen's Compensation Act and apply its provisions to invalidate the limitation against recovery for endemic diseases, is not properly before us. A party must give "reasonable written notice" in the district court proceedings in order to raise an issue concerning the law of a foreign country on appeal. Fed. R. Civ. P. 44. 1. No written notice that appellant intended to rely upon Liberian law was given in the district court.

In any event, we were to consider Liberian law in deciding this appeal, we do not see how it could change the result. While Ruff might have a cause of action against his employer under Liberian law and Coverage B of the endorsement obligates the insurer "To pay on behalf of the insured all sums which the insured shall become legally obligated to pay as damages because of bodily injury caused by accident or disease… sustained by an employee… arising out of and in the course of his employment… ." the scope of that coverage, like the scope of Coverage A, is limited by the specific provision in Section 4 that "The provisions of this policy shall not apply to injury or death due to or arising out of endemic disease."

The judgment is affirmed.

课堂案例摘要（A Case Brief for Class）

1. 当事人

（1）一审原告（plaintiff）、上诉人（plaintiff in error）：Charles Ruff, work for the Institute of International Education, Inc. as a teacher at the Arthur Grimes School of Law of the University of Liberia.

（2）一审被告（defendant）、被上诉人（defendant in error）：St. Paul Mercury Insurance Company.

2. 重要的相关事实（necessary and relevant facts）

The plaintiff got a work-connected disability because an endemic disease in Liberia. The defendant issued an employer's liability insurance policy to Ruff's employer. The plaintiff contends that he should be covered by the policy, but the defendant held that Ruff's injury was resulting from endemic disease and was excluded from coverage under the terms of the policy.

3. 双方诉求及支持各自诉求的事实和法理

（1）原告的诉求：Be entitled to benefits under the terms of an insurance policy.

（2）被告的诉求：Plaintiff's injury, resulting from endemic disease, was excluded from coverage under the terms of the policy.

（3）支持原告诉求的事实和法理：the insurer agreed to pay benefits to the insured's foreign employees as if they were injured in New York State and covered by New York Workmen's Compensation Law.

（4）支持被告诉求的事实和法理：Section 4 of the endorsement states "The provisions of this policy shall not apply to injury or death due to or arising out of endemic disease."

4. 争议焦点（issue）

Whether Plaintiff be covered by the policy?

5. 该判决所阐明的法律原则或理论

The scope of the coverage is limited by the specific provision in the endorsement, so the insured's foreign employees' injury was excluded from the coverage of the policy.

（二）案例摘要范例二[①]

Carlill v. Carbolic Smoke Ball Co.

Citation. 1 Q. B. 256（Court of Appeal 1893）

Brief Fact Summary. The Plaintiff, believing Defendant's advertisement that its product would prevent influenza, bought a Carbolic Smoke Ball and used it as directed from November 20, 1891 until January 17, 1892, when she caught the flu. Plaintiff brought suit to recover the £ 100, which the Court found her entitled to recover. Defandants appealed.

Synopsis of Rule of Law. This case considers whether an advertising gimmick (i. e. the promise to pay £ 100 to anyone contracting influenza while using the Carbolic Smoke Ball) can be considered an express contractual promise to pay.

Facts. The Defendant, the Carbolic Smoke Ball Company of London (Defendant), placed an advertisement in several newspapers on November 13, 1891, stating that its product, "The Carbolic Smoke Ball", when used three times daily, for two weeks, would prevent colds and influenza. The makers of the smoke ball additionally offered a £ 100 reward to anyone who caught influenza using their product, guaranteeing this reward by stating in their advertisement that they had deposited £ 1,000 in the bank as a show of their sincerity. The Plaintiff, Lilli Carlill (Plaintiff), bought a smoke ball and used it as directed. Several weeks after she began using the smoke ball, Plaintiff caught the flu.

Issue. Lindley, L. J., on behalf of the Court of Appeals, notes that the main issue at hand is whether the language in Defendant's advertisement, regarding the £ 100 reward was meant to be an express promise or, rather, a sales puff, which had no meaning whatsoever.

[①] 该案例摘要材料来源于 https：//www. casebriefs. com。

Held. Defendant's Appeal was dismissed, Plaintiff was entitled to recover £ 100. The Court acknowledges that in the case of vague advertisements, language regarding payment of a reward are generally a puff, which carries no enforceability. In this case, however, Defendant noted the deposit of £ 1,000 in their advertisement, as a show of their sincerity. Because Defendant did this, the Court found their offer to reward to be a promise, backed by their own sincerity.

Concurrence. In the concurrences of Bowen L. J. and A. L. Smith, L. J., the notion of contractual consideration also becomes an issue of relevance. Both of these Judges note that while the Defendant could argue lack of consideration, Plaintiff, in buying the Carbolic Smoke Ball and using it as directed, provided adequate consideration through the inconvenience she experienced by using the product.

Discussion. This case stands for the proposition that while sales puffery in advertisements are generally not intended to create a contract with potential product buyers, in this case it did because the Defendant elevated their language to the level of a promise, by relying on their own sincerity.

（三）案例摘要练习的案件判决

以下是一份有关美国冲突法规则的离婚案件的判决，全文较为简短，可在研读的基础上做一份案例摘要，作为练习。

390 A. 2d 4, * ; 1978 D. C. App. LEXIS 401, * *

Gwendolyn C. Williams, Appellant, v. Alfred Williams, Jr., Appellee

District of Columbia Court of Appeals

390 A. 2d 4

June 8, 1978, Argued

July 27, 1978, Decided

Prior History:

Appeal from the Superior Court of the District of Columbia (Hon. Richard R. Atkinson, Trial Judge)

Opinion By:

PER curiam

This is an appeal from the court-ordered conveyance of appellant's interest in certain real property located in Maryland to appellee pursuant to an award of absolute divorce on the ground of desertion. Appellant raises one issue: the improper choice of the controlling law by the trial court in its determination of the ownership of the Maryland real estate. Since we agree with the appellant that the trial court failed to apply the proper law-that of Maryland-we must remand for further proceedings consistent with this decision.

The parties were lawfully married in Texas on or about June 3, 1953, and subsequently resided in the District of Columbia. Appellant (Gwendolyn Williams) was a legal resident of the District of Columbia at the time appellee (Alfred Williams) sued for divorce. Appellee resided in Maryland. Appellant's residence was thus the basis for our jurisdiction over the divorce proceedings and subsequent distribution of property.

The real property at issue, 2007 Hannon Street, Lewisdale, Maryland, was purchased by and through the sole contribution of the husband one month before the wife's desertion although title was placed in joint ownership of the two parties as tenants by the entirety.

The trial court found that the wife "entered upon a continuous and sustained effort designed to destroy the husband and the marriage." "[She] applied pressure to compel him to sell the marital abode in Washington and purchase the Maryland property… [Her] strong insistence [sic] that the House in Washington be sold, was part of the wife's plans to get all of his money she could and leave him."

The law of Maryland differs from that of the District of Columbia upon the question of the resolution of property interests between tenants by the entirety upon divorce. The law of the District of Columbia is set forth in D. C. Code 1973, §16 – 910. See *Moore v. Moore*, 51 App. D. C. 304, 278 F. 1017 (1922). In this jurisdiction, the creation of a tenancy by the entirety in property acquired through the sole contribution of one spouse is a gift conditioned upon fulfillment of the marital vows and continuance of the married state. Thus desertion by a spouse and subsequent divorce upon those grounds may result in a divestiture of the conditional gift of a half interest in the property in favor of the innocent spouse purchaser.

The state of Maryland has rejected the *Moore* doctrine. *McCally v. McCally*, 250 Md. 541, 243 A. 2d 538, 542 (1968). Under Maryland law, in the absence of proof that the acquisition as tenants by the entirety was not a voluntary act, the transaction is presumed to create an absolute gift of one-half interest in the non-paying spouse, and the courts will not inquire into the respective contributions of the parties or attempt an apportionment. *Anderson v. Anderson*, 215 Md. 483, 138 A. 2d 880, 883 (1958); *Gunter v. Gunter*, 187 Md. 228, 49 A. 2d [* * 4] 454, 456 (1946); *Brell v. Brell*, 143 Md. 443, 122 A. 635 (1923). See also *Hardy v. Hardy*, 250 F. Supp. 956, 961 (D. D. C. 1966). Given the conflict in the law of the District of Columbia and Maryland, we must determine what law controls the resolution of the property interest in this case.

The District of Columbia has followed the recent trend adopting the "governmental interest analysis" approach to resolve choice of law questions. E. g., *Mazza v. Mazza*, 154

U. S. App. D. C. 274, 475 F. 2d 385 (1973); *Fowler v. A & A Co.*, D. C. App., 262 A. 2d 344 (1970); Tramontana v. S. A. Empresa De Viacao Aerea Rio Grandense, 121 U. S. App. D. C. 338, 350 F. 2d 468 (1965), *cert. denied*, 383 U. S. 943, 86 S. Ct. 1195, 16 L. Ed. 2d 206 (1966). This approach requires us to evaluate the governmental policies underlying the applicable conflicting laws and to determine which jurisdiction's policy would be most advanced by having its law applied to the facts of the case under review.

The District's policy interest underlying the forfeiture doctrine was the protection of the innocent purchasing spouse's interest in marital property should there later be cause to divorce a wrongdoing spouse (divorce at the time of the doctrine's establishment then being based upon fault). *Richardson v. Richardson*, 72 App. D. C. 67, 69, 112 F. 2d 19, 21 (1940); *Moore v. Moore*, supra.

The courts of Maryland have clearly explained the policy interests lying behind their rejection of the Moore doctrine:

> Not that the doctrine of *Moore* does not have much to recommend it, or that we do not view with gravity violations of the marriage bonds; but to incorporate the doctrine of divestiture of the culpable spouse... into the law of Maryland would open a Pandora's box, possibly affecting the stability of land titles long thought secure, not to mention the engrafting of complications onto divorce laws already less than perfect. [*McCally v. McCally*, *supra*, at 542.]

The *McCally* court also noted with approval, *supra* at 542, the reasoning of *Hardy v. Hardy*, *supra* at 960, where the District Court ruled that the District of Columbia's policy of forfeiture ran counter to Maryland's strong policy interests in "certainty, convenience, and uniformity" of land transactions within its borders.

In our case, both parties had moved into Maryland upon purchase of the disputed property as a marital abode. The District of Columbia only obtained jurisdiction over this case because the wife deserted her husband and moved into the District, where the husband then sued for divorce. The District can have scant interest in insisting upon the application of its policy toward an innocent purchaser spouse to protect a Maryland resident when Maryland real property will be affected and that state has expressed such a strong interest in land title stability and would not protect the innocent spouse. Since (既然) "the only relationship of the District of Columbia to this claim is that it provides a forum with jurisdiction over [appellant,] [that] is hardly a reason for the forum to prefer its own notions of policy to those embodied in the [Maryland] law.... " Tramontana v. S. A. Empresa De Viacao Aerea Rio Grandense, supra, at 346 – 47, 350 F. 2d at 476 – 77. We hold that Maryland law should have been applied by the trial court to the resolution of the interest in Maryland real estate between the parties.

While the law of Maryland may not have been fully developed as yet by the cases, it is clear that the Maryland law's presumption of an absolute gift by creation of a tenancy by the entirety can be rebutted by proof of fraud, coercion, or undue influence in procuring the conveyance of the property to husband and wife as tenants by the entirety. *Ensor v. Ensor*, 270 Md. 549, 312 A. 2d 286, 290 (1973); *Anderson v. Anderson*, supra, at 883; *Brell v. Brell*, supra. The burden of proof necessary to rebut the presumption is "by clear and convincing evidence." *Klavans v. Klavans*, 275 Md. 423, 341 A. 2d 411, 416 (1975).

Although the trial court's findings of fact make reference to an intent to defraud by the appellant wife, we cannot say that the trial court has made the requisite determinations which would be required under Maryland law to defeat her interest as a tenant by the entirety in the Maryland real estate. Accordingly, we must reverse the judgment ordering appellant to convey her interest in the property to appellee, and remand for further proceedings consistent with this opinion.

So ordered.

第七章　备忘录与律师法律意见

律师介入涉外商事法律服务，所发挥的重要作用是参与商业谈判，从法律角度对合作方案进行可行性论证，对双方谈判形成的合作方案以协议文件的方式固定下来，对合作事务处理中所遇到的法律程序和法律障碍提供法律咨询，出具法律意见。因此，参与商事谈判、制作备忘录、出具律师法律意见，是涉外律师实务技能的重要构成部分。

第一节　商事谈判与备忘录制作

一　商事谈判中的律师业务

谈判是利益各方为解决问题、争议而互相协商的过程。商务谈判是商业利益各方为解决商业利益、纠纷而互相协商、妥协的过程。在谈判过程中，双方都会设法以在策略上对自己最有利的方式来表明自己的情况，一方面企图发现对方的真实态度，另一方面避免泄露自己的真实态度。初步的沟通，会使双方争议问题变得更加明确，各方的优势和劣势变得更加明显，最终由一方或双方作出让步，形成最终的谈判结果。

律师在商务谈判中的事务就是协助商务谈判的完成。为商业谈判提供好的律师服务，需要律师了解其在商业谈判中所扮演的角色和地位，并把握好律师参与商务谈判的要点。

（一）律师在商业谈判中的角色和作用

律师在商业谈判中扮演配角，商业谈判中谋求利益的双主或多方主体是主角。律师在参与商业谈判时，一定要区分什么问题是商务问题，什么问题是法律问题。商务问题可以直接交给客户决定，律师甚至不需要发表法律意见。而法律问题上，律师虽然同样没有最终的决定权，但往往会有较大的建议权。律师发挥法律服务的作用主要体现在，有些商事问题的解决的确依赖于法律问题的解决。

例如，客户为收购一个公司而进行商事谈判，往往面临着收购工作步骤安排方面的问题，第一步支付定金以后，当把股权转让、股东会决议等办理股权转移登记的文件提交登记部门办理后,收购方是支付全部股权转让款还是只支付一部分?如果收购方支付了全部款项但公司股权还没有变更到收购方名下时,该股权仍然有可能被转让方的债权人查封,所以稳妥的做法是收购方尽可能地少付款,等股权转让完毕后再付清。但是对方则当然希望尽可能多地获得付款,以免办理完毕股权交割后还迟迟收不到股权转让款而陷入被动。在这种情况下,律师可以提出建议,将需支付的股权转让款交由第三方进行托管,设立共管账户,即保障收购方将所有款项提前拿出来保障转让方后续能够拿到款项,又可以使得收购方的款项在获得股权前全部支付到转让方名下从而在股权被查封后一无所获。

(二) 律师参与商务谈判的要点

律师所接触的商务谈判,有的是拟开展合作双方进行的商务谈判,有的是为解决争端所进行的商务谈判,这两类谈判中谈判双方的出发点有所不同,但最终都是需要达成共识而坐下来进行商讨。谈判不但是解决合作双方具体合作方案的方法,还是解决分歧的最佳方法,即使在提起诉讼以后还可以继续通过谈判达成和解。事实上,在律师办理的民事案件中,相当部分是完全可以通过谈判解决的,只不过委托人与对方当事人因发生过冲突便产生了强烈的反感情绪而不愿意谈判,或者办案律师没有认识到本来可以通过谈判顺利解决双方纠纷而盲目顺从了委托人的不良情绪,或者有的承办律师根本不具备运用谈判技巧化解矛盾和分歧的能力,导致过多的案件没有经过谈判或者谈判破裂率高,最终不得不通过诉诸法院来解决;相反,统计结果表明,在美国、英国等西方国家,90%以上的民事案件是通过谈判达成和解而结案的,在已经起诉的案件中,又有50%以上最终是双方谈判而庭外和解的。在中国,据统计最终在法院立案起诉的民事案件中,也有60%左右的案件是通过双方调解后达成调解协议或撤诉而结案的。

律师参与谈判要注意的问题,主要有以下四个方面。

1. 律师对谈判所涉行业要熟悉

在谈判前的准备阶段,律师的主要工作是了解委托人对谈判项目的意图,收集有关信息资料、法律依据和有关政策,同时还要弄清谈判对手的资信和经营状况。在此阶段应要求委托人积极协助提供有关资料,密切配合律师工作。律师参与商务谈判常有的一个障碍就是对谈判所涉的行业不够了解,甚至一点儿也不了解。例如拟参与收购煤矿项目的谈判,如果律师对煤矿相关的法律、法规、政策、地方的规范性文件等不了解,对小煤矿实践中具体是怎么运作的不了解,则可能就难以提出有价值的法律咨询意见。如果律师参与收购房地产开发企业,而对房地产开发的一套流程的实务操作不懂,对开发中所涉的税费,对相关审批手续等不懂,则显然就难以控制交易流程中的法律风险。举例而言,在一起土地收储协议的谈判中,被收购企业希望将协议措辞调整为土地收购,而不希望描述为土地征收。作为土地整理储备机构的律师,就需要为当事人提供建议表明这两者在法律上有何区别。然而需要提醒当事人注意的是，在土地征收方面，国家有免除被征收土地的土地增值税的政策，如果把整理收购的事项描述为土地收购，而被认定为系土地转让，则无法享受该项免税政策。在这种情况下，律师通过自己所了解的一项政策规定给当事人阐明了调整协议文本措辞背后的法律风险。

在进行谈判方案的可行性研究时，律师不只限于法律方面，还要主动与技术经济方面的专家配合，使项目的可行性研究形成一个整体，同时还要进行风险预测和防范对策的研究。然后就调查分析研究的结论与委托人交换意见，介绍这类项目的传统做法和惯例，商定需要就哪些问题与对方交换意见，并根据委托人确定的意图与对方进行意向接触，进一步了解对方的动机和目标计划。同时要确定委托人的最大让步和争取达到的最优惠条件及最高目标。通过与委托人反复商讨后，就可以确定合同的形式和基本条款。这些准备工作是否充分，对于谈判是否能取得预想效果起着决定性作用。律师一定要审慎、周密地进行谈判前的准备工作。

2. 律师不宜作为主谈人并要善于保持沉默

商务谈判，比方说一个并购项目，要组建一个包括商务人员、法律人员、财务人员、技术人员，有时还包括翻译人员在内的团队，这样的人员配置能更好地控制风险。团队人员不易过多，一般控制在四五个人之内。谈判是商务活动，律师的工作只是为其控制风险以及对相关法律问题进行把关。律师并不具备商业判断的综合能力。但有些当事人并没有商业谈判的专业人员，他们会要求律师作为主谈人。这种情况下对标的品种、数量、价格等商务条款不是律师关注的重点，但律师应当充分注意到合同中约定不明的情况并在谈判中一一加以明确，特别是要防止条款上存在漏洞或约定不明而使当事人权益处于不明确状态。即便是律师作为主谈人，也应注意律师提供的意见仅供最终决策者决策时参考，绝不可越俎代庖在谈判现场未经委托方确认同意对方临时提出的条件。

在正式谈判阶段，律师的主要工作是对照研究双方的合同（或协议）草本，找出双方的分歧意见，对第一轮谈判要解决的问题，双方的观点和意图都应做到心中有数，然后与委托人磋商制定谈判方案。正式谈判时，律师是充当主谈判的法律顾问，要密切注意谈判的进展，对对方的意见和让步的程度应迅速作出反应，拟定新的具体方案提供给主谈判人。

商务谈判中有一个技巧如果运用好可以事半功倍，那就是沉默。沉默虽然无语，但却是一种进攻性的谈判策略。人对长时间沉默会感到很不舒服。你向对方抛出一个问题，他回答后，你不搭腔，他会觉得可能是他没有表达清楚或者没有表达全面才导致你沉默。为了避免沉默带来的尴尬，他就可能会披露更多信息。你保持沉默的时间越长，你越有可能获得更多信息。老练的谈判高手深谙此道。然而律师一定要注意不能觉得自己作为律师能言善辩而在现场喋喋不休。如果不注意在必要的时间保持沉默，则很容易掉进对方陷阱。

3. 事先确定谈判提纲

律师如果是主谈人那事先就得和当事人协商好整个项目的谈判提纲；如果只是负责法律方面的谈判，那就得把需要谈判的法律方案列成提纲，不能有所遗漏。对于己方的谈判提纲事先就要做到心中有数，坚持什么，在哪些方面可以妥协让步，所以谈判提纲要做到可进可退，关键条款和节点要得到当事人的确认。律师对经济条款和技术性条款，要尊重委托方和主管机关及专业顾问的主张，没有把握证明他们的意见有漏洞，就不宜参加意见。但有关是否符合法律的条款，律师应有主导意见。

在谈判过程中，律师应及时综合谈判双方意见，改写事先拟定准备好的合同（协议）或章程。对谈判期长的项目，或经过多轮谈判而尚未有结果的项目，可写出谈判纪要，其内容应限于反映谈判经过和双方的观点和意向，不能作为肯定权利义务的法律文件。在谈判的最后阶段，律师的主要工作是起草合同文书，正确反映双方意见。

4. 以促成交易为原则

商务谈判属于非诉讼业务，非诉讼律师不像诉讼律师那样当面锣对面鼓地对抗，需要更多的时候表现为合作性。律师的职责是为当事人控制风险，但律师的服务价值的体现需要以促成交易为前提，如果只想着控制风险，不能提出双方均可接受的风险分配方案，则最后生意没有谈成，律师的服务费用都可能没法收取。只有项目谈成了，律师才可能继续发挥服务作用。

为了尽量促成交易，在达成谈判成果文件过程中要尽量尊重对方，对方方案中于我方无损的内容应尽量保留。我方在谈判中已同意的条款，只要不严重损害我方利益，又不违首先提出谈判的方案和合同（协议）、章程的草案。如果谈判方案在我方内部来不及充分酝酿，合同草案来不及提出，谈判中只得就对方所提草案来讨论，这时，我方不宜采取逐条讨论的方式，而应只对对方草案中的分歧点发表意见，并应力争改写合同。这样才能变被动为主动。

链接：一则有关谈判艺术的传闻

基辛格堪称 20 世纪的谈判大师。一次，基辛格主动为一位穷老农的儿子做媒，想试试自己的折中之技。

他对老农说："我已经为你物色了一位最好的儿媳。"老农回答说："我从来不干涉我儿子的事。"

基辛格说："可这姑娘是罗斯切尔德伯爵的女儿（罗斯切尔德是欧洲最有名望的银行家）。"

老农说："嗯，如果是这样的话……"

基辛格找到罗斯切尔德伯爵说:"我为你女儿找了一个万里挑一的好丈夫。"罗斯切尔德伯爵忙婉拒道:"可我女儿太年轻。"

基辛格说:"可这位年轻小伙子是世界银行的副行长。"

"嗯……如果是这样……"

基辛格又去找到世界银行行长,道:"我给你找了位副行长。"

"可我们现在不需要再增加一位副行长。"

基辛格:"可你知道吗,这位年轻人是罗斯切尔德伯爵的女婿。"

于是世界银行行长欣然同意。基辛格功德无量,促成了这桩美满的婚姻,让农夫的穷儿子摇身一变,成了金融巨头的乘龙快婿。

二 律师起草备忘录

在涉外律师法律服务中,律师经常接触到的一个法律文书的概念就是 MEMO,或者叫 Memorandum of Law。MEMO 本身至少有这样几种情形:其一,在涉外律师事务所工作时,当主任律师接到一项法律业务后,可能会安排事务所内的助理律师(Associates lawyer)草拟一份法律备忘录(MEMO);其二,当我们向法院提交起诉状(complaint)或答辩状(answer)时,通常需要就法律和事实递交一份陈述状(MEMO);其三,在庭审(court proceeding)中,向法院提交一项动议(motion)时,也需要我们递交一份支持该动议的法律陈述状(memo of points and authorities);其四,当我们代理客户在参加一起国际商事仲裁(arbitration)时,仲裁机构也往往会要求当事方提交MEMO,以阐明自己的观点;其五,当我们代表国家在国际法院(International Court of Justice)参加诉讼时,国际法院也会要求当事国提交一份"memorial",这实际上也是一种 MEMO;其六,在律师对客户所咨询的某法律事项出具咨询意见时所出具的法律意见书,在英文中也是作为 MEMO 出现的。

上述 MEMO 的各种适用情形,我们在本章主要介绍两种,一种是作为谈判双方达成的一致事项确认为书面文件的备忘录,另一种是对某专门法律事项出具的律师事务所内部的法律意见(本章第二节)。

(一) 备忘录的结构

备忘录,可以作为记载交易框架、各方就该交易已达成一致和尚未达成一致的事项、各方下一步应该采取的行动等内容的书面文件。典型的备忘录结构包括首部 Preamble、前言(鉴于条款)Preliminary Statements、所达成一致的事项 Issues Agreed、尚需进一步磋商的事项 Open Issues、下一步行动 Next Steps、通用条款 Boilerplate Clauses、签字页 Signature Page、附录及附件(如果有)Schedules and Annexes。

律师负责或参与起草备忘录,可以运作自己的法律知识为双方在备忘录中确定法律上可行的交易框架,保障后续交易安排的可操作性。律师在起草备忘录时,要注意清楚地表达各方当事人的意思,对哪些事项是双方确定下来准备作出承诺的、哪些事项是仅有初步的想法有待于再行确认的要加以区分,避免就当事方无意承担的义务作出承诺。同时要注意确定项目进程,明确签署备忘录以后要开展的工作在什么时间由何当事方负责实施。

在备忘录起草中,特别需要注意的一个问题是区分有约束力的条款和无约束力的条款。对于双方确定达成共识并愿意在备忘录中确定下来的条款,可以将其确定为有约束力的条款;对于有一方倡议,另一方未作反对表示但亦不愿意作明确承诺的事项,可以确定为无约束力的条款。通常情况下,有约束力的条款主要包括保密条款、独家谈判权安排的条款、提供有关文件和信息以便于对方进行尽职调查的条款,还包括某些在备忘录中已经确定为达成一致的具体商务事项条款、下一步要开展的工作条款等。无约束力的条款可以是双方对合作项目具体方案的展望,为确定其无约束力,需要有专门的条款明确这些条款确无法律约束力。但是应当注意,虽然无法律约束力,但一旦这些条款在备忘录中出现,通常各方会认为对方有诚信的义务在后续继续遵循这些条款进行谈判(这一点与意向书类似)。如果对于备忘录中已经记录的事项,尽管已事先明确其无法律约束力,但只要有一方拟在后续的谈判中作出变更,通常需要充分地给出合理的解释以取得对方的谅解,否则可能会被对方认为是不诚信的,甚至基于某些国家的法律规定还要由此承担不诚信而带来的民事责任。

(二) 合作备忘录的范例

Memorandum of Understanding on Cooperation

<u>合作备忘录</u>

This Memorandum of Understanding on Cooperation ("MOU") dated the [·] Day of March, 2017 is made

本合作备忘录(以下简称"备忘录")由以下双方于<u>2017 年 3 月 [·]</u> 日签署:

Between:

(1) JHB Holdings, LLC, an affiliate of Jamie H. Brown Partners, L. P. formed by the principals of Jamie H Brown Partners, L. P. and organized under the laws of Delaware ("Party A"); and

甲方:JHB 控股有限公司,其为 Jamie H. Brown Partners, L. P. 的关联企业,由 Jamie H. Brown Partners, L. P. 的股东持有,依美国特拉华州法律设立;和

(2) Tianjin Tonghai Investment Co. Ltd., a company wholly owned by the Municipal Government of Tianjin and organized under the laws of the People's Republic of China ("Party B").

乙方:天津同海投资有限公司,其为天津市政府全资拥有的企业,按中华人民共和国法律设立。

(Each is a "Party"; both are the "Parties")

(每一方当事人简称为"各方",两方当事人合称为"双方")

Whereas Party A and Party B desire to cooperate in establishing, sponsoring, and managing a new China related private equity fund in RMB to be established under the laws of the People's Republic of China (the "RMB Fund"),

鉴于双方有意愿合作,共同设立、发起以及管理一家新的从事与中国有关的、按中华人民共和国法律成立的私募股权投资的人民币基金(以下简称"人民币基金"),

It is Hereby Agreed that both Parties will cooperate in developing the RMB Fund under the principles and terms set forth below:

双方特此同意将按照以下原则和条款进行人民币基金方面的合作。

1. The key objectives of the RMB Fund are intended to be:

该人民币基金欲达到以下主要目标:

Through its portfolio investments, support the strategic readjustment of China's economic growth model, by upgrading Chinese industries on global value chains, enhancing their global competitiveness, and supporting their global participation;

通过基金的投资活动,提升中国企业在全球产业链中的地位,提高中国企业的全球竞争力,帮助中国企业走向跨国经营,从而支持中国经济发展模式的战略性再调整;

Attract global businesses, international financial institutions and multi-national corporations to the Tianjin Binhai New Area ("TBNA"), by leveraging the municipality's experimental financial policies granted by the central government, and making Tianjin an action center and launch pad for globalized consolidation efforts (both inbound and outbound) initiated, participated, or led by Chinese companies;

用好用足中央给予天津的金融先行先试的政策,将天津打造成中国企业发起、参与、主导全球化的产业整合并购(对内投资和对外投资)的桥头堡,以此吸引全球商务、国际金融机构以及跨国企业落户天津滨海新区(以下简称"滨海新区");

Develop domestic private equity business in the strategic global buy-out area and build local teams with global capabilities;

在具有战略性的全球并购重组领域,发展本土私募股权行业,培养具有全球操作能力的本土团队;

Promote a globally significant deal making "ecosystem" in TBNA with a catalyst fund, and future forums, think tanks, and capital markets; and

通过这样一个带有催化、辐射效应的基金及其今后伴生的论坛和脑库,以及不断发展的资本市场,在滨海新区营造适于开展跨境重大并购投资的"生态环境";以及

Achieve attractive financial returns for investors.

为投资者带来丰厚的投资回报。

2. The tentative name of the RMB Fund will be "JHB Capital" or another name mutually agreed upon by the Parties. The size of the first RMB Fund will be targeted at RMB 20 billion.

该人民币基金名称暂拟为"JHB资本",或其他双方今后共同商定的名称,首期基金规模为人民币200亿元。

3. The RMB Fund intends to focus on portfolio investments that are solely internal to China or global/cross-border but have a China focus or are China centric, based on the following considerations:

人民币基金拟投资中国国内项目或围绕、侧重于中国的全球跨境项目。投资将基于如下策略考虑:

Initiating, facilitating, and participating in merger and acquisition driven opportunities with a China focus;

策划、促成以中国为侧重点的跨国并购与重组交易,并参与由此而来的投资机会;

Creating new global platforms merging together China assets and global assets;

打造新型的全球化企业平台,整合国内和国际的资产;

Creating value for portfolio companies through combining, optimizing, and expanding operations on a global scale;

通过在全球范围内整合、优化和扩展业务来实现投资增值;

Leveraging access to global companies that can be used as consolidation platforms or acquisition targets; or

发挥与全球公司的广泛关系,将其作为产业整合的平台,或境外并购的对象;或

Investing in domestic companies to enhance their readiness for global expansion.

投资国内企业,加强其国际扩展、跨国经营的准备。

4. In connection with the cross-border M&A driven opportunities in which Chinese companies or assets play a major role, the RMB Fund may (1) invest in RMB in companies and assets inside the People's Republic of China (the "PRC"), (2) invest in RMB selectively in companies and assets in Hong Kong, Macau, and Taiwan, or (3) convert the RMB to other currencies and invest in companies and assets in other countries outside of the PRC, provided there is a China focus to such investments. For purposes of this MOU, the PRC shall exclude Hong Kong, Macau, and Taiwan.

对于中国公司或其资产发挥重要作用的跨境并购所带来的投资机会,人民币基金将可能采取的方式为:(1)直接以人民币对中华人民共和国(以下简称"中国")境内的公司或资产投资,(2)直接以人民币试点性地对港澳台地区公司或资产投资,或(3)购汇以外币对海外其他国家的公司或资产投资,前提是项目以中国为主题。为达

到本备忘录的目的，中国仅指不包括港、澳、台在内的中国内地。

5. The RMB Fund should offer co-investment opportunities to Party A, its affiliated funds, Party B, and related sponsoring LPs in USD-based investments outside of the PRC. It can also invite other major Chinese investors with substantial USD funds to invest.

人民币基金在中国境外以美元为币种的投资项目中，应给予甲方、其关联基金、乙方以及相关发起人 LP 共同投资的机会。人民币基金也可邀请具有巨额美元投资需求的中国主要投资机构共同投资。

6. The RMB Fund may consider investing in the following industries, as long as the investments fit with the investment focuses above: manufacturing, green tech, energy and resources, chemicals materials, technology, information services, healthcare, financial services, and business services.

人民币基金可考虑投资以下行业，只要投资项目符合以上目标：先进制造、节能环保、能源资源、化工材料、高新技术、信息通信、医疗保健、金融服务和物流商务。

7. The RMB Fund will give priority considerations to companies based in TBNA in creating and structuring its investment opportunities.

人民币基金将优先考虑重点帮助滨海新区的公司创造和设计相关的投资机会。

8. The Parties will use their commercially reasonable efforts to have a more detailed plan for the RMB Fund by the end of May 2017.

双方将尽商业上合理的努力，在 2017 年 5 月底前完成人民币基金更详细的方案。

9. The target IRR for the RMB Fund is 12%.

人民币基金的目标回报率是 12%。

10. The term of the RMB Fund will be 10 years with extension options, with a 5-year investment period from the final closing.

人民币基金期限为 10 年，可续期，投资期为最终交割完成后的 5 年。

11. Except for special needs or as may be required by applicable law and regulations, neither Party shall disclose to any third party the contents of this MOU or any subject matters contained herein for a period of five years from the date hereof, without the prior written consent of the other Party.

除特殊需要或法律法规另有要求之外，各方未经另一方事先书面同意，不得向第三方泄露本备忘录（或其所涉事宜）的内容。此保密条款在本备忘录签订后五年内有效。

12. Nothing in this MOU grants either of the Parties any rights in any intellectual property of the other Party.

本备忘录没有授予任何一方对另一方的任何知识产权的主张、权利。

13. No Party may assign this MOU without the prior written consent of the other Party.

任何一方未得到另一方书面认可不得将其在本备忘录项下的权利义务转给他方。

14. This MOU may be amended, superseded or extended only by an instrument in writing signed by each of the Parties. No amendment to or variation of this MOU shall be valid unless such amendment or variation is agreed by both Parties hereto in writing.

本备忘录须经双方同意并签字，方可以修改、取代或延期。未经双方书面同意，对此备忘录的任何补充修改均为无效。

15. This MOU is signed in Mainland of Chinese. Therefore, the interpretation should follow the law of Chinese Mainland.

本备忘录签署地为中国大陆，并按中国大陆法律解释。

16. This MOU represents the entire understanding between the Parties with respect to the subject matter hereof. Except with respect to the obligations set forth in Sections11 through 15, this MOU is not intended to be binding on the Parties. The parties shall not be legally obligated by any of the terms hereof, other than Sections 11 through 15 hereof, unless and until definitive documentation in form and substance satisfactory to the Parties is executed and delivered by the Parties.

本备忘录代表了双方就有关事宜的全部理解。除了第 11—15 条下的义务，本备忘录无意对各方形成约束力。除了第 11 至 15 条下的义务，双方不受其他条款的法律约束，除非双方日后订立签署形式和内容令双方皆为满意的正式文件。

In Witness Whereof, the Parties have executed this MOU in four (4) duplicates in English and Chinese versions and both language versions shall have equal legal validity.

本备忘录以中英文起草，一式四（4）份，各文本具有同等效力。双方授权代表签字，见证作实如下。

Party A 甲方

Signed by

for and on behalf of

JHB Holdings, LLC

JHB 控股有限公司

in the presence of：

Party B 乙方

Signed by

for and on behalf of

Tianjin Tonghai Investment Co. Ltd.

天津同海投资有限公司

in the presence of:

第二节 律师内部法律意见

律师内部法律意见，即 internal or office memorandum，或称内部法律备忘录，指的是在律师事务所内，助理律师根据合伙人或其他高级律师的要求，就特定案件中所涉及的法律和事实争议（issues）进行分析，提出相关意见，以供决策者参考。由于 Office Memo 用于律师事务所内部参考，所以要求写作者以客观（objective）、中立（detached）和全面（comprehensive）的角度分析当事人在案件中的利弊（positive and negative information），最后根据法律和相关事实预测法院或仲裁机构对该案件可能作出的判决，并根据此种预测提出解决问题的最佳方案（recommendation）。

一 律师内部法律意见的制作步骤

律师内部法律意见，是律师向彼此传递有关法律专题研究信息的最常见方式。通常，初级律师会通过律师内部法律意见来为高级律师总结其所研究而得出的客户所需要的法律方面的信息。而在很多英美国家的法学院，撰写律师内部法律意见也是学生法律写作课程的重要内容。大多数的律师内部法律意见有两个功能，分析客户的具体法律问题或回答客户所面临的具体情况下的问题。在写作律师内部法律意见前，律师需要研究该具体法律问题所适用的强制性（有约束力的）判例法和有说服力（不具有约束力）的判例法所确定的法律环境，同时也需要浏览行政机关所发布的行政规章或规定。

在完成研究过程后，律师将从所适用法律的视角来解释客户所面临的情况。一份律师内部法律意见会总结律师的分析，并提供律师得出结论所依赖的事实。律师内部意见的重点应该是对客户是否可以合法地参与某项事务提出建议，或者对某一法律问题的最终处理结果作出预测。

阅读律师内部法律意见的人，不必再阅读出具该意见时所考虑的判例、法规或规章。律师内部法律意见的关键点在于把相关的法律概括为可快速认知、格式简短的要点以简洁地向阅读者说明情况。要使任何一位对该案件相关法律并不熟悉的律师，在对律师内部法律意见做简要浏览之后，能够给客户提供有根据的建议。确保律师内部法律意见遵循规定的格式，是为了便于阅读者很快找到他（或她）需要的信息。

大多数律师内部法律意见的格式都是一样的，包括：标题、问题、简短的回答、事实陈述、讨论和结论。制作律师内部法律意见的第一步是概括形成问题。"问题"往往是律师内部法律意见的第一个标题，这个部分要对所拟研究的法律问题进行一句话的简短描述，可以写成一个问句。第二步是写一个"简短回答"部分。直接回答法律问题，简单描述得出的答案所依据的法律，本节通常不应超过两句或三句话。第三步是写一份简短的"事实陈述"部分。本节应以中立的、叙述性的形式描述客户提供的事实。它应该只包括与这个问题有关的事实，并且应该尽可能简短。第四步是写"分析"部分。这是律师内部法意见的主体。它必须清楚地适用你研究过的案例法。当提到判例法或其他法律（例如法规和规章）时，应予以准确的引用。但不应该引用任何二手资料，如法律百科全书。第五步是建议部分，如果您必须确定客户的情况是否可行，请在本节中对为什么客户会获胜或失败进行分析讨论。你的建议应仅建立在你对法律问题的分析基础上，律师内部法律意见的目标是中性地评估一个法律问题，而非明确倡导一个立场。

二 律师内部法律意见制作中应注意的问题

按照律师内部法律意见的写作步骤，一份规范的内部法律意见要阐明法律问题，给出简要回答，然后就法律问题涉及的事实加以概括，经过分析之后给出有说服力的结论。对这五个部分，在制作中应注意以下问题。

（一）"法律问题"的写作应注意的问题

在这一部分的写作中，要注意所提出的问题应准确陈述该法律意见所要解决的问题。这个问题应当使用客观的语气描述，并且足够具体。这一问题通常是一句话，例如"是否……"（英文写作中的 Whether 或者 Does）。虽然所提出的问题很短，但它必须尽可能简明地提到所适用的法律范畴和有关的法律原则，并且将你的案件中最具有法律意义的事实纳入其中。一个完整而准确的问题应当是尖锐的，它应当直指法律问题的核心。尽管问题通常是被制定好的，让它们能以是或否进行回答（或可能是或否），但对于有些问题的确无法这样简单回答。所以，在你拿不清问题时，不要运用有绝对意义的词，如 must（必须）。

当你开始写法律意见时，你可能还无法确定哪些事实是最具有法律意义的。随着写作的进展，你的思维可能会变得更清晰，更有条理。你可以根据与问题相关的法律（如法规或判例法）来确定哪些事实具有法律意义。因此，许多人在几乎全部写完法律意见的"分析"部分以前，不会写出问题的最终版本（或简要的答案）。

（二）"简要的回答"的写作应注意的问题

简要的回答包含了对前述所提出法律问题的清晰答案（如一个预测）和对这个答案的解释。简要的回答可以起到两个作用：它为读者提供了一个容易理解的、底线的预测以及相关法律和事实的核心；它为读者提供了更全面的阅读大纲或后续讨论部分的摘要。简要的回答可以成为一个路线图，帮助读者在"分析"中找到具体方向。

在这一部分，可以直接用你的结论作为简要的回答的开头，例如：是的，不，可能是的,等等(如果这个问题可以这样回答)。然后给一个简要的(通常不超过4—5个句子)对你的结论的原因的解释,将法律法规应用于你的案例的事实。

（三）"事实"写作应注意的问题

事实部分包含了你随后的法律分析所依据的所有事实前提。当然,在你的分析部分中引用的所有事实都应该是事实部分里记叙的事实内容的一部分。工作很忙的、有法律经验的阅读者会重视这一节的简洁性,因此,尽量只呈现那些具有重大法律意义的事实或有必要澄清问题的那些事实。同时,备忘录作为一份独立的文件,可能会向律师所的任何一个同事传送以便他们理解,因此,事实部分应该总是包含对相关事实的全面而连贯的记叙,无论备忘录的主要读者是否已经了解这些事实。

事实的陈述要尽量有条理,可以完全按时间顺序叙述事实,也可以把最重要的事件或事实放在第一位。如果事实很复杂,也可以把事实集中到离散的主题中,选择你认为会让读者印象最清楚的叙述方式。你的事实部分,一定要说明正在被提起的法律诉讼程序,并且一定要描述已经发生的所有法律诉讼。

律师内部法律意见的写作是预测性的写作,当你叙述事实时,应该尽量保持客观和公正的语气。这并不是说你应该忽略那些有情感影响的事实。更确切地说,一份律师内部法律意见的事实部分不应该以一种表达对某一特定理论的偏好的语气来写。另外,不要在事实部分对事实发表评论,也不要讨论法律如何适用于他们。

写好事实部分,前提是律师要从客户那里获取到全面的事实情况。这就要求律师做好记录。当与客户进行开会沟通时,进行严谨的笔录。如果我们不了解这个事实的全面情况,以及一些细节,那么所做的法律研究就很可能会丧失重要的依据,或者忘记、遗漏一些很重要的法律分析。例如"时间"方面,做诉讼案子有关的律师法律意见,时效就是很重要的,如果我们遗漏掉时间这个细节,这个非常具体的客观事实,那么有可能事实上我方具有非常有利的因素,但是由于遗漏了时效这个细节,结果实际上有些条件的时效已经丧失了。当客户根据这份律师意见,去打官司,花了人力、物力,可能会产生不良后果。

（四）"分析"部分写作应注意的问题

在这一部分,要对第一部分提出的问题深入进行法律分析。例如,重申所提出的关键事实和问题,并介绍相关的法律规则;明确具体适用法律及其效力、生效时间、适用范围。这一部分律师工作的关键在于,要在了解基本情况的基础上,发现和找出法律问题。

有些情况下,客户可能在提出工作要求的时候就提出了一个很明确的法律问题。但更多的情况是,客户是将情况或项目的内容告诉了律师,然后要求律师来分析其中的法律问题,或者他告诉律师分析某个法律问题,但是因为客户往往不是法律专家,于是在他要求律师就某些问题进行法律分析的时候,会遗漏某些东西。比如客户询问的只是审批问题,那么律师作为法律方面的专家,应该有提醒的义务以及能力,告知客户,您提出的某些情况,可能还涉及以下问题:税务、劳动、土地、外汇,因为在实际情况中,这些法律问题通常都是相关的。能否准确地找出法律问题,很大程度上取决于律师对该律师法律意见所涉及法律领域的熟悉程度的高低。围绕客户所希望达成的目标及其所具备的条件、所担心的问题,律师要能够推演整个法律环节中可能面临的状况,找出顺利实现工作目标过程中可能存在的漏洞,总结给出最终答案之前所需要解决的悬疑,从而得出关键的法律问题是什么的答案。

在分析法律问题的过程中,我们还需要注意,所分析的一定是客户所需要的所咨询的。有的情况下,客户要求你做 A 和 B 的内容,但是可能写着东西的时候,我们就完全忽略了所要求的,按照自己所想的一个方向,准备了一篇指向于 C 的法律意见。应该注意的无论是客户还是所内的同事,在对方给你布置任务的时候,他在一定程度上是清楚问题的方向的,你一定不要自己去加工,去臆想,去换一个自认为合适的题目,而忽略了原本的要求。

在这一部分,要注意如何将构成规则的关键案例组合在一起,然后确定法院应用该规则的标准。有时候,某些主流的法律权威观点可能并不适用于客户的个案,这时要考虑采取适当的方式进行反论证,以表明在法律实践面前有些法律规定、既有判例本身适用于本项个案所得到的结果并不明确,从而得出针对该项个案的事实,律师不能十分肯定地预测到案件结果的分析结论。

对于可能在问题解决中适用但未公开的法律法规,律师可以匿名咨询当地相关政府部门,以获得这些规范性文件;对于有冲突的法律条文,也应匿名咨询相关部门,并将这项内容写入律师意见。当政府部门有不同意见时,告知客户相关情况,建议客户与有冲突内容的政府主管负责人进行交流,避免因法律适用分析错误而给客户造成损失。

(五)"结论"的写作应注意的问题

结论部分包含了对整个律师内部法律意见的要点的总结。在前面部分,可能还需要厘清一些看似矛盾的事实:有些事实似乎符合法律规定,但有的人可能认为这些事实并不符合法律规定。而在结论部分,就需要去权衡两者,确定本律师内部法律意见所持的立场,并就法院将如何适用法律作出结论。在这一部分,要明确告知客户做法,并为其提出相关建议。

结论要尽可能传达出这样的信息:你完全有信心,法院会根据律师内部法律意见的预测作出裁决,或者,考虑某些状况,可能会发生某些问题。或者你可以表达你有多大程度的信心。请记住,阅读者将根据律师的语气和手头的数据来判断你的可信度。

三 律师内部法律意见的范例

这是一份某法学院网站上的律师法律内部法律意见范本,讨论的问题是一份商品低价抛售的广告是否构成要约,从而商店可被未购得该商品的购物者追究违约责任的问题。

Sample Memo[①]

To: Gaby Duane

From: Clark Thomas

Re: Loman's Fashions-Breach of contract claim (advertising circular)

Date: April 26, 2002

Question Presented

Under New York law, did Loman's Fashions' description of a designer leather coat in an advertising circular constitute an offer to sell the coat which became a binding contract when the text of the advertisement indicated that the coats were a "manufacturer's closeout" and that the early shopper would be rewarded, and when a shopper signified her intent to purchase the coat according to the advertised terms?

Short Answer

No. Where, as here, the text of the advertisement merely stated that the sale was a "manufacturer's closeout" and that the "early" shopper would "catch the savings," the advertisement was not an offer to sell the coat which could be converted into a binding contract by conduct signifying an acceptance of the advertised terms.

Facts

Loman's Fashions, a retailer of women's and men's outerwear, distributed a circular in November advertising a manufacturer's closeout of designer women's leather coats for $59.99, coats that regularly sold for $300.00. The ad announced that the store would open at 7 a.m. on Friday, November 30, and stated that the "early bird catches the savings!" After about fifteen minutes, all the advertised coats had been sold. At 7:30 a.m., a shopper inquired about the coats and was told that there were none left, but she complained that Loman's was obligated to sell her a comparably valued designer leather coat at the advertised price. The store manager declined, and the shopper filed a complaint in Small Claims Court, alleging that Loman's had breached a contract by failing to sell the advertised leather coats at the advertised price.

---

① 此范例材料来源于 http://www.law.cuny.edu/legal-writing/students/memorandum/memorandum-3.html。

Loman's president, Willi Loman, stated that the store occasionally gives rain checks when it is possible to replenish supplies of an item that Loman's can purchase at a discount. In this case, the manufacturer had discontinued the line of coats and Loman's was not prepared to sell other, designer leather coats at such a drastic markdown. Loman expressed concern that, if the shopper's interpretation were to hold, Loman's would have to reconsider its marketing strategies; she had assumed that the advertised terms applied while supplies lasted. She asks whether Loman's would have any contractual obligation under these circumstances.

Discussion

Loman's Fashions has been sued by a shopper for a breach of contract for its failure to sell a designer leather coat that had been advertised for sale at a substantially marked-down price. Loman's contends that the advertisement was intended to apply while supplies of the item lasted, and that is it not obligated to sell the shopper a comparably valued coat at the advertised price. The issue in this case is whether a retailer's advertisement will be considered to be an offer that may be turned into a binding contract by a shopper who signifies an intention to purchase the items described in the advertisement. A court would likely conclude that the shopper did not state a cause of action for breach of contract because the advertisement did not constitute an offer which, upon acceptance, could be turned into a contract but rather and invitation to negotiate.

In New York, the rule is well settled that an advertisement is merely an invitation to enter into negotiations, and is not an offer that may be turned into a contract by a person who communicates an intention to purchase the advertised item. Geismar v. Abraham & Strauss, 439 N. Y. S. 2d 1005 (Dist. Ct. Suffolk Co. 1981); Lovett v. Frederick Loeser & Co., 207 N. Y. S. 753 (Manhattan Mun. Ct. 1924); Schenectady Stove Co. v. Holbrook, 101 N. Y. 45 (1885); People v. Gimbel Bros., Inc., 115 N. Y. S. 2d 857 (Manhattan Ct. Spec. Sess. 1952). The only general test is the inquiry whether the facts show that some performance was promised in positive terms in return for something requested. Lovett, 207 N. Y. S. 2d at 755. However, a purchaser may not make a valid contract by mere acceptance of a "proposition." Schenectady Stove Co., 101 N. Y. at 48. Nor does the purchaser have the right to select an item which the seller does not have in stock or is not willing to sell at a reduced price. Lovett, 207 N. Y. S. at 757.

An offer to contract must be complete and definite in its material terms; a general advertisement that merely lists items for sale is at best an invitation to negotiate unless it promises to sell an item in return for something requested. In Schenectady Stove Co., for example, the plaintiff delivered to defendant a catalogue of prices containing a statement of terms of sale, but the catalogue did not state the amount of goods which plaintiff was willing to sell on those terms. Under these circumstances, the Court of Appeals held that no contract was ever made between the parties with respect to an order that defendant submitted because the plaintiff had not made an offer that was complete and definite in all material terms. Hence, it was not possible for the defendant to make a valid contract by mere acceptance of a "proposition." 101 N. Y. at 48. Similarly, in Lovett, a department store advertised that it would sell, deliver, and install certain "well known standard makes of radio receivers at 25 percent to 50 percent reduction" from advertised list prices. The plaintiff had demanded a particular model of radio that was not listed in the ad, and the defendant had declined to sell it at the reduced price. 207 N. Y. S. at 754. The court held that an advertisement by a department store was not an offer but an invitation to all persons that the advertiser was ready to receive offers for the goods upon the stated terms, reasoning that such a general advertisement was distinguishable from an offer of a reward or other payment in return for some requested performance. Id. at 755 – 56. The court further held that, even assuming the plaintiff's "acceptance" turned the offer into a contract, the purchaser did not have the right to select the item which the defendant did not have in stock or was not willing to sell at a reduced price. Id. at 756 – 57.

Loman's advertisement did not contain a promise to sell the leather coats in exchange for some requested act or promise. By its terms, the advertisement announced that it had a stock of coats to sell, and described the coats as a manufacturer's closeout selling at a substantially reduced price. Nor did the ad give the public an option to choose any comparably priced leather coat if the advertised coats were no longer available. As the court noted in Lovett, a prospective purchaser does not have the right to select items that the retailer does not have in stock or is not willing to sell at a reduced price. Lovett, 207 N. Y. S. at 757.

The claimant here might argue that the advertisement did not contain limiting language, for example, that the coats were for sale while supplies lasted. However, the ad indicated that the store, opening for business on the day of the sale at 7 a. m., was catering to early morning shoppers. By announcing that "the early bird catches the savings," the ad could fairly be read to mean that the supplies were not unlimited.

Conclusion

On these facts, the court will probably find that the claimant has failed to state a cause of action for breach of contract because the ad did not constitute an offer but merely an invitation to negotiate.

四 律师对外出具的法律意见范例

在律师内部法律意见的基础上,如果律师所主任律师认为该法律意见达到了向客户出具的水平,则可以更换抬头后直接提供给客户使用。因此,律师事务所对客户所委托出具的某专项问题的法律意见,在格式内容和要求上几乎与律师内部法律意见完全一致。在此,提供一份由一家外国律师事务所提供给国内公司的律师法律意见供学习参考。

Legal Memorandum

To:Tianjin Tonghai International Trade Corporation Ltd.

From:Kevin Law Office

Date:May 9, 2017

Case:Tianjin Tonghai vs. JHB

Re:Enforcement and Bankruptcy Procedure under Turkish Law

Ⅰ. **Statement of Assignment**

We have been asked to prepare a legal memorandum on the question of whether the legal procedures conducted for Tianjin Tonghai International Trade Corporation Ltd. ("Tianjin Tonghai") in Turkey have met the requirements of the short-term export credit insurance policy issued by China Export & Credit Insurance Corporation ("Sinosure").

This memo includes the facts provided us with by the representatives of Tianjin Tonghai, a detailed explanation of the bankruptcy process of JHB Energy Co., Ltd. ("JHB") under Turkish law, legal transactions conducted on behalf of Tianjin Tonghai by our law office, a brief summary of the current situation and the conclusion.

Ⅱ. **Facts**

i. Tianjin Tonghai carried out coal intermediary trade to Turkey, but the buyer has not paid any amounts of 3 contracts since 2015.

ii. Tianjin Tonghai Company insured short-term export credit insurance from Sinosure.

iii. Under the short-term export credit insurance policy of Sinosure, Sinosure covers the following commercial risks under non letter of credit payment, (1) Bankruptcy of a buyer or his incapability to pay the debt; (2) Refusal by the buyer to pay the proceeds after accepting the goods; (3) Refusal by the buyer to accept the goods.

iv. The Article 13 of the policy states, for Sales contract with payment guarantee or existence of disputes between trade parties, The Insurer will follow the following principles to assess the loss and claims, (1) For Sales contract with payment guarantee, unless approved in writing by the insurer, before the guarantor guarantees payment according to the agreement, or the insured apply for arbitration towards the guarantor or filed a lawsuit in the guarantor's country (region) towards the guarantor and obtained effective arbitration award or court judgment and had applied for execution. The insurer will not assess the loss and make compensation; (2) When the buyer refused to pay the payment or reject the goods because of trade disputes, unless approved in writing by the insurer, the insured should conduct arbitration or filed a lawsuit in the buyer's country (region) fist. Before obtaining effective arbitration award or court judgment and had applied for execution, the insurer shall not assess the loss and make compensation.

v. The 3 copies of the contracts Tianjin Tonghai holds are traded with the buyer THC International Trading Ltd ("THC"). JHB provided a 100% guarantee of all debts of THC with a letter of guarantee but issued 3 pieces of promissory notes with the value of 80% of the amount payment.

vi. JHB received all the goods and issued the Delivery Note.

III. Bankruptcy and Liquidation of Jhb

There are multiple ways to commence a bankruptcy proceeding under Turkish Law. In general, the process begins with the creditors' filing their claims against the debtors to the execution offices or the debtors' applying to the court and demanding their own bankruptcy. However, in our case, the creditors did not commence any kind of bankruptcy proceeding. Instead, JHB made an application to the İstanbul Anadolu 6th Commercial Court to postpone its bankruptcy in accordance with Article 377 of Turkish Commercial Code ("TCC") and Article 179 of the Enforcement and Bankruptcy Law.

Article 377 of TCC set forths that the Board of Directors or any of the creditors shall request the postponement of the bankruptcy by presenting a reconstruction project, which shows objective and real sources and precautions including contributing to cash capital, to the court. In this case, Article 179 and 179/b of the Enforcement and Bankruptcy Law shall be implemented.

Article 179 of the Enforcement and Bankruptcy Law set forths that if the directors, representatives or liquidators of stock corporations and cooperatives declare to the court that the company is heavily indebted according to the interim balance sheet calculated by way of probable selling prices of the assets and the court recognises such case, it may declare the bankruptcy without any necessity of prior execution process. However, one of the persons responsible for administration and representation may demand the postponement of bankruptcy by presenting to the court in the place where the company headquarters is located for a long period of improvement project showing that the improvement of the financial situation of the company or cooperative is possible. The improvement project shall indicate all the objective and actual resources and measures, including the intvesting of new cash resources and how to cover all operating expenses and work capital during the postponement period.

In the light of the articles mentioned above, JHB's directors filed the request to postpone JHB's bankruptcy for one year up to five years. This request was made along with an improvement project; and the commercial court appointed a commission of trustees and experts to review JHB's current financial statute and feasibility of such improvement project. After the reports of the trustees and expert commission, the commercial court decided that JHB's capital cannot improve and declared bankruptcy at the date of February 10, 2016.

In accordance with the Article 165 of the Enforcement and Bankruptcy Law, the bankruptcy verdict rendered by the commercial court comes into effect at the exact moment when the decision is announced by the judge. Appeal against conviction doesn't constitute any delay nor impediment for the liquidation process under the Article 164 of the Bankruptcy Code. Once the decision of bankruptcy is rendered, all debts of the debtor become due and the decision is conveyed to the bankruptcy office. In other words, all the transactions required for the dissolution/liquidation process continues to be made by the bankruptcy office as free and clear of the appellate procedure.

In accordance with the Article 184 and 191 of the Enforcement and Bankruptcy Law, the insolvent's all attachable assets and rights constitute the bankrupt's estate within the commencement of the bankruptcy and the insolvent loses its control over the assets thereafter. The bankruptcy administration conducts the liquidation process.

In compliance with the Article 195 and 232 of the Enforcement and Bankruptcy Law, all the creditors may apply to the bankruptcy office for the registration of their claims and the bankruptcy office prepares a list of credits (namely, the ranking scheme). This list indicates all the debt claims submitted to the bankruptcy office, including disputed claims and legal entity's receivables from the third parties. In other words, the rejection or acception of a claim is disclosed within the list's announcement and notification to the creditors. After the determination of the assets and liabilities of the bankruptcy estate, the bankruptcy office commences the liquidation process. The assets are sold within public auctions or bargaining according to Article 241 of the Bankruptcy Law. When the sale process and the collection of the receivables is finalized, the collected amount is distributed to the creditors equally in accordance with the list drawn up by the bankruptcy office in compliance with the Article 247 and 250 of the Bankruptcy Law.

IV. Legal Actions Conducted to Date

Legal actions conducted up to present are as below:

Commencement of an execution proceeding against JHB with 3 promissory notes: Under Turkish Law, the creditor has the right to commence an execution proceeding against the debtor for his credit arising from a check, bill or promissory note. In other words, it is not required to take a civil action before courts in order to collect the debts arising from the promissory notes. Although taking a civil action is another way of collecting the receivables, commencing a proceeding with promissory notes is much faster and easier than taking a civil action, because of the fact that promissory notes are considered as one of the most "certain credits". If the debtor does not object the creditor's claim in 5 days following the receival of notification, the credit becomes certain and the creditor may confiscate and sell the assets of the debtor by using the force of execution offices. As for civil actions, it takes 3 – 4 years approximately and the enforcement process starts only after the court renders its decision. Therefore, it could be easily said that no one practicing law in Turkey chooses to start a trial rather than commencing an execution proceeding if there are promissory notes subjected to the case.

• Intervened in the case of JHB regarding the suspension of bankruptcy.

Intervening in a case regarding the suspension of a company's bankruptcy enables the creditors to submit their receivables to the court, to watch the process closely and have the right to speak for the benefit or to the detriment of the company.

• Application to bankruptcy office for the credits arising from 3 promissory notes.

• Application to bankruptcy office for the credits arising from the sales contracts (20% of the guaranteed amount mentioned under the vi/Facts section).

V. Current Situation

As Kevin Law Office, we have made all the applications necessary for the collection of receivables of Tianjin Tonghai under Turkish Law. We are now waiting for the preparation of the ranking scheme by the bankruptcy office. After the announcement of such ranking scheme, we will be able to see whether the existence of Tianjin Tonghai's credits are accepted or not. In the event of rejection, a registration action set forth in the Article 235 of Enforcement and Bankruptcy Law may be brought against the bankruptcy office in order to ensure the claims to be accepted. Such case presented for the registration takes 1 or 2 years approximately.

VI. Conclusion

You may kindly find below our conclusions in the light of our explanations above.

• In Turkey, most of the debt recovery procedures will go in the enforcement procedure without trial if the debt arising from promissory notes, because it is much faster and more beneficial for the creditor.

- The execution proceeding commenced for Tianjin Tonghai did not cause JHB's bankruptcy. It is possible for the creditors to demand from court a company's bankruptcy; but in our case JHB commenced the process with the intention of suspending its bankruptcy, but failed to do so. Other creditors intervened in the case of suspension of bankruptcy in the exact way we did for Tianjin Tonghai to watch the process closely and protect its rights.

- If Tianjin Tonghai had no promissory notes from the very beginning in this case, we would start the recovery procedure according to the letter of guarantee and take a civil action against JHB or start another kind of execution proceeding; but promissory notes are more definite proofs of Tianjin Tonghai's credits, in contrast with the letter of guarantee. In such case, we cannot say it will lead to JHB directly into bankruptcy; because of the fact that JHB caused its bankruptcy by its own will and action. On the other hand, if JHB had not started the bankruptcy suspension trial, we would be able to demand its bankruptcy with following a different legal process if it was in line with the benefits and wishes of Tianjin Tonghai.

- All the applications that can be made for the collection of receivables of Tianjin Tonghai under Turkish Law is completed; but the bankruptcy and liquidation process for JHB is still ongoing. In the event of rejection of credits, a registration action set forth in the Article 235 of Enforcement and Bankruptcy Law may be brought against the bankruptcy office in order to ensure the claims to be accepted. Such case presented for the registration takes 1 or 2 years approximately.

- We are of the opinion that the legal procedures conducted for Tianjin Tonghai in Turkey have met the requirements of the short-term export credit insurance policy issued by Sinosure.

Should you have any further queries, please do not hesitate to contact.

Best regards,

Kevin Law Office.

第八章 非诉涉外律师业务要略

非诉讼律师业务涉及案件诉讼仲裁之外的律师业务，在涉外律师业务中，律师除代理涉外仲裁和诉讼案件之外，还有广泛参与涉外经济贸易等客户的经营行为，为客户开展涉外的投资、贸易、融资等商事活动提供多样化的法律服务。律师开展非诉业务与诉讼业务存在着很大的不同。对于诉讼律师而言，往往只需要熟悉较为高层次的法律就可以了，但是非诉业务的律师，可能还需要进一步了解客户开展经营活动所涉及的各种政府规章、细则、规章制度等规范性文件，熟悉经营事务办理中的详细流程，从而才能为客户提供具有价值的法律建议。而在涉外律师业务中，非诉业务律师需要熟练掌握有关涉外法律法规，并通晓外商投资、国际贸易、知识产权保护等法律知识，同时又具有优秀的外语表达能力。因篇幅所限，本章有关非诉涉外律师业务的内容不会对开展具体业务过程中所需要把握的具体法律规定等相关法律知识进行详细介绍，而主要着眼于律师从事常见跨国投资与并购业务、国际贸易与知识产权业务、证券与其他商事业务等非诉涉外法律服务领域中，律师所应关注的要点问题，以帮助律师减少自身的服务风险，提高服务水平，从而为客户创造物超所值的法律服务效益。

第一节 跨国投资与并购业务

中国的"入世"给中国企业的发展带来了巨大的机遇，同时也吸引了不少的外商来华投资，在这一过程中，越来越多的外国公司在中国新设或通过并购进行企业投资，中国公司为取得更大的市场份额也需要在境外投资并购、上市等，为了在跨国投资与并购业务中提高工作效率，防范法律风险，需要专业的法律服务。

一 境内新设外国投资公司业务的法律服务

目前，在我国境内进行直接投资设立外商投资企业，仍旧以《中华人民共和国中外合资经营企业法》、《中华人民共和国中外合作经营企业法》、《中华人民共和国外资企业法》（三部法律合称为三资企业法）和《中华人民共和国公司法》为主要法律依据。《中华人民共和国外国投资法（草案）（征求意见稿）》已经发布，经立法程序通过后将会对新设外国投资公司的法律规定做出修订。目前在设立程序方面，依照《外商投资企业设立及变更备案管理暂行办法》（商务部令 2016 年第 3 号）的规定，对外商投资企业的设立及变更，不涉及外商投资准入特别管理措施的，由审批改为备案。这一调整是为了落实国家外商投资管理改革，推动全面实行准入前国民待遇加负面清单管理制度的进行。在备案完成后，外商投资企业可以向备案机构领取《外商投资企业设立备案回执》或《外商投资企业变更备案回执》，从而取代原外商投资企业批准证书。

（一）设立外商投资企业的一般流程

以外商独资企业的设立为例，外国自然人、法人或其他组织来中国境内以新设公司方式进行直接投资，仍需向行政主管部门办理较为复杂的审批或备案程序。首先进行企业名称预核准，然后提交企业设立申请书、指定办理设立事宜的代表或委托代理人的授权委托书及身份证明、项目申请报告书、企业章程、经营合同（两个或者两个以上外国投资者共同申请设立的外资企业的情况下）、董事会成员名单、法定代表人委派书、董事会及监事会成员委派书、投资者的合法开业证明文件、投资者开户银行出具的资信证明、环保部门审批意见、项目用能申报登记意见、企业场地落实证明或厂房租赁合同、其他在营业执照获得前需获得的行业许可证明文件等。其中投资者的合法开业证明文件（外方投资者为自然人的须提供身份证明复印件，中国台湾客商需提供台胞证复印件）需要办理公证认证。

所谓投资方开业证明，即国外公司的登记注册文件，在国内一般叫营业执照，在国外多数国家可以称为注册证书或商业注册证，英文 Certificate of Incorporation，证明公司注册登记情况。办理投资方开业证明公证认证的流程一般是：境外当地公证人公证，该国外交部或其授权派出机构认证，中国驻该国使领馆认证，如果中国在该国没有使领馆，则须拿到第三国的中国使领馆认证。对于中国香港、澳门，须经中国委托公证人公证，然后送中国法律服务（香港/澳门）有限公司加章转递。投资者为自然人的，其身份证明文件亦须办理上述公证认证。如果提交的是外文文件，须同时提交加盖翻译单位印章的中文译本。

上述材料提供后，可获得外商投资企业的审批或备案文件，进一步办理营业执照，获得一个统一社会信用代码，可进一步办理刻制印章备案手续、开立银行账户、办理纳税鉴定等税务手续、涉及进出口贸易的须办理对外贸易进出口许可证及海关注册登记、外汇登记证、社会保险登记等劳动用工备案手续。

（二）常见行业新设外商投资企业的法律服务要点

因各国对外来投资管理的要求，对不同的行业进行直接投资会在设立外商投资企业一般流程的基础上作出不同的特殊安排。对此，在提供涉外律师服务中应有所了解。以下，以外商在中国开展房地产行业的投资、融资租赁业的投资为例，对外商投资企业的设立和运营要求加以介绍。

1. 关于外商投资房地产经营行业的政策要求

按照《外商投资产业指导目录（2017年修订）》（中华人民共和国国家发展和改革委员会、中华人民共和国商务部令第4号），房地产行业未被列入鼓励类、限制类或禁止类清单，即外商投资房地产行业在市场准入的基本方向上未做不同于内资的限制或禁止，但在具体管理政策上仍有一些特别的规定。

《关于规范房地产市场外资准入和管理的意见》（建住房〔2006〕171号）及《关于调整房地产市场外资准入和管理有关政策的通知》（建房〔2015〕122号）的规定，境外机构在境内设立的分支、代表机构（经批准从事经营房地产的企业除外）和在境内工作、学习的境外个人可以购买符合实际需要的自用、自住商品房。境外机构和个人在境内投资购买非自用房地产，应当遵循商业存在的原则，申请设立外商投资企业；经有关部门批准并办理有关登记后，方可按照核准的经营范围从事相关业务，即外商投资境内房地产开发进行经营，需要先设立外商投资企业，商业形式可以采用外商投资企业的所有形式即外商独资、中国合资、中外合作，但在具体项目中应符合相关限制性规定，如根据产业指导目录，电影院的建设经营需要中方控股的中外合资企业形式。

在按照上述商业存在原则新设外商投资房地产企业时，由于政策要求先行取得临时的商务主管部门的外商投资企业设立的备案文件和临时的营业执照，在确定获得可开发土地并付清土地使用权出让金以后方可设立正式的开发商业，在工作流程安排上各省份略有不同。由于目前国有建设用地使用权出让都是公开进行，外国投资者需要先报名参加竞买。有的省份在一定时期允许外国投资者以境外机构或个人的身份进行竞买国有建设用地使用权的报名，并在外汇管理部门严格监管下接受以外汇资金作为竞买保证金或由资信较高的国际商业银行提供保函作为土地竞买保证金，在竞买成交后签署合同前要求设立完毕外商投资企业，以在中国设立的外商投资企签署土地出让合同并在付清出让金办理土地登记后取得正式的外商投资企业的营业执照。但有的省市不允许以境外机构或个人的名义报名参加土地竞买，需要先行由外国投资者向商务主管部门及登记机关申请获得临时的外商投资企业营业执照，并以临时设立的外国投资企业作为竞买人参加土地出让的竞买，竞买保证金可以以外币缴纳，如果竞买不成则原路退回。竞买成功后签署土地出让合同缴纳土地使用权出让金，然后换发正式的营业执照，办理房地产开发经营企业资质，开展房地产开发经营。

对于外商投资房地产经营企业，目前政策还要求项目投资依项目建设进度分期投入的，公司需要提供资金用途和分期投入的承诺。开发项目资本金未达到项目投资总额35%的，不得办理境内、境外贷款，外汇管理部门不予批准该企业的外汇借款结汇。外商投资房地产企业的中外投资各方，不得以任何形式在合同、章程、股权转让协议以及其他文件中,订立保证任何一方固定回报或变相固定回报的条款。境外投资者通过股权转让及其他方式并购境内房地产企业,或收购合资企业中方股权的,须妥善安置职工、处理银行债务并以自有资金一次性支付全部转让金。对有不良记录的境外投资者,不允许其在境内进行上述活动。

2. 外商投资融资租赁公司设立程序和法律要点

外商投资融资租赁公司,由商务部外资司及其授权的省级商务部门和国家级经济开发区负责审批和监管,自 2009 年总投资 5000 万美元以下的外商投资融资租赁审批权限由商务部下放到 31 个省级商委和 180 多个国家级经济开发区后,外商投资融资租赁的数量呈井喷增长现象。

根据商务部《外商投资租赁业管理办法》(商务部令 2005 年第 5 号),以及商务部于 2013 年 7 月 11 日发布并实施的《商务部办公厅关于加强和改善外商投资融资租赁公司审批与管理工作的通知》,结合《中华人民共和国公司登记管理条例(2014 修订)》的要求,在新设立外商独资或合资融资租赁公司方面应满足的条件包括:①对外方投资者的要求。申请设立融资租赁公司的投资者须为公司、企业或其他经济组织。外方投资者或其境外母公司应资信良好,在境外已合法注册并从事实质性经营活动。投资各方应向审批机关提供其经会计师事务所审计的最近一年的审计报告,审计报告显示资不抵债的不符合申请资格。外方投资者的总资产不得低于 500 万美元。存续未满一年的投资者暂不具备申报条件。符合条件的外方投资者境外母公司以其全资拥有的境外子公司(SPV)名义投资设立融资租赁公司,可不要求存续满一年。②组织形式。须以中外合资、中外合作或外商独资的形式设立,采取有限责任公司或股份有限公司的形式。注册资本不低于 1000 万美元,但实施认缴资本制。合同/章程无须规定"投资总额",批复文件中也无"投资总额"项。基于此,在外债额度方面,外资融资租赁外债额度不再受《外债管理暂行办法》"外商投资企业举借的中长期外债累计发生额和短期外债余额之和应当控制在审批部门批准的项目总投资和注册资本之间的差额(即投注差)以内"的规定限制。外方投资比例应不低于 25%。经营期限一般不超过 30 年。(3)高管人员要求。指总经理、副总经理、业务主管、财务主管、风险控制主管、运营主管,应具有相应专业资质(指具备其分管业务领域专业知识并取得相关执业证照)和不少于 3 年的从业经验(指融资租赁公司或相关金融机构的管理经验)。

二 外资并购业务的法律服务

外资并购是外国投资者对境内企业进行兼并或收购,与新设公司一样,都是国际直接投资的重要形式,根据《关于外国投资者并购境内企业的规定》(商务部令 2009 年第 6 号)第二条的规定,外国投资者并购境内企业,系指外国投资者购买境内非外商投资企业股东的股权或认购境内公司增资,使该境内公司变更设立为外商投资企业

(即"股权并购");或者,外国投资者设立外商投资企业,并通过该企业协议购买境内企业资产且运营该资产,或者,外国投资者协议购买境内企业资产,并以该资产投资设立外商投资企业运营该资产(即"资产并购")。实务中,中国香港、澳门、台湾的投资者对境内非外商投资企业进行股权并购或资产并购、特殊目的公司对境内非外商投资企业进行的股权并购或资产并购亦适用《关于外国投资者并购境内企业的规定》。

(一)参与外资并购业务的法律知识要点

作为并购律师,在为并购项目提供法律服务时,需对外资并购业务的基本法律规定加以了解,特别是学会在对并购交易环节中的限制性法律规定加以掌握的基础上,做好合同设计与疑难环节法律问题的处理。

1. 了解股权并购与资产并购的差异

外交并购主要通过股权并购或资产并购来实现,这两种方面具有不同的特点。在对两者的特点予以充分了解的基础上,可以对并购方式加以选择。这两者的不同特点主要包括:①两者的主体和客体差异。股权收购的主体是收购公司和目标公司的股东,客体是目标公司的股权。而资产收购的主体是收购公司和目标公司,客体是目标公司的资产。②两者的负债风险差异。股权收购方式下,因为目标公司的原有债务对今后股东的收益有着巨大的影响,因此在股权收购之前,收购公司必须调查清楚目标公司的债务状况。而在资产收购中,资产的债权债务状况一般比较清晰。需要指出的是,《关于外国投资者并购境内企业的规定》对资产并购设置了公告和通知程序,要求出售资产的境内企业应当在投资者向审批机关报送申请文件之前至少 15 日向债权人发出通知书,并在全国发行的省级以上报纸上发布公告。③两者在税收方面存在差异。资产并购方式下,对于出售方,有形动产交易涉及增值税、消费税管理等;不动产、无形资产交易涉及增值税(营业税)和土地增值税(费)管理。对于收购方来讲,在选择以在华外商投资企业为并购主体的情况下,主要涉及并购资产计价纳税,包括流转税和所得税。而股权并购方式下,对于出售方来讲,通常情况下,转让各类所有者权益,均不发生流转税纳税义务。按照《财政部、国家税务总局关于股权转让有关营业税问题的通知》(财税〔2002〕191 号)的规定,自 2003 年起,对不动产资本化后的股权转让不再征收营业税,出售方仅可就转让所有者权益所得和债转股所得缴纳企业所得税。出售方为个人的,对所转让股权按照"财产转让所得"税目缴纳个人所得税。对于收购方来讲,在并购主体为企业所得税纳税主体的情况下,涉及长期股权投资差额的税务处理。根据国税总局发布的《关于外国投资者并购境内企业股权有关税收问题的通知》,外国投资者通过股权并购变更设立的外商投资企业,如符合《外商投资企业和外国企业所得税法》及其实施细则等有关规定条件的,可享受税法及其有关规定所制定的各项企业所得税税收优惠政策。④第三方的同意与批准要求的差异。根据我国《合资企业法》的规定,"合营一方向第三者转让其全部或者部分股权的,须经合营他方同意",因此股权收购可能会受制于目标公司的其他股东。资产收购中,影响最大的是对该资产享有某种权利的人,如抵押权人、商标权人、专利权人、租赁权人等。对于这些财产的转让,必须得到相关权利人的同意,或者必须履行对相关权利人的义务。值得提出的是,某些重大合同可能涉及控制性条款,而这些条款可能要求股权或资产的出让须取得该合同当事人的同意。⑤相关证照转让后果的差异。在资产转让的情况下,受让方通常无法直接获得目标公司的资质、牌照。而在股权收购当中,通常情况下,收购方能够自然取得目标公司的原有证照。

2. 关于交易双方情况的基本了解

通常,外资并购服务律师要对交易双方进行充分的了解与认识,特别是双方的合作基础、在交易中所处的地位、通过交易拟达到的目标、交易项目的性质等。在外资并购中,外国投资者与中国出售方交易的双方,通常对并购项目会有不同甚至对立的认识与期望,外国投资者通常会希望进行详细的尽职调查,希望获得更多的交易安全方面的保障,希望获得较大的管理权。而中国出售方则希望尽早收到收购款,担心在收购前对商业秘密的披露和保密问题,希望在收购后保证对其员工的聘用,希望基于评估结果取得公平的价格。

3. 并购中涉及的国有资产管理问题

在外资并购涉及国有资产时,通常会涉及更多的申请与审批程序,包括对国有资产的评估与转让审批、公开交易等。国有企业产权转让给外国投资者的程序在2003年1月1日起实施的《利用外资改组国有企业暂行规定》(国家经济贸易委员会、财政部、国家工商行政管理总局、国家外汇管理局令第42号)中作出了具体规定。在交易方式上,虽然《利用外资改组国有企业暂行规定》中已规定,但改组方应当优先采用公开竞价方式确定外国投资者及转让价格,在《企业国有产权转让管理暂行办法》《关于规范国有企业改制工作意见》《中华人民共和国国有企业资产法》等政策文件和法律法规实施之后,外资并购国有企业一般均要求通过公开征集、竞价转让方式确定外国投资方,国有产权转让程序中须提交律师事务所出具的法律意见书。

4. 有关转让限制问题

作为并购律师,在外资并购项目中需要特别注意目标资产或股权存在的转让限制。转让限制可以分为两大类,即法律规定的转让限制与合同约定的转让限制。法律规定的转让限制通常包括产业政策限制,反垄断政策限制,在资产转让方式下存在于资产上的抵押担保等限制,在股权转让方式下来自其他股东的限制(须取得其他所有股东的书面同意),等等。合同约定上的法律限制通常存在于出售方与第三方签订的合同,比如合同中约定,出售方在一定条件下未经该第三方同意不得处分资产或转让股权。

对于上述限制,有些限制是可以通过对法律法规以及规范性文件的审查确定的,比如产业政策方面的限制;有些是通过尽职调查即可发现,例如资产或股权上存在的第三方的权利;而对于合同约定方面的限制,假设出售方没有披露,则收购方律师是很难发现其中的限制,而这种未披露可能对交易产生一定的法律影响,甚至可能是决定性的影响。对于这种限制,一方面,并购律师应该要求出售方最大程度披露其与第三方签订的所有重大合同,另一方面应该在并购合同中的承诺与保证条款、违约责任条款等条款作出相应的规定,以防止收购方因此可能受到损失。

5. 关于并购价款的支付

外资并购中,投资者最为关心的问题之一便是外资并购的资金来源,即可以用什么样的资产在中国境内进行并购。普遍意义上来说,《关于外国投资者并购境内企业的规定》规定:"作为对价的支付手段,应符合国家有关法律和行政法规的规定。外国投资者以其合法拥有的人民币资产作为支付手段的,须经外汇管理部门核准;外国投资者以其拥有处置权的股权作为支付手段的,按照本规定第四章办理。"(即按照关于"股权并购"的规定办理)外资并购中,由于并购对象、并购主体的不同,支付手段会出现一定的差异。

如果并购的对象是国有企业,根据《利用外资改组国有企业暂行规定》的规定,外国投资者应当以境外汇入的可自由兑换货币或其他合法财产权益支付转让价款或出资。经外汇管理部门批准,也可以用在中国境内投资获得的人民币净利润或其他合法财产权益支付转让价款或出资。此外,《利用外资改组国有企业暂行规定》允许了"债转股"这一出资或对价支付形式。

如果并购的对象是上市公司的非流通股,则根据《关于向外商转让上市公司国有股和法人股有关问题的通知》:"外商应当以自由兑换货币支付转让价款。已在中国境内投资的外商,经外汇管理部门审核后,也可用投资所得人民币利润支付。"根据中国证监会法律部的解释,外商投资企业要收购法人股和国有股,也应该按照此文的要求。由此可见,无论是境外投资者、投资性公司还是境内的三资企业,收购上市公司的国有股或法人股只能用现金形式支付,其来源于两部分:一是自由兑换的货币;二是投资所得的人民币利润。

外国投资者通过其境内设立的三资企业进行并购,其收购资金有些不同。《关于外商投资企业境内投资的暂行规定》并没有明确应当用什么资金进行投资。外商投资企业可以根据《公司法》的规定,用各种法律明确准许的资产形式对被并购企业进行增资;如果属于股权受让,则可以用股权买卖双方所能接受的各种合法资产形式,包括股权或债权等;外商投资企业以其净利润投资,无须取得外汇管理部门的同意;其所投资的企业,如无"向中西部地区投资,被投资公司注册资本中外资比例不低于百分之二十五"的情况,被投资企业不享受外商投资企业待遇。

转让价款的支付时限:《关于外国投资者并购境内企业的规定》第十六条规定:

"外国投资者并购境内企业设立外商投资企业,外国投资者应自外商投资企业营业执照颁发之日起 3 个月内向转让股权的股东,或出售资产的境内企业支付全部对价。对特殊情况需要延长者,经审批机关批准后,应自外商投资企业营业执照颁发之日起 6 个月内支付全部对价的 60% 以上,1 年内付清全部对价,并按实际缴付的出资比例分配收益。"《利用外资改组国有企业暂行规定》中对转让价款的支付时限亦作了同样的规定。但后出台的两份国企改制新规定则对此有不同规定。《关于规范国有企业改制工作的意见》,特别是《企业国有产权转让管理暂行办法》规定,转让国有产权的价款原则上应当一次付清,如金额较大,一次性付清确有困难的,可以采取分期付款的方式,受让方首期付款不得低于总价的 30%,并在合同生效之日起 5 个工作日内支付;其余款项应当提供合法担保,并应当按同期银行贷款利率向转让方支付延期付款期间利息,付款期限不得超过 1 年。

(二) 律师提供并购服务的工作流程

律师参与外资并购的法律服务,通常会跟踪整个收购工作流程,从双方当事人启动项目进行初步接触开始,直到双方的交易完成交割。在此过程中,律师可提供的服务主要包括以下内容。

1. 初步意向文件的起草与签署

并购双方经过初步接触后,通常会考虑先行签署一份意向书,为后面的并购活动提供一个合作框架,以保证后续活动的顺利开展。通常还会在达成意向书的同时,签署一份保密协议或在意向书中包括保密条款。保密协议确定的保密义务对象,除了作为信息接受方的买卖双方以外,还包括为并购提供服务的咨询顾问、律师和会计师及其他受雇中介机构和人员。同时会约定,如并购交易终止,信息接受方负有返还或销毁对方提供的资料的义务。在意向书中,双方可以约定独家谈判条款,约定没有取得对方同意,一方不得与第三方公开或者私下进行并购谈判,否则视为该方违约,并要求承担违约责任。意向书的条款是否具有法律约束力,通常按买卖双方的实际需要而定。因此,律师需要注意在意向书中规定意向书本身具有何种法律约束力。通常认为,意向书一般不具法律效力,违反意向书所承担的责任为缔约过失责任。但意向书保密条款具有法律效力,所有参与谈判的人员都要恪守商业机密,以保证即使并购不成功,并购方的意图也不会过早地被外界知道,目标公司的利益也能得到维护。

2. 进行尽职调查

为了尽量减小和规避并购风险,在并购开始前对目标公司进行调查是十分重要的,其目的是了解目标公司各方面的情况,发现潜在的责任与风险。从而为并购方案的制定与修改、合同的制作、并购价格的调整等提供依据。作为出售方律师而言,也要对并购方的主体资格进行审查,从资信情况、支付能力和经营实力等角度对并购方的行为能力先作个确认,确认其有无交易资格。商务部等国家六部委联合发布的于 2006 年

9月8日起施行的《关于外国投资者并购境内企业的规定》第三十条第一次提出要做尽职调查,外国投资者以股权并购境内公司,境内公司或其股东应当聘请在中国注册登记的中介机构担任顾问。

通常,尽职调查的种类可分为法律、财务与专业性的调查,其分别由律师、会计师与有关专家完成。尽职调查的主要内容包括并购主体、重大合同、贷款与担保、相关证照、资产(包括土地和建筑物)、劳动事宜、环保事宜、知识产权、诉讼与仲裁、保险等。在尽职调查过程中,作为收购方律师的主要职责是确定目标公司已经获得相应的许可、批准和登记;确认法律文件是否完整;确定是否存在须征得第三方同意的事项;确定是否有特殊的合同义务;确定合同权利是否得到法律保护;确定潜在的法律责任;就尽职调查的范围与收购方的法律顾问磋商;协助出售方收集和整理相关文件;在向收购方交付前审查相关文件;就向收购方提供的文件作出记录;等等。

鉴于大部分供调查的文件材料都是由目标公司提供的,而目标公司存在提供虚假文件的可能性。并购律师应对其提供文件中的最关键问题进行再次核实,例如,其合法主体性应到工商局核实,其房产权属应到房管局核实等。法律尽职调查完成后,并购律师要给收购方制作一份真实的、可靠的尽职调查报告,不能有任何虚假和水分,要将风险充分地向收购方予以揭示,即使收购方可能因此而放弃收购。

3. 参与商务谈判确定并购工作步骤

在尽职调查有了初步的结论之后,并购当事人进入谈判回合。并购当事人根据调查了解到的实际情况开始进行有针对性的谈判。这个回合是由一轮又一轮的谈判组成的。这个过程中并购当事人的相互了解会进一步加深,知己知彼的境界在逐渐提升,各自的相同与不同之处会逐步地显现出来。

并购工作步骤是买卖双方的路线图。买卖双方在尽职调查、谈判中形成的一致意见将逐步形成清晰的工作安排,这主要涉及实体和程序两个方面。实体性的内容主要包括并购目的、主体及其历史沿革、并购标的、价款及其确定依据、支付方式和期限、债权债务的处置、职工的安置、权利义务的安排、利益风险的分配等;程序性的内容主要包括并购当事人的内部决策程序、外部报批或报备等并购程序,以及内部程序和外部程序之间的先后关系等。其中的许多内容在进一步具体化之后会成为并购合同的有机组成部分。这些步骤安排有时特别重要。外资并购的实质是外国投资者以并购的方式在中国设立或变更设立外商投资企业。根据中国目前的法律规定,对外商投资企业的设立尚需要行政审批。此外,根据《关于外国投资者并购境内企业的规定》,以并购的方式成立外商投资企业的需要承担垄断申报和审查义务。因此,外资并购所涉及的审批主要包括成立外商投资企业的行政审批制度和外资并购的垄断审查制度。此外,外资并购涉及国有资产变动的,则需要国有资产部门的同意或备案,这就使得在涉及外资对国有企业进行并购时,要将双方的协议程序与国有资产管理中的产权转让程序结合起来，既保障双方协议安排、并购价格在公开交易程序中确定能够大致符合双方预期，又要在最终获批并依法定程序确定国有资产的受让方之前不违背国有资产产权转让程序的要求，同时还要能够结合商务主管部门对外资并购国内企业的流程安排。

4. 制作并购文件并签署执行

并购协议是整个并购行为进行的基础，是并购双方就所有的并购问题达成一致意见的体现，同时，它也是实际并购操作的准则和将来争议解决的根据。为确保并购的顺利进行和减少今后不必要的纠纷，一份内容详尽明确、语言直接无歧义的并购协议是必不可少的。如果是股权并购，这份并购协议的主要内容实质上是一份股权转让合同或增资协议，如果交易通过国有产权交易程序实现，往往还会签署一份国有产权交易部门要求的格式化的产权交易合同。

并购协议一般由三个部分构成：首部、主文和附件。首部主要用来写明并购当事人的各种基本情况，主要包括名称、地址、法定代表人姓名、国籍等；主文是并购协议的核心部分，主要包括以下几个内容：陈述条款、保密条款、先决条件条款、补偿保证条款、争议解决条款、法律适用条款及定义条款等。附件主要包括财务审计报告、资产评估报告、土地转让协议、政府批准文件、财产清单、职工安置方案等；这些主要条款是并购协议精髓所在。在制作这些并购文件时要注意，双方首先应就文件制作的语言达成一致（通常是中文和/或英文）。在文件修订过程中，任何一方对文件修改处提出修改意见，尽可能地说明拒绝接受或需要进一步修改的理由，以推动尽快达成一致的认识。

文件签署后，要按照并购步骤的安排各自办理相关手续，完成必要的审批或备案流程。在协议履行过程中要做好相关的交割事项。出售方与收购方通常在并购协议中约定交割的先决条件，只有满足预定的先决条件，才能进行交割。否则，交易双方有权退出交易，即解除合同。交割行为主要包括交付文件、支付对价、变更登记（所有权转移）。交割交付的文件包括目标公司的法定登记文件（如公司章程、议事程序）、董事会决议、支付工具（如用银行汇票支付现金对价）、税务补偿保证、目标公司有能力开展业务的证明文件，出售方的原始董事会记录、账簿、存货簿、股权转让登记簿和公司印章等；交割时间可能交易主协议签署时同时交割或在签署后交割。前者较易避免交易风险，但因法律或实际情况可能无法实现（如未能及时取得第三方同意）；后者存在过渡期间的交易风险。

为有效安排交割行为的进行，双方可以在交割之前制定交割时间表。交割时间表应包含：①交割前应完成的各项工作；②交割时应提交的各种文书证照；③交割时应签署的所有文件；④交割后所有后续行为的安排。

三 中国企业海外投资的法律服务

近年来,中国从政府到企业以及个人层面的海外投资持续火热。展望未来,扩大和深化对外合作,推动中国企业走出国门开展海外投资,培育世界级跨国公司,在促进我国经济增长和社会发展、推动产业结构调整、实现互利共赢共同发展等方面都将发挥更大的作用。同时,我们也应注意到,在我国企业海外投资经营的意愿和能力不断上升的同时也面临诸多外部环境的风险和挑战,迫切需要提高法律服务水平。

中国企业进行海外投资,不但须考虑有关投资的业务前景、项目融资等问题,更须顾及投资地的法律法规、税务政策及营商环境。企业在落实投资前,应对有关项目进行多方面评估,例如往海外投资设厂生产、设立中转仓库或分销设施,便须深入了解投资地的商业环境、劳工政策、环保要求等,才能认清风险并作出相应措施,以保证顺利开展投资项目。即使简单如前往香港开设公司,亦须预先了解香港入境政策以利于安排管理人员来港,同时要清楚香港地区的税务政策以符合法律要求,以享受有关优惠政策。中国企业进行海外投资也广泛采取并购的方式,而前往海外并购的复杂程度不亚于一般海外新设企业的直接投资,除了解当地法规政策以外,投资者还需要深入了解并购项目的股权、财务和资产等实际情况。如果前往较冷门的投资地点投资,部分国家的法律制度不够完善,又可能缺乏与国际接轨的商业惯例,交易风险就可能相对更大,更需要专业的服务。中国律师为企业开展境外投资提供的相关服务,主要包括以下几个方面。

(一) 海外投资项目的前期法律咨询

在中国企业在选定境外投资的目标对象之前,律师可协助企业了解国家相关的指导政策——主要为境外投资产业和国别导向政策。主要参考的文件为《境外投资产业指导政策》(发改外资〔2006〕1312号)和商务部、外交部、国家发展和改革委员会发布的《对外投资国别产业导向目录(一)、(二)、(三)》。了解上述指导政策,对于后续顺利获得国内审批机关的批准,是非常重要的。为了帮助企业了解和熟悉世界主要国家的投资环境积极稳妥地推进企业国际化进程,自2009年起商务部研究院会同我国驻外经商机构,驻外使馆同志们共同编写发布了《对外投资合作国别(地区)指南》,并且每年定期更新,客观介绍了165个重点国家和地区的政治、经济、法律、政策、商务成本以及文化习俗等各方面的情况,帮助企业研判市场潜力和市场机会,对企业在当地开展经营给予帮助。该指南文件可以登录商务部网站,国别指南栏目下载阅读。

为防止企业盲目投资、贸然进入陌生的国度,通过前期调查对东道国政治风险和法律环境予以充分的了解尤为重要。政治风险通常包括东道国国有化、征收、汇兑限制、战争、内乱以及东道国违约。根据伯尔尼协会 ("Berne Union", the International Union of Credit & Investment Insurers，即"国际信用和投资保险人协会"）统计，汇兑限制和东道国违约是近年政治风险中发生频率比较高的风险种类。防范政治风险是各国多边、双边投资保护协定的主要内容。目前中国已与东盟签订了中国—东盟投资协定，与世界上130个国家和地区签订了双边投资保护协定。从国家层面就规避政治风险给予中国企业一定的支持。中国企业也可以通过购买政治风险保险、针对重大项目与东道国单独签订稳定协议、多元化融资以及引进东道国当地有实力的合作伙伴等方式从企业层面规避政治风险。

法律环境方面涉及海外并购中的国家安全风险限制、违法征收等法律和政策风险。这方面的例子有，一家浙江民营企业在2003年以股权收购方式购买了俄罗斯哈巴罗夫斯克的一处林场，经过多年开发当森林资产估值飙升时，林场公司被俄方以涉嫌违法为由查封，公司资产被强制拍卖，森林经营权被提前收回。这是中国企业在海外投资中遇到的重大的法律风险。至于美国，威胁国家安全的收购案例遭阻拦不计其数。另外还要注意相关国家的最低工资标准，罢工与涨工资等劳资关系风险，生态环境保护风险、专利和商标使用权、所有权分离等知识产权风险、人身安全风险和商业贿赂风险以及舆论危机等。

（二）海外投资项目境内外审批事项的协助办理

中国企业在进行境外投资之时，需要由境内相关部门审批同意。相关的手续主要包括发改委、商务部门以及外管局的审批或备案或前期报告或确认手续。如果涉及国有企业，还需国资委的审批或备案。中国律师可协助整理相关的审批流程、应提交的资料，协助与相关审批部门进行沟通，以使企业顺利获得相关审批文件。境外投资项目中，牵涉的手续繁多，因此需要根据各种手续的先后顺序，统筹规划，整理出一套切实可行的项目进程表。尤其是中国境内的审批与境外交易的进展密切相连，如未能协调好二者，将导致巨大的麻烦。

例如，对于境外收购项目，我国法律要求境内企业在对外签署约束性协议、提出约束性报价及向对方国家/地区政府审查部门提出申请前，境外投标项目在对外正式投标之前，应向国家发改委报送项目信息报告并取得国家发改委的确认函后，方可在确认函的有效期内开展实质性工作；此外，在获得国家或地方发改委审批核准之前，企业不能对外签署最终交易文件。由此，上述发改委的确认及审批手续，对境外并购的谈判进程将造成实质性影响。在境外并购项目谈判进程紧张的情况下，如果因为境内审批耽误太长时间，将会使境内企业错失并购的良机。因此，要提前与发改委以及其他审批机关沟通好，获得审批机关的理解与支持，从而能够灵活处理相关事宜［如能先对外签署好协议（协议中约定获得发改委批准为合同交割条件而非生效条件），后补报发改委审批］。

在境外，投资企业如想开展经营，往往须取得一系列的与投资活动相关的东道国政府的各项运营许可,如企业设立、土地获得、员工雇用、设备材料进出口、环境许可、建设许可、融资、外汇汇兑等。以环境许可为例,在大多数国家开采自然资源,环境影响评估、环境保护计划以及持续的环境保护报告一般是取得开采自然资源的环境许可的必要前提,根据经验,这是一个费时费力的过程。这些境外所需办理的审批或许可,应尽可能委托当地熟悉法规政策的律师事务所办理,但中国的服务律师仍可参与沟通和流程审核。

（三）项目交易结构的选择与融资安排

在境外投资项目中,需要特别解决好交易结构的问题。在交易结构的设计上,可根据具体情况分别设计不同的交易模式,如直接收购境外公司股权；在境外设立子公司,以该子公司收购境外公司股权。不同交易结构的设计,牵涉到不同的问题,如融资、审批等方面的问题,需要予以综合把握与平衡。在交易机构的设计上,税法问题是很重要的一方面。尽管一些较大的境外投资项目中,境内企业通常也会聘请会计师/税务师,帮助他们做税务筹划,以节省成本,但是相关税务操作的法律依据及法律风险判断,很大程度上,还需要依赖律师的意见。关于境外投资项目,主要涉及企业所得税法的问题,可参照的法规主要是《财政部、国家税务总局关于企业境外所得税收抵免有关问题的通知》(财税〔2009〕125号)。

境外投资项目,还可能涉及境内的反垄断审批问题。根据中国反垄断法的规定,中华人民共和国境外的垄断行为,对境内市场竞争产生排除、限制影响的,同样适用《中华人民共和国反垄断法》。因此,境外投资可能涉及经营者集中,从而需要与商务部沟通乃至向商务部提交反垄断审查文件。

境外投资项目中的融资问题,也非常重要。如果收购资金是境内企业在境外的自有资金,境内律师通常需要从中国法律的角度审核该境外自有资金来源的合法性；对于境内企业向境外银行的借款,需要境内律师审核该交易在中国法律项下的合规性。境内企业向境外银行借款,目前操作上可行的方式包括：境内企业在境外设立子公司,然后以该子公司的名义向境外银行借款,同时境内企业作为母公司（在此情况下,境内的个人也可以同时提供对外担保）向境外银行提供担保,不过该等对外担保需要在外管局办理审批登记；内保外贷的模式。如果海外并购使用的是来源于境内的资金,则在该等资金的出境方面（包括境外投资所需前期费用资金的购汇汇出、境内机构从事境外收购项目的收购保证金或押金的购汇汇出、境外投资资金的购汇汇出）受到外管局的审批。此外,如果是境内企业自有资金,中国律师需要核查该等资金来源的合法合规性。如果是银行借款,需要密切注意银行内部审批与整个境外投资交易流程的协调。

第二节 国际贸易与知识产权业务

我国在加入 WTO 之后,与国外的经济贸易活动更加广泛和经常化。随着对外贸易量的增加,中方企业与外国企业的国际货物贸易、服务贸易和知识产权贸易的业务数量及由此产生的纠纷数量也在随之增加。在国际贸易与知识产权业务中涉及众多的国际条约、国际惯例的大量适用,这对我国律师是一个很大的挑战,当然也给我国的律师业走向成熟和现代化提供了良好的契机。

一 国际贸易业务的非诉法律服务

国际贸易活动中的律师业务在日益频繁和更加广泛的国际贸易活动中,涉及有关法律事务的方面异常复杂和繁多。在律师实务中越来越广泛地接触《关税和贸易总协定》《服务贸易总协定》《与贸易有关的知识产权协议》《联合国国际货物销售合同公约》和我国的《对外贸易法》及有关的国际贸易组织决议等。国际贸易活动广泛地存在于货物、服务、技术等各个领域,需要在国际贸易合同的谈判、签订、履行以及发生纠纷后的调解、国际仲裁与诉讼、国际贸易的支付、有关贸易方政府对贸易的管制措施、有关国际经济组织状况的了解以及反倾销、反补贴调查等许多方面做大量而繁复的工作。就关于政府管理贸易方面的法律业务、国际仲裁与诉讼业务,将在其他专章中介绍。就日常的国际贸易中律师能够参与的法律实务而言,主要包括以下方面。

(一) 律师参与国际贸易活动中有关的合同协议的谈判和签订过程

对国际贸易相对方进行必要的资信调查,调查并咨询贸易相对方所在国的贸易法规和相关政策。代理或协助贸易委托方与对方进行签订合同或协议的谈判,依据有关国际贸易法规、针对不同的贸易项目,把握好对贸易委托方有利的相关条款,掌握主动权,以充分维护委托方的利益。在合同条款确实符合国际贸易法的相关规定、遵循了国际贸易惯例的前提下与贸易相对方签订合同或协议。

一些企业在从事国际贸易活动的过程当中,由于法律意识的欠缺,也不注意寻求专业人士的帮助,总是想当然地做事,尤其是在和已经有长期业务往来的客户的交往过程中,不注意法律风险的防范,长此以往,定会埋下较大的隐患。在国际货物买卖合同的订立过程中应当注意以书面的形式签署合同,虽然随着现代通信技术的不断发展,很多公司采用电子邮件与客户进行商事交往,限于技术的原因,目前这种形式证据的证明效力还存在较大争议,所以公司在发送正式文件时应谨慎使用。因为书面合同具有较强的确定性和较高的证据效力,所以在国际货物买卖合同的订立过程中,建议当事人特别注意采用书面合同来确定双方的权利和义务,而且最好保存书面合同的正本直至合同履行完毕后一定时间。对于合同的修改也应该以书面形式来进行，而不能以电话沟通了事。

在签署合同过程中还要注意，签约方名称要准确，签约日期、地点要写明。在合同的订立过程中，合同的首部签约双方的名称第一次出现时应当写全称，并且应当与商业登记文件上的企业名称以及在合同上所加盖的公司印章的内容一致，以免引起争议。如果合同采用代表人签字生效的方式，那么准确写明签约方名称就更重要了，最好同时将签约方的营业登记文件的复印件经盖章确认后作为合同的附件。此外，在合同中一定要注意写明签约日期与地点，这些内容对国际货物买卖合同的法律适用、诉讼管辖等有很大的影响，尤其是在合同中未明确约定适用的法律和管辖地点的情况下，更是有着至关重要的影响。

在合同签署中要注意把握签署好品质条款。品质条款是货物买卖合同中的重要条款，它是当事人提出索赔的依据，如果卖方所交货物的品质与合同不符，买方有权拒收并可提出索赔。如果合同中品质条款不明确，或没有约定品质条款，买方则可能失去索赔依据。实践中，合同双方当事人关于货物品质、规格问题发生争议是比较常见的，所以在品质条款中对货物规格、型号、颜色、材质等进行明确具体且操作性强的约定是非常重要的。品质条款的制定应该注意科学性、严密性和准确性，并且应该便于执行。一切空洞的词语应该避免使用，如"上等材料""一流工艺""优质产品"等均不宜使用，因为无法据此确定卖方所交货物是否违反合同规定。对于有些复杂的产品（如成套设备），鉴于技术规格复杂，内容繁多，在合同中难以评述的，可以列入附件，并注明是合同的组成部分。对于凭样品交货的合同，要注意对样品的选择，不要一味为了达成合同而提供质量过高或过低的样品，而且应该做好样品的封存工作。当然，国际贸易合同一旦形成质量纠纷，对于买方来讲，因货物已在境外，取证难度和证明损失的难度非常大。

（二）律师参与国际贸易合同或协议的履行及其发生纠纷后解决争议

在国际贸易合同的履行过程中代理律师要注意贸易相对方是否依约履行合同，如是否依约在船上交货、是否依约交付了有关单据及单据与货物是否相符等。如合同的履行发生纠纷，律师可与对方协商和解、进行调解或通过国际仲裁或诉讼的方式解决。在解决贸易纠纷过程中，代理律师要全面把握合同的履行情况及对方的违约情况，如货物的遗失是在风险转移之前还是之后、委托方不履行合同是否因对方预期违约所造成、委托方拒收货物是否因对方的货物与单据不相符或不符合合同的约定等。在国际贸易进行票据结算和国际贸易支付过程，律师可协助审查票据的合法有效性，是采取的汇付、托收、信用证哪一种支付方式，如信用证是可撤销的还是不可撤销，是否"单单相符""单证相符"等。

国际贸易纠纷通常类型包括：①买方付款后收不到货物或收到的货物不合格；②

卖方发货物无法收回货款或全部货款等；③因知识产权、经销关系或代理关系而产生的纠纷等。处理国际贸易纠纷的方式主要有以下途径：①纠纷双方自行协商，如能通过此种途径解决，双方还可能今后继续合作；②由律师向对方签发律师函，要求对方履行合同，律师也可以参加之后的索赔谈判；③如双方有仲裁条款，依据仲裁条款进行仲裁；④如没有仲裁条款，向有管辖权的法院起诉进行索赔；⑤如另外一方涉嫌诈骗，可向警方报案，要求采取刑事措施追究对方犯罪责任，特别是在货物的一致性问题上很难做到完整的证据链接。

在通过民事诉讼或仲裁方式解决贸易纠纷的具体方式的选择上，仲裁是解决国际货物买卖合同纠纷的一种比较经济、快捷的方式。仲裁协议是合同当事人自愿将其争议提交仲裁机构裁决的协议，它是当事人向仲裁机构提请仲裁的前提条件。仲裁协议须约定明确，如仅约定因合同履行发生的争议提交仲裁裁决是不够的，必须写明具体由哪一个仲裁机构进行仲裁，最好将仲裁适用的仲裁规则和法律也进行有效约定。

二 涉外知识产权业务的非诉法律服务

当今世界，随着知识经济和经济全球化深入发展，知识产权日益成为国家发展的战略性资源和国际竞争力的核心要素，国家和国内外企业都在充分利用知识产权制度维护其竞争优势。与之相适应，律师在为企业提供知识产权法律服务方面，也有着越来越广阔的服务空间。主要提供的法律服务包括以下方面。

（一）知识产权调查和企业知识产权战略咨询

知识产权尽职调查，指基于特定的商事需求，委托第三方专业机构或人员对目标公司的知识产权进行全面性调查及系统性梳理，为委托方或预期投资者提供目标公司可能影响预期商业计划或其他关键因素的知识产权信息，最终形成专业性综述报告的非诉讼法律服务活动。知识产权尽职调查的目的基本相同，主要有两个：一是梳理目标公司的知识产权状况，包括权利内容、权利归属、权利来源、权利负担、权利价值等；二是分析目标公司知识产权存在的风险，包括实施风险、交易风险、管理风险等。律师参与知识产权的尽职调查，可根据委托方的期望和目标，准确把握被调查对象的权利保护状况、知识产权管理制度等，以期形成满足需求的调查成果。

在对委托人所面临的知识产权制度环境予以充分了解的基础上，律师可以协助企业制定和实施知识产权战略。知识产权战略主要包括专利战略、商标战略、商业秘密战略等。知识产权战略应当根据企业自身的特点来制定，比如有的企业具有核心技术的优势，那么围绕核心技术可以考虑选择专利战略或商业秘密战略，专利有保护期限且需要公开技术方案，商业秘密的保护是无期限的。如果该核心技术是不易反向研究获得的，则优先考虑以商业秘密的形式予以保护；如果围绕核心技术的竞争对手颇多，则当机立断地实施专利战略，以抢先占领市场为目的，无须等到研制出最佳、最成熟的技术方案。因为专利的价值在于其保护范围的大小，而不在于专利是否具有最优的技术方案。专利的保护范围是否恰当是至关重要的法律问题，既要确保专利的新颖性和创造性，使其符合授权的标准，又要使专利得到有效的保护，最大限度地体现专利的市场价值。专利是技术与法律的集合体，普通的专利代理人或律师对专利的维护难以提供最优的专业服务，因此既懂法律又懂技术的专利律师的意见是不可或缺的。

（二）律师代理商标注册及解决侵权纠纷等商标法律事务

2012 年 11 月 6 日，司法部、国家工商行政管理总局联合发布《律师事务所从事商标代理业务管理办法》。根据该《办法》，自 2013 年 1 月 1 日起，凡在国家工商总局商标局办理备案的律师事务所，均可从事商标注册申请、商标注册驳回复审等商标局和商标评审委员会主管的商标代理业务。加之律师事务所之前无须备案即可继续从事的商标国际注册、商标行政复议、商标诉讼、商标纠纷调解仲裁等商标代理法律事务，意味着律师事务所可全面介入商标代理业务，其服务客户包括代理中国申请人到国外办理商标国际注册以及在申请注册过程中的各种法律事务，也包括代理外国申请人到中国申请商标注册及其他商标法律事务。

另外，律师还可代理商标权海关备案、代理解决商标侵权纠纷、代理进行商标侵权投诉等法律事务。律师也可为企业申请著名商标和驰名商标的认定提供服务。著名商标可以提升品牌影响力并为申请驰名商标做准备，并在区域范围内活动的行政保护，符合条件的商标持有人可以主动向工商局申请认定。驰名商标有行政认定和司法认定两种，行政认定是在出现商标异议、商标争议及因侵权行为向工商部门投诉时三种情况下提出驰名商标的申请认定。司法认定是在侵权诉讼案件中向法院提出的认定驰名商标的申请，但目前司法实践中法院的态度谨慎，采取"因需认定"的原则，并不必然对驰名商标的申请作出认定。律师可以提供的服务包括：协助企业组织申请著名商标的材料、为企业申请驰名商标提供实施规划、为企业选择恰当的方式申请驰名商标。

（三）为企业提供专利法律服务

律师可以对企业专利战略的运用提供咨询意见，指导企业运用基本专利战略、专利网战略、专利出售战略、专利汇出战略、产品出口专利先行战略、专利诉讼战略、防御专利战略等。律师可以对企业专利申请提供咨询意见，对企业的核心技术的知识产权保护方式提供意见，对专利权利要求的保护范围审核并提供法律建议，提供最新专利信息。

在专利申请业务中，律师在分析企业的交底技术后，可根据相关技术检索结果，协助确定专利的发明点，审核申请人或专利代理机构撰写的权利要求书，确定权利要求书中的必要技术特征，分析独立权利要求与从属权利要求的设定是否合理，从而确保专利具有恰当的保护范围。专利申请人对国务院专利行政部门驳回申请的决定不服的，律师可以代理专利复审，还可代理进行专利行政复议、指导客户向专利管理部门提出行政请求、代理专利侵权诉讼、代理专利无效案件、专利权归属纠纷、专利权合同纠纷、代理客户进行海关知识产权保护备案、指导企业进行专利转让和实施许可。

（四）知识产权海关保护的律师服务

在为企业维护自身知识产权方面提供的法律服务中，寻求知识产权海关保护已经日益被企业关注和重视。适宜配合海关行政职能进行保护的情况，可首先将知识产权在海关总署备案。虽然海关也可以在知识产权没有备案的情况下依权利人申请而采取知识产权保护措施，但在这种情况下，海关仅对涉嫌侵权货物做短暂扣留，而不对是否存在侵权事实做实质性判断。根据《中华人民共和国知识产权海关保护条例》规定，如果在货物被扣留后20天内未收到法院协助执行的通知，海关应放行货物，因此保护力度非常有限。但如果企业事先在海关总署取得了知识产权备案，海关则可依职权对其所扣留的货物是否侵权进行实质性调查，并最终作出结论。

海关对知识产权的保护职权仅限于与进出口货物有关的，受中国法律、法规保护的商标权、专利权、著作权，而广义知识产权所包括专有技术、商业秘密等，并不在海关的保护范围之列。其中，商标权的表现形式具有可视性的特点，因而海关判断进出口货物是否侵权相对容易，进而使商标权取得实质性保护效果的可能性较高。而对专利权与著作权而言，判断货物是否侵权难度较高，海关很难仅凭借自身能力即在短时间内直接作出结论，因此大大影响了海关保护这两种权利的力度。此外，涉嫌侵犯专利权的货物收发货人可在权利人提出知识产权海关保护申请时提供反担保，进而使涉嫌侵权货物实际放行成为可能，因此也很难达到权利人利用海关职权阻止涉嫌侵权货物进出境的目的。

进出口货物种类庞杂繁多，有相当部分涉及知识产权，但被海关查扣的侵权货物则多集中于化妆品、烟草制品、机电产品、五金机械、服装、鞋类等类别。其主要原因是这些产品在我国出口商品结构中占有重要比例，而且这些产品之上的商标更可能具有较高的社会影响力、辨识度更高。为提高查获率，企业应尽量向海关提供涉嫌侵权货物的通关线索。每日通关的商品不计其数，而海关监管力量非常有限，实际查验率很低，单纯依赖海关主动工作就达到保护目的是不现实的。如果企业能够向海关提供涉嫌侵权货物的准确物流线索，则可以帮助海关准确查扣涉嫌侵权的货物，显著提高保护力度。

基于上述分析，知识产权海关保护职能有一定的局限性，在此之外，仍有必要采取民事诉讼、寻求工商行政管理部门对商标侵权行为的行政救济及刑事救济的途径来做好企业知识产权维权工作。在知识产权海关保护环节，即使海关根据权利人的申请，对涉嫌侵权的进出口货物采取了扣留措施，但是否会作出最终的认定，尤其是作出侵权认定，却是不确定的。比如，在商标已备案的情况下，海关认为凭借其自身力量很难对商标是否侵权作出判断时，或者进出口收发货人及权利人之间民事关系复杂，海关认为不考虑背景关系而仅对商标做简单比对即作出决定存在风险时，海关都很可能给出"不能认定是否侵权"的结论，继而等待权利人去法院提起诉讼，如果海关没有及时收到来自法院的协助执行通知，则只能放行货物。而在商标未备案时，海关更是只能最多扣货 20 天，在此期间如果没有收到法院的协助执行通知，海关必须放行货物。也就是说，在很多情况下，海关对货物的扣留其实并不能一步到位达到保护知识产权的目的，而最终还是要依赖民事救济途径来彻底解决。但海关对涉嫌侵权货物的扣留，至少为实施民事救济手段提供了证据保全方面的帮助，还是很有价值的。

同时，海关对知识产权的保护职能仅限于货物进出境这个单一环节，而工商行政管理部门的职权则为更广泛。工商行政管理部门认定侵权行为成立的，可以责令侵权人立即停止侵权行为，并可没收、销毁侵权商品和主要用于制造侵权商品、伪造注册商标标识的工具，对违法经营额 5 万元以上的，可以处违法经营额 5 倍以下的罚款，没有违法经营额或者违法经营额不足 5 万元的，可以处 25 万元以下的罚款。对 5 年内实施两次以上商标侵权行为或者有其他严重情节的，会从重处罚。此外，权利人和侵权人也可以在工商行政管理部门的协调下就赔偿数额进行协商。工商行政管理部门解决侵权问题的效率是比较高，且效果比较好的。另外，如果权利人发现有单位或个人侵犯其权利时，可以向公安机关报案，并根据刑事诉讼程序，由国家追究侵权人的法律责任。同时，根据《刑事诉讼法》第二百零四条规定，知识产权权利人也有权在有证据证明犯罪嫌疑人有轻微侵犯知识产权的犯罪行为时，直接向人民法院起诉。刑事救济途径当然是最强有力的救济途径，即使最终不能认定刑事犯罪，公安机关的侦查工作无疑也会对权利人采取民事救济途径提供包括证据保全方面的帮助。实践中，海关也会向公安机关移交知识产权涉罪案件。

第三节　证券与其他商事业务

除前述国际投资与贸易的法律服务内容以外，律师可从事的涉外非诉法律服务事项还包括国际贷款业务、涉外证券业务、破产清算业务、海事海商业务、国际工程承包等专项业务。在这些业务领域提供律师服务，不但要了解涉事国家国内的法律规定，还要对相关国际条约、国际惯例、跨国合作机制等加以充分的了解。本节主要围绕涉外证券业务及破产清算业务，对律师服务过程中应把握的要点问题加以梳理。

一　境外首发并上市业务中的律师法律服务

证券法律业务是指律师事务所接受当事人委托，为其证券发行、上市和交易等证券业务活动，提供的制作、出具法律意见书等文件的法律服务。在涉外证券法律服务中，为国内企业提供境外上市的法律服务是重要的内容。境外上市是指国内股份有限公司向境外投资者发行股票，并在境外证券交易所公开上市。

我国企业境外上市主要有直接上市与间接上市两种模式。境外直接上市即直接以国内公司的名义向国外证券主管部门申请发行的登记注册，同时发行股票（或其他衍生金融工具），向当地证券交易所申请挂牌上市交易。即我们通常说的 H 股、N 股、S 股等。H 股，是指中国企业在中国香港联合交易所发行股票并上市，取 Hongkong 第一个字"H"为名；N 股，是指中国企业在纽约交易所发行股票并上市，取 New York 第一个字"N"为名；同样 S 股是指中国企业在新加坡交易所上市。通常，境外直接上市都是采取 IPO（首次公开募集）方式进行，即将首次发行股票和上市相结合的境外首发并上市。

间接上市的模式是指国内企业在境外注册公司，由境外公司以收购、股权置换等方式取得国内资产的控制权，然后以该离岸公司的名义在境外证券交易所上市。间接上市主要有两种形式：买壳上市和造壳上市。其本质都是通过将国内资产注入壳公司的方式，达到拿国内资产上市的目的，壳公司可以是上市公司，也可以是拟上市公司。如果壳公司已经是上市公司，则属于对上市公司的收购，与首次发行股票并上市有所不同。中国企业间接上市的模式还有一种被称为"新浪模式"（VIE 架构）。VIE，即 Variable Interest Entity，最初是一个财务概念，其实际含义是不通过持股的方式来实际控制一家公司，从而实现合并财务报表。VIE 结构这个词在中国，通常是指境外特殊目的公司通过其在中国的全资子公司（WFOE）以协议控制的方式控制一家内资公司，从而实现该境外特殊目的公司对内资公司的并表，进而得以基于此在境外融资或上市。用于控制内资公司的协议包括控制权、利润转移协议、股权质押协议等一系列合同。因为新浪是第一家采取此种方式在境外上市的企业，所以也被称为新浪模式。1999 年新浪在美国纳斯达克挂牌上市时，当时中华人民共和国工业和信息化部（MIIT）规定互联网内容提供商的牌照（ICP）只能由内资公司拥有，所以新浪在海外的上市公司投资到内地形成的外资公司只能与持有经营牌照的内资公司以合约关系而非控股关系来实现控制。这种协议控制模式后来逐渐扩展到传统产业，成为中国企业间接上市的主要模式之一。

中国企业在海外上市通常较多采用直接上市与间接上市两大类，但也有少数公司采用存托凭证和可转换债券上市。但这两种上市方式往往是企业在境外已上市，再次融资时采用的方式。

中国律师可为境外上市提供的法律服务，主要包括：①开展境内尽职调查；②协调公司与有关各方（包括财务顾问、境外律师、国际会计师等）的（法律）关系；③协助公司私募融资，为公司境外上市做前期准备，包括但不限于为拟上市公司私募重组的工作方案提供咨询和论证意见，参与公司与境内外机构投资人谈判，协助制订相关股权转让或/及增资扩股方案,制定相关协议及法律文书,根据需要依法出具相关法律意见书;④审阅上市招股书的中国大陆法律问题,依据中国大陆法律法规出具法律意见书;⑤协助回答海外股票交易所有关公司上市的中国大陆法律问题。

境外上市过程中,律师所起的作用贯穿于公司上市过程的始终,从前期准备到上市申报,及至在上市挂牌后续工作中,律师都发挥着重要作用。由于律师执业受到国家或地区地域的限制,一般应有两家以上的律师事务所为发行人、境内企业以及券商提供法律服务,包括发行人及境内权益公司聘请的中国律师和境外律师,以及券商聘请的中国律师和境外律师;境外律师除拟上市地的律师外,还包括发行人注册地的律师(如注册地非上市地)。

(一)中国律师在境外上市前期的服务

由于发行人的权益公司在我国境内,且该境内权益公司是外商投资企业,因此,境外上市必然涉及我国的公司法、外商投资法、外国投资者并购境内企业的规定,以及国家对公司管理所制定的一系列法律、法规及规范性文件。在上市预备期,中国律师应适时介入上市的前期工作,其工作范围包括为境内外公司重组提供法律意见、为重组后的公司规范化运作提供法律意见。律师可对公司进行上市前的法律辅导,确认公司实现规范化治理和运营,保证企业法人主体的存续不存在法律瑕疵,其主营项目符合我国《外商投资产业指导目录》、筹资项目的立项手续及生产许可手续符合国家相关规定、公司有健全的法人治理结构、公司财务管理合规、劳动管理制度合规、企业资产产权清晰、不存在重大违法行为并妥善处理已经存在或潜在的诉讼、仲裁。

中国律师还可以配合企业选定拟上市的证券交易所,并协助公司的股东和管理层对拟上市所在国的证券法律体系、证券监管机制、股票上市条件、申报程序及重大信息披露等制度作详尽了解。律师还可以协助公司寻找及选择境外中介机构,并进一步发现并处理股票上市可能存在的任何法律障碍。

(二)中国律师在发行人上市申报过程中及上市后的服务

中国律师在发行人上市申报过程中应就发行人内权益公司所涉及的中国法律事宜出具相关备忘录、综合法律意见书、物业法律意见、专项法律意见书,并就证券发行地审核机构提问所涉及的中国法律意见出具法律意见书。在审核阶段,证券交易所通常会提出问题,需要公司或各中介机构予以回答。律师在此阶段中,一般仅就证券交易所明确向律师提出的问题逐一发表法律意见。

中国企业境外上市,通常还需要办理国内的相关审批备案等手续。从我国现行的法规来看,对中国企业境外上市的监管立法缺乏统一性,对不同类型的公司、在不同的国家上市所适用的法律规范可能都有所不同。律师在提供法律服务时应熟悉相关国内的规范。以"红筹企业"上市的相关规定为例,就"红筹企业"而言,基本是背景特殊或享有特权的国有企业。红筹企业境外上市,为绕过证监会的监管,经常采取利用境外"壳公司"间接上市的方式。内地企业境外"买壳""造壳"的收购资金基本上是从内地调拨，因而造成了国有资产的流失。为了规范境外上市的审批，1997年6月20日，国务院公布《国务院关于进一步加强境外发行股票和上市管理的通知》，其中明确表明：限制内地企业买壳上市，买壳上市必须经内地证监委和证券委审批；造壳上市则以三年为限，规定地方和部门企业资产在内地达三年以上的，可以先行在港上市，再到国务院备案。由于涉及资产管理，所以要经财政部批准。而就民营企业来说，境外上市的法律监管主要分三个阶段。第一，"无异议函"时期。"无异议函"是2000年中国证监会颁布的规定，但实际上，"无异议函"实施后，许多民营企业境外上市均选择设立离岸公司的形式，并将大部分资产注入离岸公司，这使监管部门的监管形同虚设，最终废弃了"无异议函"制度。第二，《外国投资者并购境内企业暂行规定》时期。"无异议函"制度取消后，对外经济贸易合作部（即现在的商务部）2003年4月颁布的《外国投资者并购境内企业暂行规定》成为民营企业海外间接上市的重要法律规范。该规定为民营企业转型海外控股提供运作基本法则的同时，也规定了一定的限制。该规定的出台加速了民营企业境外上市的步伐。第三，2005年以来。2005年，国家外汇管理局先后发布《国家外汇管理局关于完善外资并购外汇管理有关问题的通知》《关于境内居民个人境外投资登记及外资并购外汇登记有关问题的通知》《国家外汇管理局关于境内居民通过境外特殊目的公司融资及返程投资外汇管理有关问题的通知》，即11号、29号、75号文件。是从客观上不批准民营企业境外上市到重启境外上市之门的过程。到2014年国家外汇管理局发布了《关于境内居民通过特殊目的公司境外投融资及返程投资外汇管理有关问题的通知》（汇发〔2014〕37号），替代了2005年75号文件，为境内居民境外投融资和返程投资打开多扇窗口。

在发行人上市后，中国律师可继续依据中国法律、法规及规范性文件的相关规定，对发行人境内权益公司的合规性经营提供规范性意见，包括审核应予披露的重大事项、为财务报告中涉及境内权益公司的相关法律问题提供法律意见。

二 国际债券发行的法律服务

随着我国经济体制改革——尤其是企业制度改革的深入，企业的自主权必将越来越大，在资金来源方面则表现为企业自筹资金渠道的多元化，而发行企业债券便是其中一种渠道。近年来境内企业以红筹方式海外上市，以及外商投资控股公司在境外但其主要资产和业务在中国境内的情形越来越多，在该等情形下的境外注册公司在境外发行债券时往往需要中国律师提供相关服务。上述情形的企业境外发行债券的共通点是债券发行主体及债券发行行为在境外，但境外主体在境内有子公司或资产等相关权益，或其在中国境内有主要业务。也正是因为如此，需要中国律师提供相关法律服务。该等法律服务的一般内容包括审阅债券募集说明书中的有关中国法律问题，草拟与发行主体有关的中国法律、法规概述，出具中国法律意见书。

中国律师一般审阅债券募集说明书中风险因素、中国子公司有关信息、中国法律法规等相关部分。中国律师需要对中国相关法律、法规有全面了解，同时结合公司实际情况，验证债券募集说明书的相关部分是否表述正确。中国律师草拟法律、法规部分时需注意相关行业的管制法规（如汽车行业的生产许可、排放要求、召回制度，也如房地产行业的房地产开发一般制度、宏观调控政策、外资从事房地产开发的特别规定）以及与债券发行相关的法规。

在发行各类债券均须向审核机构提交法律意见书，律师在债券发行中的作用不言而喻。律师事务所及其指派的律师从事债券发行法律业务时，应当根据项目及发行人的实际情况，编制核查和验证计划，明确核查和验证的事项，通过面谈、书面审查、实地调查、查询、函证、计算、复核等各种方法，明确债券发行所依据的文件资料的真实性、准确性、完整性。

律师参与债券发行业务，应当具备为委托人提供相应服务的专业能力。债券发行业务往往较为复杂，除需要法律专业知识外，还可能涉及公司运作、财务会计、金融证券等方面的基础知识。律师事务所应配备专业的团队为客户提供服务，出具的文件必须符合法律法规和证券监督管理机构的要求，内容简洁、准确、条理清楚，对于现有法律法规没有明确规定的事项或者律师已尽勤勉义务仍不能对其法律性质或其合法性作出准确判断的，应当出具保留意见。律师在接受委托人为其发行债券提供法律服务的委托后，首先展开的工作是进行尽职调查，通常的做法是律师根据出具法律意见书所发表法律意见的内容起草尽职调查材料清单，由发行人按照清单所列内容向律师提供材料，律师进行审查。一份详尽而合适的调查清单，不仅能够得到发行人现状的详尽资料、记录、文件等，而且还可以极大地方便后续的律师工作。

搜集资料和法律核查并非尽职调查工作的全部，律师尽职调查的宗旨是及时地发现发行人历史沿革与经营现状中所存在的、需要按照发改委或中国证监会的要求进行及时规范与改进的地方，并与保荐人和其他中介机构协商处理的办法和方案，以使发行人的各个方面最终在申报材料上报前符合中国证监会和拟上市交易所的有关规定。律师还需协助发行人审查和验证募集说明书等发行申请文件；起草承销协议、债券人会议议事规则、债券受托管理协议、专项偿债账户监管协议等法律文件；出具法律意见书及专项鉴证意见；参与起草发行审核部门的反馈回复等。

律师工作贯穿了债券发行的全过程，律师的参与对债券发行方案的制定、申报材料的起草修改、法律障碍的解决等方面起到重要的作用。律师只有勤勉尽职，熟悉企业债券和公司债券发行的相关法律法规，才能为公司提供优质的法律服务。

三　外资企业破产清算的法律服务

外资企业经营期限终止须清算或因资不抵债需破产清算时，往往需要律师提供相关法律服务。应当了解的是，在我国外商投资企业的破产不属于仲裁机构的受案范围，如有争议应在法院解决。而办理外资企业的破产清算法律业务，应关注的问题包括以下五个方面。

（一）外资企业注册资本需缴清后进入清算程序

破产程序持续时间较长，从清算组开始接管，到结束都至少需要一年以上的时间。律师在对其进行破产清点相关司法程序时需要注意的是，有些外资企业注册资本并不是一次缴清，而是分期出资，因此对于企业破产时的注册资本是否缴清需要格外注意，应在缴清后办理相关程序。

（二）外商投资企业非破产清算的法规依据

在2008年之前，外商投资企业的非破产清算均应当遵照1996年7月9日所实施的《外商投资企业清算办法》办理，然而在2008年1月15日，该办法已被国务院予以废止。随后，商务部办公厅于2008年5月5日发布了《商务部办公厅关于依法做好外商投资企业解散和清算工作的指导意见》（商法字〔2008〕31号），同时，国家工商行政管理总局、商务部又于2008年10月20日下发了《关于外商投资企业解散注销登记管理有关问题的通知》（工商外企字〔2008〕226号）。根据上述两份文件，目前，我国外商投资企业的非破产清算应当适用《公司法》《公司登记管理条例》的有关规定。除此之外，若外商投资法律和行政法规有特别规定而公司法未做详细规定的，适用特别规定，例如，中外合资的公司还应适用《中外合资经营企业法实施条例》第九十、九十五条规定，中外合作的公司还应适用《中外合作经营企业法实施细则》第四十八条规定，外商合资或外商独资的公司还应适用《外资企业法实施细则》第七十二、七十三条关于外商投资企业解散清算的有关规定。

（三）外资企业破产程序的启动

自2007年6月1日《中华人民共和国企业破产法》实施后，在我国注册的外商投资企业的破产也需要按照该规定处理。因此，外资企业的破产程序与中资企业的破产程序基本一致。按照《中华人民共和国企业破产法》的规定，若外商投资企业不能清偿到期债务，并且资产不足以清偿全部债务或者明显缺乏清偿能力的，可以依法启动破产程序。

破产程序的启动需要向人民法院提出申请，若外商投资企业不能清偿到期债务，其本身可以向人民法院提出破产清算申请，债权人也可以向人民法院提出破产清算申请；如果企业在清算过程中，发现资产不足以清偿债务的，清算责任人应当向人民法院申请进入破产清算程序。法院在收到破产申请后，将依法进行审查，若符合受理条件的,人民法院将自收到破产申请之日起十五日内裁定受理。破产案件受理后,法院将指定破产管理人接管拟破产企业的财产、印章和账簿、文书等资料;管理人还应当调查拟破产企业的财产状况;整理拟破产企业的债权与债务;组织召开债权人会议。此时,拟破产企业或者债权人均可以依照破产法的规定,向人民法院申请对拟破产企业进行重整或者在法院组织下进行和解。

(四)破产企业清算期间员工费用问题

《企业破产法》第一百一十三条对于破产财产应优先清偿破产费用和共益债务后,按照第一破产人所欠职工工资、医疗、伤残补助、抚恤费用等;第二破产人欠缴的除所欠职工工资、医疗、伤残补助等项规定以外的社会保险费和所欠税费;第三普通破产债权。但是对于清算期间员工的开支问题,即在破产企业清算终结前职工费用问题并无明确细则,容易让员工受到生活困扰,甚至存在不安定因素。因此,需要律师争取破产公司有关部门以及社会劳动部门的支持,解决职工清算终结前的费用问题,以免引起不必要的麻烦。另外,在非破产清算程序中,商务主管部门在办理备案时一般还需要拟解散的外商投资企业出具一份《关于员工安置(处理)方案的说明》,企业在该份说明中应当详细描述目前企业员工的状态、公司解散时员工的补偿方案、是否存在尚未解决的劳资纠纷等内容,最后拟解散的企业必须在该说明中承诺不会因企业清算而侵犯劳动者的合法权益。

(五)破产企业的无形财产价值界定

根据我国现行的破产法规定,破产财产应该包括以下几个部分,即手里破产申请时破产企业所有的财产,包括有形财产、无形财产、货币和有价证券以及投资收益。对于有形财产的界定已经相对明确,但是在无形财产的评估上,并无法律细则,给律师清算的无形财产评估造成一定困难。因此对于无形财产的评估须结合物价部门相关审批标准意见进行。

中国境内的外资企业不仅受到国内法律的保护,也受到国内法律的管辖。随着我国市场化程度的不断加深,市场经济运行机制也逐步完善,外资企业破产问题也变得越来越多,清算问题也逐渐复杂,此外由于周期较长,在清算前以及清算过程中等都应该注意一些细节问题,以此保障外资企业破产清算的顺利进行。

第九章 律师参与涉外诉讼仲裁业务

随着经济全球化的不断发展，涉外诉讼的数量也不断地增多。其中，我国的涉外诉讼很多都是涉外民事商事案件的诉讼，也有很多涉外民商事争议通过仲裁解决。这些涉外诉讼仲裁如果是由位于国内的中国法院或机构管辖，则中国的律师通常会具有作为律师担任双方当事人中的任意一方的代理人的资格。而如果涉外诉讼仲裁是在国外进行的，需视该国外法院或仲裁机构的要求确定中国律师是否可以作为代理人或以律师的身份出庭。在中国律师在国外的诉讼中不具备代理当事人出庭的资格或未获得当事人委托作为出庭律师时，中国律师仍然可以在国外的诉讼中发挥协助当事人参加诉讼的作用。

第一节 涉外诉讼仲裁案件代理需知

由于涉外诉讼仲裁案件的涉外性，律师在办理涉外诉讼仲裁案件时，应当熟悉其与国内诉讼仲裁案件办理中的差异，掌握涉外诉讼程序的特殊要求。

一 涉外诉讼仲裁案件分类

《最高人民法院关于适用〈中华人民共和国涉外民事关系法律适用法〉若干问题的解释（一）》（法释〔2012〕24号）第一条规定："民事关系具有下列情形之一的，人民法院可以认定为涉外民事关系：（一）当事人一方或双方是外国公民、外国法人或者其他组织、无国籍人；（二）当事人一方或双方的经常居所地在中华人民共和国领域外；（三）标的物在中华人民共和国领域外；（四）产生、变更或者消灭民事关系的法律事实发生在中华人民共和国领域外；（五）可以认定为涉外民事关系的其他情形。"而基于涉外民事关系发生的涉外民事诉讼的涉外因素，通常是指具有以下三种情况之一，即（一）诉讼主体涉外，即诉讼一方或者双方当事人是外国人、无国籍人或者外国企业和组织；人民法院在审理国内民商事案件过程中，因追加当事人或者第三人而使得案件具有涉外因素的，属于涉外民商事案件。（二）作为诉讼标的的法律事实涉外，即当事人之间的民事法律关系发生、变更、消灭的事实发生在国外；（三）诉讼标的物涉外,即当事人之间争议的标的物在国外。

涉外诉讼仲裁案件根据管辖地,可以进一步区分为我国法院处理的涉外诉讼案件、我国仲裁机构处理的涉外仲裁案件、国外法院处理涉及我国当事人的诉讼案件、国外或国际仲裁机构处理涉及我国当事人的仲裁案件。

二 代理国内涉外诉讼案件

随着中国与世界各国的合作和交流日益广泛和频繁,在中国境内从事贸易、投资等经济活动的外国人越来越多。当外国人(包括自然人和企业)在中国遇到民事纠纷时,可以向中国法院提起诉讼,行使诉讼权利来保障自己的合法权益。凡在中国领域内进行民事诉讼活动,在法律程序上,必须遵守中国《中华人民共和国民事诉讼法》及其相关的司法解释。我国《民事诉讼法》采用了同等原则和对等原则来确定中国人与外国人诉讼权利与义务之间的关系,即该外国人所在国家的法院限制中国公民、法人和其他组织的民事诉讼权利时,中国法院对其相应的民事诉讼权利也加以限制;如果外国人所在国家的法院赋予中国公民与该国公民同样的诉讼权利,中国法院也将一视同仁。因此,进行诉讼之前,外国人应首先了解母国对中国公民的诉讼权利是否加以限制来确定自己的诉讼权利在中国是否能够得到充分的实现,从而决定是否要选择诉讼这一法律救济方式。

(一) 国内涉外诉讼程序应注意的问题

外国人如何在中国法院起诉或应诉呢?以外国自然人为例,在相关法律文书的出具方面,如果是原告,应向人民法院递交由原告本人签名的起诉状。具有诉讼主体资格的材料:原告是外国自然人的,应提交用以证明自己身份的护照等身份文件;本人在中国境外不能到人民法院起诉或应诉的,应提交经过公证、认证的身份证明复印件。也就是说,如果外国自然人在中国境内,程序相对简单,外国自然人提交护照的复印件。如果本人到庭,一般仅提供复印件即可。如果不能到庭,通常情况下,该护照复印件最好经过国内公证处公证。在现实中的操作中,大陆各地法院做法不一致。另一种情形是外国自然人不在中国境内,那么该外国自然人的身份证明复印件应经所在国公证机关的公证和中国驻当地使领馆的认证。在委托律师出具授权委托书时,外国人在中国参加诉讼,如果委托律师代理,必须委托中国律师。外国人在中国领域内没有住所,委托我国律师或者其他人代理诉讼,从我国领域外寄交或者托交的授权委托书,应当经所在国公证机关证明,并经我国驻该国使领馆认证,或者履行我国与该所在国订立的有关条约中规定的证明手续。外国人也可以在中国公证处对授权书进行公证。同时,外国人在人民法院法官的见证下签署授权委托书,人民法院也应予以认可。

在证据材料方面,如果证据来源于国外,同样要履行公证认证手续。在所提交材料的语言上,当事人向人民法院提交的书面材料是外文的,应当同时向人民法院提交中文翻译件。外方当事人在仲裁或诉讼过程中书面文字必须使用汉字,外文要翻译成中文。庭审中外方当事人使用外语陈述的,必须由现场中文翻译。当事人可向我国法院申请提供中文翻译,费用由当事人承担。

在国内进行涉外诉讼,在诉讼前,律师应注意先查阅母国与中国是否有相关的条约或者协定,如果有,该外国当事人在中国的民事诉讼活动将遵守条约或协定的约定,也就是说,在中国的民诉法与该条约或协定规定不一致时,该条约或协定优先适用。在诉讼时,还要选择有管辖权的法院。对于合同或者涉外财产权益纠纷,如果当事人书面约定争议管辖的法院,该约定的法院所在地与争议有实际联系并且不违反中国民诉法中级别管辖和专属管辖的规定,则该约定条款有效,该法院对其争议纠纷有管辖权。作为涉外诉讼的被告应注意,如果在收到应诉通知书等法律文书后,没有向法院提出管辖异议,并应诉答辩的,视为承认该法院为有管辖权的法院。外国当事人可在诉讼中或者诉讼开始前申请财产保全措施,并向法院提供相应的担保,法院将在收到申请后的48小时内作出裁定。对于裁定准许诉前财产保全措施的,申请人应在裁定作出后30日内提起诉讼。逾期不起诉的,法院将解除财产保全。

涉外当事人要注意上诉期间,如果双方当事人在中国境内都没有住所,有权在判决书、裁定书送达之日起30日内提起上诉;双方当事人分别居住在我国领域内和领域外的,居住在我国领域内的当事人有权在判决书送达之日起15日内,裁定书送达之日起10日内提起上诉;居住在我国领域外的当事人有权在判决书、裁定书送达之日起30日内提起上诉;如果双方在中国境内都有住所,则有权在判决书送达之日起15日内、裁定书送达之日起10日内提起上诉。

在申请外国承认和执行法院判决方面,中国法院作出的发生法律效力的判决、裁定,如果被执行人或者其财产不在中国境内,当事人请求执行的,可以直接向有管辖权的外国法院申请承认和执行,也可以由法院依照缔结或者参加的国际条约的规定,或者按照互惠原则,请求外国法院承认和执行。

(二)关于准据法的选择和外国法的查明

各国民事立法的差异,对同一涉外民事案件适用不同国家的法律,往往导致不同的结果,此即国际私法上的法律冲突问题。法院审理涉外民事案件时,需要运用冲突规范来确定各类涉外民事关系应适用的法律,从而达到解决法律冲突的目的。我国《民法通则》《涉外民事关系法律适用法》等法律法规就此作了相应的规定。

《涉外民事关系法律适用法》所确定的国际私法规则在内容上较为合理、全面和完善,具有相当程度的先进性,对意思自治原则、最密切联系原则、保护弱者原则都有很好的体现。该法创新性地以经常居所为主要联结点,对民事主体、婚姻家庭、继承、物权、债权、知识产权等方面所作的法律适用具体规定,既总结了改革开放以来的涉外民事审判经验,也顺应了当代国际私法的发展潮流。

在依据冲突规范明确了应当适用哪一国的实体法后，还需要解决如何查明该外国法的存在和如何确定其准据法内容的问题，这一过程被称为外国法的查明。外国法的查明如何维护涉外民商事案件中当事人的正当权益同样起着关键作用，直接关系着涉外民商事案件的判决结果。在外国法查明的责任分配上，《涉外民事关系法律适用法》区分了法院和当事人的查明责任，规定"当事人主动选择适用外国法时，由当事人负主要的查明责任；除此之外根据其他冲突规范的指引适用外国法时，法院负有主要的查明责任"。由此对法院及当事人查明外国法的责任作了划分，明确了法院可以依职权查明外国法，但同样没有免除当事人查明外国法的义务。在查明的途径问题上，《涉外民事关系法律适用法》并未作详细规定，但是《最高人民法院关于适用〈中华人民共和国涉外民事关系法律适用法〉若干问题的解释（一）》（法释〔2012〕24号）第十七条规定，"人民法院通过由当事人提供、已对中华人民共和国生效的国际条约规定的途径、中外法律专家提供等合理途径仍不能获得外国法律的，可以认定为不能查明外国法律"。同时，2005年12月26日最高人民法院发布的《第二次全国涉外商事海事审判工作会议纪要》提及，当事人提供外国法，可以通过法律专家、法律服务机构、行业自律性组织、国际组织、互联网。但在司法实践上，当事人提供的外国法律内容还需要由法院进行审查，且看似合法的途径获取的外国法资料并不必然能够使其在证明力方面获得法院的认可。

如果法院认为当事人提供的外国法资料不能充分证明所需证明的法律主张，除了就此认定外国法不能查明外，法院也会在当事人提供资料的基础上，进一步查找外国法内容。《中华人民共和国涉外民事关系法律适用法》规定了在外国法无法查明情况下如何处理，即直接适用内国法作为准据法。但是在直接适用内国法之前，尚存如何判断外国法无法查明的问题。最高人民法院在2011年施行的《关于适用〈中华人民共和国涉外民事关系法律适用法〉若干问题的解释（一）》中对此做出说明，即仍然区分两种情况（1）法院负主要查明责任的情形下，通过各种合理途径仍不能获得外国法；（2）当事人负主要查明责任的情形下，当事人在合理期限内无正当理由未提供，视为不能查明；（二）法院对外国法的主动查明。

三　代理国内涉外仲裁案件

涉外仲裁是争议本身具有国际性、涉外性的仲裁事项，其争议发生在涉外经贸或者海事活动之中。普通的民事纠纷，如婚姻、收养、监护、继承案件，劳动纠纷以及行政争议不属于涉外仲裁的范围。在争议各方已就争议解决方式达成书面仲裁协议的情况下，可提交仲裁协议明确写明的仲裁机构进行仲裁。涉外仲裁裁决是终局的。争议各方既不得向任何行政机关和机构要求复议，也不得向任何国家的法院提起诉讼。

在我国，中国国际经济贸易仲裁委员会和中国海事仲裁委员会是受理涉外仲裁的最主要机构，负责审理绝大部分涉外仲裁案件。中国国际经济贸易仲裁委员会现在执行的规则是2015年1月1日开始执行的。根据现行《中国国际经济贸易仲裁委员会仲裁规则（2015版）》第3条的规定，该仲裁委员会根据当事人的约定受理契约性或非契约性的经济贸易等争议案件。这些案件包括：①国际或涉外争议案件；②涉及香港特别行政区、澳门特别行政区及台湾地区的争议案件；③国内争议案件。近年来，有些地方仲裁委员会，如北京仲裁委员会也开始受理涉外案件。

律师在代理涉外仲裁时，在接受委托之初，应注意审查仲裁协议的效力。在实践中，有些仲裁条款的起草者为了给客户留有余地，同时将人民法院和仲裁机构作为解决争议的机构列入仲裁条款供当事人临时选择，或者同时提出国内的一家仲裁机构和国外的一家仲裁机构由当事人临时选择。根据最高人民法院关于仲裁法的司法解释，前者因为违背了仲裁法律关于选择仲裁就必须排除法院管辖的基本原则，所以是无效的。而在后一种情况下，如果两家仲裁机构都是明确具体的，而且两者之间是"或者"关系，则协议仍然有效。在办理律师的委托授权手续时，按照中国国际经济贸易仲裁委员会的仲裁规则，提交仲裁申请时无须提供经过中国驻外使领馆认证的律师委托手续，只要有当事人的委托授权书即可，而且在很多情况下，甚至无须中文译文，这一点大大方便了中国律师的工作。但是，实践经验表明，在立案工作完成后，为了方便启动将来的法院执行程序，律师应建议外国客户另行履行委托手续的认证手续，这主要是因为法院与仲裁机构是两个系统，有些地方的法院会坚持履行我国法律关于外国当事人在中国进行诉讼程序的有关规定。如不早做准备，未雨绸缪，到时可能会耗费不必要的时间，给执行工作带来困难。

在仲裁员的选择方面，选择仲裁员时要特别注意仲裁员的背景和口碑。在仲裁语言方面，根据中国国际经济贸易仲裁委员会的仲裁规则，当事人对仲裁语言有约定的，从其约定。当事人对仲裁语言没有约定的，以中文为仲裁语言。仲裁委员会也可以视案件的具体情形确定其他语言为仲裁语言。在实践中，有些外国当事人以争议合同是用英文起草，或者争议各方基本是以英文进行通信为由要求仲裁文字为英文，这些要求通常不能得到中国国际经济贸易仲裁委员会的批准。但仲裁庭开庭时，当事人或其代理人、证人需要语言翻译的，可由仲裁委员会仲裁院提供译员，也可由当事人自行提供译员。在资料和证据的提供方面，也不像法院诉讼那样必须对国外形成的证据材料做公证、认证和翻译。当然，对于当事人提交的各种文书和证明材料，仲裁庭或仲裁委员会仲裁院认为必要时，可以再要求当事人提供相应的中文译本或其他语言译本。

四 参与国外诉讼仲裁案件

中国律师参与在国外进行的诉讼或仲裁案件，或者依当地法律规定取得当地的律师资格出庭，或者只能协助中国客户做好协助外国律师的工作。国内客户无论是作为原告还是作为被告，都需要特别关注跨境诉讼仲裁本身的特殊性。

在启动国外诉讼仲裁程序以前，首先要做好证据收集和保全。实践来看，中国企业在外国诉讼和仲裁中败诉的一个重要原因在于在发生纠纷前或者发生时未能保留好证据或者不注重证据的制作和收集。这需要律师凭借其专业直觉判断哪些情况是需要通过证据方式加以保留的，如对于往来邮件进行公证、对于双方电话进行录音等，为将来的争议解决打下坚实的基础。

办理国外诉讼仲裁案件还应注意选择合适的争议解决机构、仲裁员并协助中国客户选择合适的外国律师。由于跨境诉讼往往涉及多个不同国家法院的管辖权，不同国家司法机关的管辖将适用不同的程序法，这对于最终的判决结果具有非常重大的影响，所以如果中国客户作为原告提出诉讼，需要律师为中国企业选择合适的管辖法院提供有价值的建议。而在国际仲裁中，律师在帮助中国企业选择合适的仲裁员时可以发挥指导作用，在仲裁中可以帮助中国企业理解不同于我国的国际仲裁规则。由于仲裁所具有的民间性，仲裁员是由双方当事人自行挑选的，仲裁员选择的合适与否直接决定了仲裁裁决结果。律师通过其法律共同体的联系，能够对仲裁员的性格因素、政治倾向、知识结构等进行全方位的了解，进而能够帮助中国企业选择合适的仲裁员。

在跨境诉讼仲裁中，除聘请国内律师帮助外，中国客户通常还需要选择合适的外国律师。专业能力强、责任心重的外国律师对于中国企业赢得国际诉讼和仲裁具有非常重要的作用。经过几百年的发展，国外的律师行业已经呈现出分工极细、专业分明的特点。不同的外国律师及律师事务所的专业方向、行业背景都是不同的。由于国外法律分工极其细致，不同出庭律师的专业领域、收费方式等差别很大。如何根据不同案件类型选择合适的国外律师，需要中国律师基于其经验帮助中国企业作出准确判断。

在跨境纠纷中，往往会适用外国的法律，中国律师在为中国当事人解释外国法律方面具有一定的优势，例如可以运用自己的语言优势和对中国法律的理解对照，帮助中国当事人准确了解外国法律的内容。与中国法律制度相比，有时外国法律制度的规定在中国没有相同的规定，这就需要中国律师从专业角度剖析外国法律，向中国当事人准确传达外国法律的含义，并就中国类似的制度加以介绍，从而加深中国当事人的理解。在外国法律中，有时一些重要的法律原则是由判例形成的，中国律师还需要从司法判例角度全面把握外国法律，帮助当事人深入理解外国法律的适用。在全面把握案例可能涉及的外国法律的基础上，帮助当事人确定诉讼策略。

中国律师虽然不作为代理律师，但仍可以协助中国当事人制订诉讼策略，在跨境诉讼和仲裁中控制成本。参加国际诉讼或者仲裁，不但耗费时间和精力，往往还需要支出大量的费用，包括法院诉讼费、仲裁费及律师费等。经常有中国企业因高昂的诉讼费用而不参加诉讼或中途退回，也有虽胜诉但花费巨大而只能算是惨胜的情况。在某中国企业与外国企业之间的知识产权诉讼中，中国企业虽然最终胜诉，但由于不同文化习惯的差异，国外律师的收费方式、习惯和国内律师差异极大。基于案情选择合适的国外律师及合理的律师收费方式，对于案件最终的成本控制极为重要。中国企业需要依靠中国律师基于其专业知识和法律共同体的信息沟通，帮助当事人选择最为合理的诉讼方案及收费方式，从而帮助当事人节约诉讼费用。在诉讼过程中，也可以采取必要的和解策略，以节约诉讼费用。

五　外国仲裁裁决承认和执行

取得外国仲裁裁决以后，如确定需向中国法院提请承认和执行，无论是外方当事人还是中国当事人，都可以委托中国律师代理该执行案件，而被申请执行一方也可以委托中国律师申请法院不予承认和执行该仲裁裁决。就具体的管辖法院而言，如果被执行人是自然人的，由其户籍所在地或者住所地所在的人民法院管辖；被执行人是法人的，由主要办事机构所在地中院执行；住所、户籍或者主要办事机构没有的由财产所在地中院执行。在具体执行的规则方面，由于中国是《承认及执行外国仲裁裁决公约》即通常所说的《纽约公约》的成员，中国法院对源于《纽约公约》成员国的仲裁裁决依照《纽约公约》和我国《民事诉讼法》等有关规定执行，或者可以按照其他可以适用的国际条约、国际惯例乃至互惠的原则办理外国裁决的承认和执行事项。

（一）《纽约公约》对承认及执行外国仲裁裁决的条件的规定

《纽约公约》是目前国际上关于承认与执行国际商事仲裁裁决的最重要、影响范围最广的公约，几乎所有主要国家皆是该公约的成员国。较之此前的有关公约，《纽约公约》扩大了承认和执行外国仲裁裁决的范围，减少了承认和执行外国仲裁裁决的先决条件，也简化了相关手续。我国于1986年加入《纽约公约》，该公约于次年在我国生效。《纽约公约》以排他的形式规定了承认及执行外国仲裁裁决的条件，即除非属于下列情况之一，被申请执行国皆应承认、执行外国仲裁裁决。这些情况包括以下方面。

（1）仲裁协议无效。有效的仲裁协议是仲裁的前提和基础。判断一份仲裁协议是否有效，应当根据所依据的准据法。但是《纽约公约》同时规定，凡是满足以下六项要求的，缔约国就应当承认该份仲裁协议的效力：①以书面形式完成；②协议内容是为了处理当事人之间已经发生的或者可能发生的争议；③这种争议与一个确定的法律关系有关；④这种争议属于仲裁范围；⑤当事人双方具有行为能力；⑥根据特定的准据法，仲裁协议是有效的。

（2）仲裁过程违反正当程序。《纽约公约》所谓的违反正当程序至少包括：①未给予适当通知；②未能令当事人进行充分申辩，使其丧失了公平陈述的机会。

（3）仲裁员超越权限。

（4）仲裁庭的组成和仲裁的程序不当。

（5）裁决不具有约束力或已被撤销、停止执行。

(6) 争议事项具有不可仲裁性。从国际通行的法律实践看，仲裁事项通常不包括涉及家庭关系和人身关系的争议。即使是商务纠纷，有些案件也通常不通过仲裁进行解决。这些案件包括：①涉及专利、商标权和著作权的纠纷；②涉及破产的纠纷；③涉及证券的纠纷；④反不正当竞争、反托拉斯案件。

(7) 违背被申请承认和执行国的社会公共利益。这里所谓"社会公共利益"并无通行的定义和标准，一般是指被普遍接受的善良风俗和道德准则，以及最根本的社会利益和法律准则。由于世界各国在文化宗教、政治制度、法律体系等各个方面存在分歧，各国法院在诠释"社会公共利益"时具有一定的裁量权。

我国《民事诉讼法》第二百六十条第二款是"社会公共利益条款"，即人民法院认定该仲裁裁决违背社会公共利益的，不予执行。该条款是法院主动审查仲裁裁决的依据。"社会公共利益条款"是世界各国法院用以保护本国或本国当事人利益的弹性条款。依据《纽约公约》，对于外国仲裁裁决的执行，执行地国法院可以主动适用社会公共利益或公共政策条款。我国是该公约的缔约国，在执行外国仲裁裁决确实违反我国的社会公共利益或公共政策时，我国法院应当适用公共利益条款。我国现行人民法院作出不予执行或者不予承认和执行涉外仲裁和外国仲裁裁决需要报告的制度，体现了人民法院对于适用公共政策或者公共利益条款的谨慎态度。

（二）我国有关外国仲裁裁决和涉外仲裁裁决承认与执行程序中的内部报告制度

为加强对地方法院关于承认和执行外国仲裁裁决工作的监督，我国最高人民法院在1995年8月28日发布《关于人民法院处理与涉外仲裁及外国仲裁事项有关问题的通知》，要求凡起诉到人民法院的涉外、涉港澳和涉台经济、海事海商纠纷案件，如果当事人在合同中订有仲裁条款或者事后达成仲裁协议，人民法院认为该仲裁条款或者仲裁协议无效、失效或者内容不明确无法执行的，在决定受理一方当事人起诉之前，必须报请本辖区所属高级人民法院进行审查；如果高级人民法院同意受理，应将其审查意见报最高人民法院。在最高人民法院未作答复前，可暂不予受理。凡一方当事人向人民法院申请执行我国涉外仲裁机构裁决，或者向人民法院申请承认和执行外国仲裁机构的裁决，如果人民法院认为我国涉外仲裁机构裁决具有民事诉讼法第二百六十条情形之一的，或者申请承认和执行的外国仲裁裁决不符合我国参加的国际公约的规定或者不符合互惠原则的，在裁定不予执行或者拒绝承认和执行之前，必须报请本辖区所属高级人民法院进行审查；如果高级人民法院同意不予执行或者拒绝承认和执行，应将其审查意见报最高人民法院。待最高人民法院答复后，方可裁定不予执行或者拒绝承认和执行。该通知可以看出，事涉互惠，中国对于拒绝承认和执行外国仲裁裁决是较为谨慎的，实践中，中国法院也以裁定承认为主流或占多数，不承认为例外或少数。之后，在1998年4月23日最高人民法院《关于人民法院撤销涉外仲裁裁决有关事项的通知》、2000年4月17日最高人民法院《关于审理和执行涉外民商事案件应当注意的几个问题的通知》中这一制度又得到了进一步的明确和强调。

第二节 诉状制作与法庭文件

作为中国律师,在有关国外诉讼案件的咨询或参与到在国外的诉讼案件时,往往需要对国外的诉讼程序有基本的了解,甚至进一步为当事人起草简单的诉状类法律文书。本节以在美国参加民事诉讼案件的审理为例,就简单的民事诉讼案件可能涉及的基本的诉状制作加以介绍,并提供法庭文件供学习。

一 美国民事诉讼的基本程序

在美国有两个平行的法院体系,即联邦法院体系和州法院体系。但是两个法院体系所适用的法律程序十分接近。根据《美国联邦地区法院民事诉讼规则》,美国民事诉讼程序可以分为诉答程序、审前程序与开庭审理三个阶段。其基本程序如下。

(一) 起诉、通知被告与被告回应(Complaint filing, Service of Process& defendant's filing of answer or pre-answer motions)

在确定起诉并选定法庭后,起诉方必须递交诉状并将起诉通知书送达被告。美国和中国都是《海牙送达公约》的成员国,在司法实践中形成了一系列的送达规则[①]。

(二) 动议(Motion)

被告在作出"答辩"之外,还可以向法院提出"动议"。"动议"所依据的是联邦民事诉讼规则第12条的规定。其中,除依据12条b款(2)项至(5)项所提出的动议必须在首次答复的时候或之前提出以外,所有的动议都可以在诉讼过程中提出。例如12条b款(6)项的动议涉及内容包括:对诉讼标的无管辖权;对人无管辖权;审判地不适当;传唤令状要件不充分;传唤令状的送达要件不充分;没有陈述救济请求;没有按照19条规定合并当事人。一旦被告向法院提出联邦民事诉讼规则第12条所列之请求,原告即无法请求法院做出缺席裁判。

(三) 答辩(Answer)

《美国联邦地区法院民事诉讼规则》第12条规定,除非另有法律规定,被告应当在接到传票和起诉状之日起20日内提交答辩状。如逾期仍对所收到的通知书置之不理,既无作出任何法律所允许的请求(pre-answer motions),也未进行答辩,原告就可以向法庭请求作出缺席裁判(motion for default judgment)。

---

① 程冰:《美国诉讼中的送达规则在中国内地的适用》,《中国法律(中英文版)》2012年第3期。

(四) 证据开示程序 (Discovery)

在美国民事诉讼规则中有一步骤与大部分国家不同，就是诉讼双方可以要求对方提供与案件相关的咨询 (discovery)。取得资讯的方法有三：书面质询 (written interrogatory)、口头质询 (oral deposition) 以及要求就自己拥有与案件相关证据做出确认 (request for admission)。这样的一个程式，特别是就自己拥有的证据要求对方做确认的程序，可以替当事人省下不少在诉讼上花费的时间，并可以帮助双方当事人把心思专注在案件关键性争点上。

诉讼代理人对对方当事人提出相关证据确认的请求不能拒绝。若对方期望取得的证据并不受任何法律所提供的特别保护 (non-privileged information)，被索求证据的一方则需要完全配合并在收到请求的 30 日内提出对方期望得到的证据。如有任何不合作的情况发生又没有合理的原因，请求证据的一方可以要求法院对不配合一方做出惩罚。

(五) 正式进入案件审理程序 (Trial)

在美国，所有的刑事案件都必须有陪审团陪审，但是民事案件是否应有陪审团陪审则是诉讼代理人决定。只要任何一方提出要求陪审团陪审，诉讼代理人就必须参与陪审团的挑选。陪审团由一群被法院随机挑选出的选民担任，担任陪审员不需要有任何法律知识，不但如此，陪审员在参与案件审理之前基本上是对案件没有任何的了解。陪审团的功用是在对案件的事实面作一个审理，之后再根据诉讼代理人所提供的事实（包括人证、物证以及法庭上所做之言辞答辩）和法官所给予的指示经由各陪审员投票对案件作出裁决 (verdict)。

除了陪审员的挑选，在开庭前的准备还包括对证人 (witness) 的甄选、面谈与为其在法庭上质询所作出的准备。在法庭中，诉讼双方都可以提供证人。无论是哪一方所提供的证人，对方当事人都可以有机会作交叉询问 (cross-examination)。证人在法庭上的目的，是经由诉讼双方律师的带领下，提供法官以及陪审团更多与案件相关的资讯。因此，证人的可信度常常成为律师攻击对方证人的方法。证人的可信度低，其所提供的资讯在法庭上的说服力也相对较低。

为加快诉讼进程、节约诉讼成本，美国有很多案件是作过做出即决判决 (Summary Judgment) 而解决的，即决判决又称即决审判、简易判决，是英美法系国家一种具有特色的民事诉讼制度，该制度允许法官可以不经开庭审理而直接对全部或者部分案件作出实体性的、有拘束力的判决。即决判决可以上诉，但如果提出的要求即决判决的动议被拒绝，则法院认为该案的审理是必要的，因此这种裁定是中间裁定，在审理结束针对实质问题作出判决前不得上诉。

(六) 上诉 (Appeal)

假如法庭已经审理完案件，而且已经根据案件的事实作出最后的判决后，不服判决的诉讼代理人（或当事人）可以向上诉法庭提起上诉。在美国，是否对案件提出上诉的决定权在当事人。如果当事人决定不提出上诉，律师必须遵照当事人的指示对案件作出善后的处理。

在美国，对案件提起上诉并不便宜并且耗时耗力。不但如此，如在上诉法院未能查出初审法院的判决有重大错误的情况下，上诉法院废弃法院判决之机会并不大。此外，由于初审法院着重的是案件事实的审查核实，并不会对案件的法律层面做太多的分析。因此，上诉法院在审理上诉案件时，并不会对案件的事实再作审理，会把主要的精力花在法律面的分析上。只有在上诉法院审理后发现初审法院对案件的事实认定上有错误，上诉法院不但会废弃下级法院的判决，同时也会将案件发回至下级法院，要求下级法院针对其认为有错的部分重新审理。

（七）发回案件至下级法院重审（Remand）

一旦上诉法院将案件发回至下级法院要求其对案件重新审理，下级法院必须依据上诉法院的指示重新审理案件而不是从头到尾地审理整件案子，并根据审理的结果作出判决。这是美国法庭处理案件的程式，参与诉讼双方并不能干涉。假如诉讼双方仍不服重新审理案件后所作出的判决，其可以再度上诉。

二 国外民事诉讼仲裁的诉辩书状范例

以美国为例，在联邦法院的官网（http://www.uscourts.gov/forms/civil-forms）上提供了各种法律文书的格式模板，包括民事案件、刑事案件及破产案件等，仅民事案件的格式文本就有69种，可供案件当事人下载使用。

以下是在美国联邦法院就合同违约提起诉讼的起诉状格式（Complaint for a Civil Case Alleging Breach of Contract）

United States District Court

for the

_____ District of _____

_____ Division

Case No.

Plaintiff（*s*）

（to be filled in by the Clerk's Office）

（*Write the full name of each plaintiff who is filing this complaint. If the names of all the plaintiffs cannot fit in the space above, please write "see attached" in the space and attach an additional page with the full list of names.*）

Jury Trial：（*check one*）'Yes 'No

$- v -$

_____

Defendant（s）

(*Write the full name of each defendant who is being sued. If the names of all the defendants cannot fit in the space above, please write "see attached" in the space and attach an additional page with the full list of names.*)

Complaint for a Civil Case Alleging Breach of Contract

(28. S. C. § 1332; Diversity of Citizenship)

Ⅰ. **The Parties to This Complaint A. The Plaintiff**（s）

Provide the information below for each plaintiff named in the complaint. Attach additional pages if needed.

Name _____

Street Address _____

City and County _____

State and Zip Code _____

Telephone Numbe _____

E-mail Address _____

B. The Defendant（s）

Provide the information below for each defendant named in the complaint, whether the defendant is an individual, a government agency, an organization, or a corporation. For an individual defendant, include the person's job or title (if known). Attach additional pages if needed.

Defendant No. 1

Name _____

Job or Title (*if known*) _____

Street Address _____

City and County _____

State and Zip Code _____

Telephone Numbe _____

E-mail Address (*if known*) _____

Defendant No. 2

Name _____

Job or Title (*if known*) _____

Street Address _____

City and County _____

State and Zip Code _____

Telephone Numbe _____

E-mail Address (*if known*) _____

Defendant No. 3

Name _____

Job or Title (*if known*) _____

Street Address _____

City and County _____

State and Zip Code _____

Telephone Numbe _____

E-mail Address (*if known*) _____

Defendant No. 4

Name _____

Job or Title (*if known*) _____

Street Address _____

City and County _____

State and Zip Code _____

Telephone Numbe _____

E-mail Address (*if known*) _____

Ⅱ. **Basis for Jurisdiction**

Federal courts are courts of limited jurisdiction (limited power). Under 28 U.S.C. § 1332, federal courts may hear cases in which a citizen of one State sues a citizen of another State or nation and the amount at stake is more than $75,000. In that kind of case, called a diversity of citizenship case, no defendant may be a citizen of the same State as any plaintiff. Explain how these jurisdictional requirements have been met.

A. The Plaintiff（s）

1. If the plaintiff is an individual

The plaintiff, (*name*) _____, is a citizen of the state of (*name*) _____.

2. If the plaintiff is a corporation

The plaintiff, (*name*) _____, is incorporated under the laws of the State of (*name*) _____, and has its principal place of business in the State of (*name*) _____.

(*If more than one plaintiff is named in the complaint*, attach an additional page providing the same information for each additional plaintiff.)

B. The Defendant（s）

1. If the defendant is an individual

The defendant, (*name*) _____, is a citizen of the State of (*name*) _____. Or is a citizen of (*foreign nation*) _____.

2. If the plaintiff is a corporation

The defendant, (*name*) _____, is incorporated under the laws of the State of (*name*) _____, and has its principal place of business in the State of (*name*) _____. Or is incorporated under the laws of (*foreign nation*) _____.

And has its principal place of business in the State of (*name*) _____.

(*If more than one defendant is named in the complaint*, attach an additional page providing the same information for each additional defendant.)

C. The Amount in Controversy

The amount in controversy-the amount the plaintiff claims the defendant owes or the amount at stake-is more than $75,000, not counting interest and costs of court, because (*explain*):

_____

Ⅲ. Statement of Claim

Write a short and plain statement of the claim. Do not make legal arguments. State as briefly as possible the facts showing that each plaintiff is entitled to the damages or other relief sought. State how each defendant was involved and what each defendant did that caused the plaintiff harm or violated the plaintiff's rights, including the dates and places of that involvement or conduct. If more than one claim is asserted, number each claim and write a short and plain statement of each claim in a separate paragraph. Attach additional pages if needed.

The plaintiff, (*name*) _____, and the defendant, (*name*) _____, made an agreement or contract on (date) _____. The agreement or contract was (*oral or written*) _____. Under that agreement or contract, the parties were required to

(*specify what the agreement or contract required each party to do*) _____

The defendant failed to comply because (*specify what the defendant did or failed to do that failed to comply with what the agreement or contract required*)

_____

The plaintiff has complied with the plaintiff's obligations under the contract.

Ⅳ. Relief

State briefly and precisely what damages or other relief the plaintiff asks the court to order. Do not make legal arguments. Include any basis for claiming that the wrongs alleged are continuing at the present time. Include the amounts of any actual damages claimed for the acts alleged and the basis for these amounts. Include any punitive or exemplary damages claimed, the amounts, and the reasons you claim you are entitled to actual or punitive money damages.

_____

Ⅴ. Certification and Closing

Under Federal Rule of Civil Procedure 11, by signing below, I certify to the best of my knowledge, information, and belief that this complaint: (1) is not being presented for an improper purpose, such as to harass, cause unnecessary delay, or needlessly increase the cost of litigation; (2) is supported by existing law or by a nonfrivolous argument for extending, modifying, or reversing existing law; (3) the factual contentions have evidentiary support or, if specifically so identified, will likely have evidentiary support after a reasonable opportunity for further investigation or discovery; and (4) the complaint otherwise complies with the requirements of Rule 11.

A. For Parties Without an Attorney

I agree to provide the Clerk's Office with any changes to my address where case-related papers may be served. I understand that my failure to keep a current address on file with the Clerk's Office may result in the dismissal of my case.

Date of signing: _____
Signature of Plaintiff _____
Printed Name of Plaintiff _____

B. For Attorneys

Date of signing: _____
Signature of Attorney _____
Printed Name of Attorney _____
Number _____
Name of Law Firm _____

Street Address　　　　　　_____

State and Zip Code　　　　 _____

Telephone Number　　　　 _____

E-mail Address　　　　　　 _____

以下是一份中国当事人在美国期货交易委员会提起仲裁上诉程序时,被告律师提交的一份答辩状(当事人为化名)。

United States of America before the
Commodity Futures Trading Commission

ZILAN HUANG,

　　　　Complainant,

　　v.　　　　　　　　　　　CFTC Docket No. 18 – R005

ROBERT H. CHAN,

　　　　Respondent.

Response Brief

Pursuant to Rule 12.401（c）, 17 C.F.R. § 12.401（c）, respondent Robert Chan（"Chan"）responds to Complainants' Appeal Brief entitled "MOTION for punish fraud in Chan IB services".

STATEMENT OF FACTS

1. On May 20, 2010, Complainant submitted to Peregrine Financial Group, Inc.（"PFG"）her completed Customer Application and Customer Agreement for her forex accounts.

2. Complainant's account was a self-directed account, and Complainant initially traded on the Currenex front-end retail platform known as Viking.

3. On February 4, 2011, Compliance Rule 2 – 48 of the National Futures Association went into effect, requiring all Forex Dealer Members to file daily electronic reports of trade data with the NFA. At that time, Viking did not have the technology to provide PFG the order data necessary to comply with Rule 2 – 48, and therefore PFG transitioned clients off of Viking before Rule 2 – 48.

4. Thereafter, Complainant failed to maintain sufficient margin in her account and her account was subsequently liquidated.

5. On December 7, 2011, Complainant filed a NFA Arbitration（11 – ARB-95）against Chan and PFG. Although Complainant's Statement of Claim listed several conflicting theories of recovery, the main gest of her NFA Arbitration alleged losses to Huang's commodities trading

account at PFG in which Robert Chan was her broker.

6. On September 28, 2012, after reviewing all of the evidence and lengthy submission by the parties, the NFA arbitrator issued an Award in Robert Chan's favor.

7. Thereafter, Complainant filed her CFTC reparation on the same causes of action concerning the same account. Complainant even attached her NFA Statement of Claim in support of her reparations complainant.

8. Therefore given the NFA Statement of Claim is virtually identical to the CFTC Complaint, the NFA Arbitration Award of September 28, 2012 resolved all issues raised by Complainant before the CFTC, Chan filed his Motion for Summary Disposition on December 3, 2014.

9. On January 26, 2015, the Judgment Officer issued an Order Granting Summary Disposition.

10. Thereafter, Complainant appealed from the January 26, 2015 Order.

Argument

Complainant's reparation complaint is barred under the theory of res judicata. The doctrine of res judicata provides that, "a final judgment rendered by a court of competent jurisdiction on the merits is conclusive as to the rights of the parties and their privies, and, as to them, constitutes an absolute bar to a subsequent action involving the same claim, demand or cause of action.'" Barth v. Reagan, 497 N. E. 2d 519, 522 (2nd Dist. 1986) (*citing* LaSalle National Bank v. County Board of School Trustees, 61 Ill. 2d 524, 528 (1975) (*quoting* People v. Kidd, 398 Ill. 405, 408 (1947)). Furthermore, "the doctrine precludes a party from raising in a subsequent action not only 'every matter which was offered to sustain or defeat the claim or demand' made in the prior action, but also 'any other matter which might have been offered for that purpose'." Id. (*quoting* Barry v. Commonwealth Edison Co., 374 Ill. 473, 478 (1940)).

The Judgment Officer correctly granted Respondent's Motion for Summary Disposition based on the res judicata effect of the NFA arbitration award in Respondent's favor on very same issues Complainant was attempting to assert in her reparation's complaint. Neither in the reparation's proceeding nor in this appeal did Complainant present any additional facts that would counteract the application of res judicata. Instead of presenting any new facts or case law in support of her position, Complainant simply restates the same evidence presented in the NFA Arbitration in the hopes that her third bite at the apple would render a different result. Complainant merely fails to address any legal principle. As a matter of law, Complainant is estopped from pursuing her Reparation claim under the legal theory of *res-judicata*.

Conclusion

For the reasons set forth above, Robert Chan respectfully requests that the Commission affirms the Order granting Summary Disposition and dismiss this appeal in its entirety.

_____
One of Respondent Robert Chan's Attorneys

下面是一例驳回起诉的动议①。

STATE OF INDIANA	TYPE YOUR COURT HERE
TYPE YOUR COUNTY HERE	
NAME OF PLAINTIFF HERE	Case No. :
Plaintiff	DEFENDANT's MOTION TO
v.	DISMISS CASE
YOUR NAME HERE EXACTLY AS	
LISTED ON SUMMONS	
Defendant	

Motion to Dismiss Case Without Prejudice

Comes now, Defendant, _____, and files a Motion for Plaintiff to Comply with Indiana Trial Rule 9.2 and states as follows:

To Dismiss this Case because Plaintiff failed to comply with Trial Rule 9.2 by not attaching the actual contract and assignment showing the Plaintiff is the Real Party in Interest.

wherefore, Defendant requests that Plaintiff's Complaint be Dismissed without Prejudice and the Plaintiff be ordered to comply with Indiana Trial Rule 9.2 within thirty days by filing an amended complaint and for dismissal with prejudice for failure to comply and all other relief necessary and proper in the premises.

Respectfully Submitted,
_____

以下是一份要求法院驳回对方动议的辩论意见：

In the Circuit Court in and for Bay County, Florida

Jodee Berry,

    Plaintiff,   Case No. : 01-2642

---

① 此动议范例参见 http://www.howtowinacreditcardlawsuit.net/example-of-a-motion-to-dismiss-credit-card-debt/, 更多动议范例可参见 http://www.likelihoodofconfusion.com/legal-publications-ron-coleman/motions-dismiss-under-frcp-12b6/, 后者主要涉及知识产权争议案件。

v.

Division: J

Gulf Coast Wings, in C.,

d/b/a Hooter's Restaurant

Defendant.

Argument for Motions to Dismiss

1. The manager of the restaurant, Jared Blair at the time, was not responsible for setting up contest and awarding the employees. The manager of the restaurant are not able to represent our company-Gulf Coast Wings, Inc., who are in charge of setting up contests and awarding the employees between several restaurants. All the statements that Blair mentioned about the contest and the award was unconfirmed by the relevant departments of the company.

2. When the Plaintiff mentioned about the announcement Blair stated about the contest and the award, they did not get any agreement about the prizes or the rewards to the winner, neither oral agreement or written contract.

3. The Plaintiff stated that "throughout the month of April, 2001, Blair repeatedly provided plaintiff and other waitresses with information regarding the contest and the award that the winner would receive. For instance, Blair told defendant's waitresses that the award might be a car, truck, or van, but that he knew it was a brand new Toyota." From the explanation of Plaintiff, Blair used the word "might", he did not actual confirm the award would be anything.

4. The Plaintiff did not inquire about the detailed information of the contest and the award under the condition that she even knew Blair's statements were knowingly false and misleading.

5. The Plaintiff stated that she relied on Blair's statements and dedicated extra time and effort to sell beer for restaurant. Actually, she relied and dedicated extra work time because of an unconfirmed award, this was a voluntary act, not in accordance with any regulation of the restaurant.

6. The Plaintiff has two counts for suing: COUNT I- breach of contract and COUNT II- fraudulent misrepresentation. Actually, there was no contract that confirmed the contest and the award between the Plaintiff and us (Gulf Coast Wings, Inc.,). Additionally, the Plaintiff believed in the manager's statement in the case of knowing that the manager has no right to provide awards representing the Gulf Coast Wings, Inc., thus there's no reason for fraudulent misrepresentation.

Conclusion

THEREFORE, neither COUNT I-breach of contract nor COUNT II-fraudulent misrepresentation from the Plaintiff is able to be verified. Moreover there is no evidence support the assumptions and complaints of the Plaintiff. For these reasons the Complaint should be dismissed, or in the alternative, that the appropriate parties be substituted or jointed as the Court deems proper.

下面是一则法院的裁定文件（申请人为化名）：

United States District Court

Eastern District of California

Audrey Le,	1: 11 – cv-00668 HC
Petitioner,	Order to Show Cause Why the Petition Should not be Granted
v.	
Eric Holder, Jr., et al.,	ORDER DIRECTING THE CLERK TO SERVE DOCUMENTS ON RESPONDENT
Respondents.	

Petitioner is detained by the United States Bureau of Immigration and Customs Enforcement ("ICE") and is proceeding through counsel with a Petition for a Writ of Habeas Corpus pursuant to 28 U.S.C. § 2241.

In the petition filed, Petitioner alleges that he is a native of Vietnam, that he is subject to a final order of removal from the United States as of June 9, 2010, and that he has been in continuous custody of ICE since December 3, 2009. (Doc. 1, p. 2). Petitioner alleges that his detention is unlawful under 8 U.S.C. § 1231 (a) and that it also violates his substantive and procedural due process rights under the Due Process Clause of the Fifth Amendment of the United States Constitution. (Doc. 1, pp. 7 – 8).

Because Petitioner may be entitled to relief if the claimed violations are proved. Respondent IS ORDERED TO SHOW CAUSE why the Petition should not be granted. Rule 4, Rules Governing 1Section 2254 Cases; see Rule 1 (b), Rule 11, Rules Governing Section 2254 Cases; Fed. R. Civ. P. 81 (a) (2). Respondent SHALL INCLUDE a copy of Petitioner's Alien File and any and all other documentation relevant to the determination of the issues raised in the petition. Rule 5 of the Rules Governing Section 2254 Cases. In the event the Petitioner is released from ICE custody during the pendency of this Petition, the parties SHALL notify the Court by filing a Motion to Dismiss the Petition or other proper pleading. Should the parties fail to notify the Court that Petitioner has been released, the parties may be subject to sanctions pursuant to the inherent power of the Court to issue sanctions in appropriate cases. See Local

Rule 110.

 Accordingly, It is Hereby Ordered:

1. Respondent is Ordered to Show Cause why the Petition should not be granted. The Return to the Order to Show Cause is due within Forty-Five (45) days of the date of service of this order. Petitioner may file a Traverse to the Return within TEN (10) days of the date the Return to the Order to Show Cause is filed with the Court.
2. The Clerk of the Court is Directed to Serve a copy of the Petition for Writ of Habeas Corpus on the United States Attorney.

The Court has determined that this matter is suitable for decision without oral argument pursuant to Local Rule 230 (h). As such, the matter will be taken under submission following the filing of Petitioner's Traverse or the expiration of the time for filing the Traverse. All other briefing in this action is suspended.

 It is so Ordered.

 Dated: _____　　　　　_____

 9j7khi　　　　　　　　　　　United States Magistrate Judge

第三节　律师参与 WTO 相关业务

 经过加入 WTO 后十多年的发展，中国已经处在全新的阶段，成为经济体中第一大贸易国、第二大对外投资国，在整个经济格局中的地位大幅上升，在国际市场扮演着越来越重要的角色。在世界范围内，中国企业和中国政府频频成为反倾销反补贴的调查对象，为维护中国企业在 WTO 规则下的合法权益，律师应广泛参与 WTO 相关法律业务。律师可以提供的 WTO 相关业务的范围，包括提供世界贸易组织法律、政策咨询服务，代理国内外反倾销、反补贴、保障措施调查，协助政府相关部门参与 WTO 争端的解决。律师可以代理中国商务部应诉外国政府发起的反补贴调查、保障措施调查，并进行相关的法律抗辩。在各类贸易救济调查案件中，律师可以代理商会、协会进行行业无损害法律抗辩。律师还可代理国内企业应诉国外发起的反倾销、反补贴、保障措施等贸易救济调查，代理商务部参与 WTO 争端解决案件。

一　律师参与应对反倾销调查的法律服务

 倾销一般被定义为国际贸易中的价格歧视或差价销售，即指厂商利用其定价能力在两个或更多国家的市场上以不同的价格销售相同产品的现象。反倾销指对外国商品在本国市场上的倾销所采取的低制措施。一般是对倾销的外国商品除征收一般进口税外,再增收附加税,使其不能廉价出售,此种附加税称为"反倾销税"。目前,我国已经成为世界上遭遇反倾销立案数量最多、受损害最为严重的国家。根据世界银行的统计,对华反倾销,以欧盟、美国等为首的发达国家和地区为主。而现如今,发展中国家也渐渐成了对华反倾销的主力。

反倾销调查是行政调查程序,各国反倾销调查机关的设置有两种模式:美国模式下,由美国商务部和国际贸易委员会分工独立进行调查,美国商务部下属的国际贸易局进口组(Import Administration, International Trade Administration, ITA)负责调查涉案产品是否有倾销事实。美国国际贸易委员会负责调查涉案产品对美国国内同类产品的产业是否造成实质损害并作出倾销是否成立的裁定。而在欧盟模式下,由一个机关既对外国产品是否在本国倾销的问题进行调查,又对本国产业是否因此而受到损害的问题进行调查。采取欧盟模式的国家还有印度、韩国和中国等。

典型的反倾销调查包括的具体程序为:①申请人提出反倾销调查申请。②调查机关审查申请人的申请并决定是否立案。反倾销机关也可以根据自身掌握的证据直接立案并发布反倾销调查通知。③立案后企业登记应诉。④初裁和实地核查。⑤终裁。⑥发布反倾销税命令。以美国为例,倾销调查可由美国商务部主动依职权提起或是由美国国内产业相关之利害关系人以书面方式同时向美国商务部及国际贸易委员会提出控诉。如果商务部决定展开调查,商务部应于联邦公报(Federal Register)上发布公告,通知涉案国政府及涉案出口商/生产商,并知会国际贸易委员会。反之,若商务部决定不展开调查,亦应将该决定公告于联邦公报上。

律师既可以代理国内产业提起反倾销调查,也可以代理出口商/生产商来应诉反倾销调查。以后者为例,律师在应对外国政府对中国出口企业和产品进行反倾销调查案件中,可以提供的法律服务主要有以下几个方面。

(一)判断企业的应诉资格并进行应对方案设计及相关法律辅导

在反倾销调查的立案公告中,一般会明确指明调查国家以及调查期的起止日期,同时对被调查产品作出描述以确定被调查产品的范围。企业首先要判决是否在调查期内和是否向调查国家出口过被调查产品,如果企业所出口的产品不属于被调查产品,或者虽属于被调查产品但在调查期内没有出口,则都不能应诉反倾销调查。应当注意的是,反倾销调查的应诉资格只与出口企业在调查期内是否向调查国家出口过被调查产品有关,即便申请人将未出口过产品的企业名字列入申请书,其仍不当然具有应诉资格。而即便未被列入,也应仔细核查是否具备应诉资格以免错过应诉机会。有应诉资格的企业一般有两种。其一是倾销调查期内自己生产并直接或通过离岸贸易公司出口涉案产品到美国的生产商;如果生产商仅先销售给中国国内贸易公司,通过国内贸易公司转售到美国,生产商与贸易商之间是中国国内销售,由贸易公司进行出口报关,生产商没有资格应诉,也无法获得单独税率或平均税率。其二是倾销调查期内从中国国内生产商采购涉案产品，并转售到美国的位于中国的贸易公司（包括位于保税区或非保税区），或位于中国香港、澳门、台湾，和其他国家/地区的离岸贸易公司也可获得单独税率或平均税率。

在核查完毕具备应诉资格以后，如企业有意愿参与调查，则应在立案公告规定的期限内提交应诉登记材料。该登记期限各国具体规定不同，一般是立案之后 20 天左右。如超过规定期限未登记参加反倾销调查程序，则企业将被判定为"不合作"而最终获得最高的全国税率。在遇到反倾销调查时，企业是否应诉以及如何应诉非常重要，律师要协助企业进行策略设计。企业不应诉往往意味着放弃该国的出口市场。以美国的反倾销调查案件为例，如经调查认定构成倾销，对企业适用的反倾销税率有单独税率、平均税率、全国税率、特殊惩罚性税率共 4 种情况。如果积极参与调查，可争取获得较低的单独税率。有时参加应诉企业过多，调查机关可以按照 WTO《反倾销协定》的规定采取抽样方式来确定强制应诉企业（一般抽取三到四家企业）及其倾销幅度，而其他应诉企业的倾销幅度将采取加权平均的方式确定给予平均税率。如果不应诉将获得较高的全国税率。美国反倾销税从终裁公布之日起将征收至少 5 年、第 5 年时如进行日落复审，发现取消反倾销将导致损害继续，将继续征收反倾销税 5 年。因此，企业决定是否应诉需要看未来 5 年，10 年，甚至更长时间的美国市场对企业的重要性。由此，律师可以结合企业实际情况和反倾销调查中的各种因素，预测应诉后可能获得的最好和最差结果，并提供不同的应诉方案，以供企业科学决策。

（二）协助填写调查问卷

在调查开始后，调查机关会向应诉企业发放调查问卷以收集确定倾销和损害所需的信息，企业要通过填写调查问卷来反映自身的销售、生产、采购等状况。律师在填写问卷阶段，要与应诉企业有关专门人员充分协调，从提出有效抗辩的角度出发，策略性地填写调查问卷。

在美国的反倾销调查中，美国国际贸易委员会会在立案后首先开展损害调查，并会向该案直接利害关系人，亦即美国国内生产者、进口商及涉案的外国出口商/制造商发放问卷。美国国际贸易委员会的问卷调查通常分为三部分，包括外国出口商/制造商在其国内、美国的营运情形及产能、存货等资料，其目的在于调查进口货物是否已/将损及其国内产业。虽然美国国际贸易委员会并不强制外国厂商一定要回复问卷，然而拒答问卷可能导致美国国际贸易委员会作出不利外国厂商的推论（例如美国产业正遭受实质损害）。

在国际贸易委员会进行损害调查的同时，商务部会进行初步倾销调查，并在国际贸易委员会作出初步裁定并公布后的 115 天内（必要时得延长为 165 天）作出初步认定。在这期间，商务部将会寄发倾销问卷给相关利害关系人。所有应诉企业需要回答有关数量金额的倾销问卷,并可提交分别税率申请表(Separate Rate Application,"SRA"①)。分别税率申请表的目的是从事实上、法律上证明公司出口不受政府控制。从 2014 年起美国商务部在 SRA 上的最新变化是国有控股企业无法通过分别税率申请,而直接适用最高的惩罚性税率,即全国统一税率。数量金额问卷分 A 至 E 共 5 种②,对非市场经济国家,调查问卷分 A 卷、C 卷、D 卷和 E 卷。A 卷为有关组织机构、会计制度、市场和商品等内容;C 卷为销售至美国的价格;D 卷为生产要素;E 卷为在美国进行后续生产的成本。另在商务部无法确实掌握出口涉案产品到美国的出口商/生产商名单时,商务部会寄发一种被称为"mini-A"的问卷给所有已知的涉案国出口商/生产商。该问卷会要求已知出口商/生产商协助提供其他涉案厂商的名单。回收 mini-A 问卷后,商务部再依回复内容选定后续指定被调查之厂商。问卷 A 的回复期限为寄发问卷后 21 天,其他问卷则为 37 天,必要时涉案厂商得(经申请)征得商务部同意后延长期限,但展延期限最长不得超过 14 天。商务部在收到调查问卷后可以再次发出补充问卷。

美国商务部通常根据数量金额问卷填报的对美出口涉案产品数量,抽取倾销调查期(提出申请前完整的两个季度)出口数量最大的前两位出口商作为强制应诉企业。强制应诉企业将按照自己的替代国结构成本和对美出口价格计算自己的倾销幅度,即单独税率。而未被抽中的企业只须回答数量金额问卷和分别税率申请表,无须回答反倾销大问卷,工作量较小,将获得强制应诉企业的加权平均税率。而未回答数量金额问卷和分别税率申请表,通不过分别税率申请表审查的企业将获得最高的惩罚性税率,即全国统一税率。举例说明,如中国共有 20 家出口商,10 家出口商回答了数量金额问卷和分别税率申请表,前两家倾销调查期出口量最大的出口商将被抽中作为强制应诉企业,将获得单独税率,如 5%、10%;其余 8 家出口商将获得这两家强制应诉企业的加权平均税率,如 7%;而剩余的 10 家没有应诉的企业,倾销调查期没有出口的企业,或者没有通过分别税率申请表审查的企业将获得最高的惩罚性税率,全国统一税率,如 100%。

(三)提供反倾销调查应诉法律服务

在反倾销调查阶段,律师可协助企业提交综合性法律意见和事实性资料,并对申诉方的意见和资料进行答辩或反驳,也可结合企业所填写调查问卷、提出的抗辩等情况,以企业产品的出口行为没有构成倾销为出发点,适时提出召开听证会;或者组织有关方面人员参加听证会,以进一步阐明支持企业应诉的观点和主张,着重补充和强调调查与抗辩的不足。在反倾销调查的环节,律师可配合国外反倾销调查机关的实地

---

① 中国适用的分别税率申请表格可下载于 https://enforcement.trade.gov/nme/nme-sep-rate.html。
② 该类问卷可下载于 https://enforcement.trade.gov/questionnaires/questionnaires-ad.html。

核查。在实地核查环节，律师的工作是协调、组织应诉企业的相关部门和人员，积极主动地接受核查。帮助企业准确掌握国外反倾销调查机关调查范围和内容，做好充分准备。并且律师也可以直接代表企业接待调查人员。虽然WTO《反倾销协定》没有具体规定实地核查，但该协定规定了反倾销调查应当在立案后一年内结束，特殊情况下不能超过18个月，因此调查机关能够安排的实地核查时间有限，通常每个企业会核查两三天，一般不会超过一个星期。在此期间，企业要充分证明其对调查问卷所填信息的真实性、准确性和完整性。

反倾销调查机关作出初裁后，在一些情况下，需要与对方进行价格承诺的谈判，这种谈判往往是以初裁的较为合理为前提的。其目的在于确保应诉企业必要的市场份额。律师在这一阶段可以参与提供谈判服务。

律师在原始反倾销调查已经完成、结果已经确定的情况下，还可提供年度复审、新出口商复审、日落复审的服务。原审终裁公布后，美国进口商以保证金的形式被征收反倾销税和反补贴税。终裁公布后一年，申请人或中国的生产商/出口商可申请提出年度复审，以改变原审的反倾销税和反补贴税税率。如果经过年度复审，发现年度复审税率比之前原审或复审税率高，美国进口商须补交差额部分；如果经过年度复审，发现年度复审税率比之前原审或复审税率低，美国海关将退还进口商差额部分。因此，原审税率或之前复审税率只是确定了保证金税率，之后的年度复审也非常重要。如果原始税率为零税率，即反倾销税率低于2%，反补贴税率低于1%，则不需要进行年度复审。如果申请人和中国出口商都认为税率合适，不提出年度复审申请或达成和解，则维持原始或之前复审税率，保证金也转变成实际征收的反倾销税和反补贴税。

对于在原审调查期没有出口的，并且与原审调查期出口商没有关联关系的企业，如在原始调查期之后有涉案产品出口，可以申请新出口商复审（New Shipper Review）。美国商务部将根据申请人的出口价格和替代国结构成本计算申请人自身的倾销幅度，并根据申请人自身的补贴情况计算补贴幅度。这与强制应诉企业进行的应诉工作一样。新出口商申请可以在周年内或半年内提出。新出口商还可选择在年度复审时申请分别税率。选择申请分别税率的，只须回答并递交前文所述的分别税率申请表。申请通过的，将获得复审中强制应诉企业的加权平均税率。反倾销税和反补贴税将在终裁公布后至少征收5年时间。终裁公布后的第5年会进行日落复审，以确定如果取消反倾销或反补贴税，损害是否继续。如损害继续，则继续征收5年反倾销税反补贴税；如损害不存在，则停止反倾销税和反补贴税的征收，案件终止。律师通过协助企业参与这些调查程序，可以最大限度地趋利避害。

律师还可以提供反倾销诉讼服务。如果有正当理由和充分的证据证明，最终裁决和行政复审决定是不公正的，建议企业向反倾销诉讼提出国的司法机关提起诉讼，请求修改或撤销原裁决或行政复审决定。例如如果中国企业对终裁结果不服，可以向美国国际贸易法院提起上诉。中国政府也可以向 WTO 争端解决机构提出上诉。

二 参与中国企业应诉美国"337 调查"法律服务

所谓"337 调查",是指美国国际贸易委员会根据美国《1930 年关税法》的相关条款(该条款在美国行政法典第 19 章第 1337 节,即 19 U. S. Code § 1337)针对侵犯美国知识产权的不公平贸易行为实施的调查,属于准司法程序。实践中,涉及侵犯美国知识产权的"337 调查"大部分都是针对专利或商标侵权行为,少数调查还涉及版权、工业设计以及集成电路布图设计侵权行为等。其他形式的不公平竞争包括侵犯商业秘密、假冒经营、虚假广告、违反反垄断法等。如今"337 调查"已经成为美国外贸法中调节外国产品进口法律制度的重要组成部分,是极其重要的贸易保护工具之一。

随着中国制造业的发展,中国向美国出口的产品与美国公司的知识产权冲突日趋激烈,"337 调查"已成为继反倾销调查后中国产品出口的主要障碍,越来越多的中国企业成为"337 调查"的牺牲品。尤其在中国加入 WTO 之后,中国企业被调查的频率日渐提高。这一方面表明我国出口产品技术含量的提升;另一方面,也和前几年国内企业怠于应诉有关。从统计数据看,"337 调查"的结果大都是庭外和解,如果被诉的中国企业不为较高的败诉率所吓倒、提高自身应诉实力和应诉自信、主动应诉的话,那么胜诉几率还是很大的,前景并非实务中表现的那样不容乐观。

"337 调查"通常应当事人的申请发起,原则上也可由联合国开发计划署(ITC)自行发起。"337 调查"虽然不是由司法机关负责,但其调查程序、调查方式与民事诉讼有许多相似之处。它由一名行政法官负责审理,一项完整的调查程序可大致分为以下阶段:立案、证据开示程序、开庭、行政法官初裁、ITC 复审、ITC 终裁和总统审查。根据调查结果,若 ITC 认定被申请人违反 337 条款,可应申请人的请求,针对被申请人发布有限排除令(Limited Exclusion Order),或在满足特定条件的前提下发布普遍排除令(General Exclusion Order),禁止侵权产品进入美国市场。此外,ITC 还可发布制止令(Cease and Desist Order),要求美国境内的批发商或零售商等停止销售相关侵权产品。

中国企业"337 调查"涉案案由,绝大多数是专利侵权。对于一起涉及专利侵权的美国"337 调查"案,应诉律师团队核心成员既要有专长于"337 调查"的诉讼律师,又要有精通涉案专利技术的专利律师,还要有熟悉"337 调查"的中国律师。中国律师在与中国企业保持顺畅沟通方面将发挥重要作用,同时可以承担案件中律师工作量较大的证据交换(Discovery)程序中的大部分工作。在涉及商业秘密的"337 调查"案件中,当事人所提供的商业秘密会在美国国际贸易委员会的调查程序中得到严格保护。"337 调查"程序中商业秘密只有进入商业秘密保护令名单的人员和特定政府官员能够接触。美国"337 调查"的商业秘密保护主要靠保护令制度执行。在调查开始后不久,行政法官一般发布一个商业秘密的保护令。其主要内容是规定有权获取该"337调查"的商业秘密的人员,以及详细规定这些商业秘密的处理等。一般而言,有权进入保护令名单可接触商业秘密的人员主要包括当事人的外聘律师和当事人的专家证人及翻译。进入保护令名单的人员违反保护令将导致严重的后果。对于外国律师而言,由于制裁很难落实,美国国际贸易委员会一般不允许外国律师接触337程序中的商业秘密。但是,对于拥有美国律师执照的外国律师,曾有裁决将同时有美国律师执照的外国律师纳入保护令名单①。

美国"337调查"制度程序复杂,但存在许多未经详细规定的事项,这就为我国企业提供了较大周旋空间。根据这一系列庞杂的规定,只要被诉企业积极应诉,原告就必须克服重重障碍力求胜诉,包括证明自己有合法有效的知识产权,证明美国还会出现使用该知识产权的产业或产品等问题。在应诉之前,被诉企业应综合考量,对企业自身进行必要的前景和成本分析,即研究判断再次诉讼中的胜诉把握、应诉费用、不应诉的损失、市场影响等,避免造成巨大成本,丧失市场,或不应诉而败诉,虽伤敌一千但自损八百,得不偿失。为了更大的胜诉概率,应该选聘有相关经验、了解中美两国相关法律法规的专业律师,并且防患于未然,在签订合同时就应该考量周全,提前做好有关知识产权的调查,从根源避免招致"337调查"。

随着中国对美出口技术的提升和出口量的增大,美国的贸易保护主义日见抬头,其撒手锏之一就是知识产权方面的问题,且存在滥用倾向,其中尤为突出的"337调查",已经成为我国企业进军美国市场的巨大障碍。这就迫切需要国内企业以积极的态度加以应对,其核心在于形成完备的知识产权保护体系,增强企业应诉能力,切实扭转被动不利的局面,为自己创造一个公平合理的国际商业环境。

三 律师参与 WTO 争端解决程序

从关贸总协定和世界贸易组织发展的历史进程来看,政府聘用律师的问题是随着争端解决机制司法性的加强而逐渐出现的。在关贸总协定最初适用时,缔约方普遍认为关贸总协定争端解决程序应该是一个有助于外交协商的机制。随着实践发展,争端解决由工作组转为专家组负责,争端解决机制越来越司法化。20世纪80年代中期,关贸总协定秘书处设立了法务部,在法律事务方面为专家组提供帮助,这使得专家组报告的质量大大提高,在作出结论时越来越注重对条约条文的解释和权利义务的确定。在这种趋势下,争端当事方需要在程序中根据协定提出对己方有利的观点和法律解释,这方面的工作是外交官员和贸易官员所不擅长的,从而为律师参加关贸总协定的争端解决提供了客观条件。

---

① 冉瑞雪:《美国337调查程序中的商业秘密保护》,《中国律师》2007年第3期。

(一) 律师参与 WTO 争端解决的必要性与作用

从实践发展来看，律师参与争端解决是很必要的。但是关贸总协定法律文件中并未对律师参与争端解决纠纷作出规定，律师是否参与由当事方决定，但是缔约国均认为关贸总协定的专家组听证会是政府代表之间的外交行为，因此律师作为非政府人员并不具有参加的身份而只能用于准备各种法律文件、提供意见等。在世界贸易组织成立后，根据争端解决机制（DSU）规定，在世界贸易组织成员发生贸易争端时，首先应该进行磋商，或者选择性地调停、调解、斡旋和仲裁。当以上方式均不能解决争端时，争端一方可以提交专家小组的成立申请，该申请通过专家组来进行系统的调查并报告。任何当事方对该报告存有疑虑，均有权进行上诉。由此可见，在世界贸易组织争端解决机制的司法化的基础上，在争端解决中，除了外交与贸易官员的加入，还纳入了相关的辩论和论证的环节，在这一过程中，当事方所提出的辩论观点、法律解释等各方面都发挥着至关重要的作用，因此当事方聘用律师的趋势逐渐增加。就律师能否参加专家组和上诉机构所举行的会谈的问题上，世界贸易组织争端解决实践对关贸总协定的做法进行了变革，这主要体现在"欧盟香蕉案"和"印度尼西亚影响汽车工业措施案"之中。经过这两个案件，关于律师能否参加世界贸易组织争端解决的各个阶段尤其是会议阶段的问题基本得到了解决，允许律师全程参加的权利已经成为世界贸易组织中新的实践惯例。

律师在 WTO 争端解决中发挥着重要作用。首先，律师可以利用世界贸易组织的争端平台进行维权，根据 WTO 争端解决机制的运作情况，律师可以为有关外贸部门提供争端预防与解决有关的法律咨询服务。在世界贸易组织争端解决机制中，律师最关键的作用就是代表各自的国家进行"起诉"和"应诉"。此外，无论在该机制的哪个环节中，律师都能起到相关的有利作用。其次，律师可以促进企业与政府的沟通，以便在贸易争端中掌握主动地位。我国大多数企业的法律意识不够强，用法律维权的意识比较弱，导致在贸易纷争中，中国企业长期处于弱势地位。相对于国外跨国公司拥有的律师团队，我国企业因涉外律师的缺少对世贸组织相关规则缺乏了解，致使在维权方面捉襟见肘。律师还能够进入专家组名单和上诉机构，扩大中国的在世界贸易组织中的话语权，更大地发挥中国的国际影响力，增加世界对中国的了解。

(二) 律师参与 WTO 争端解决时应注意的问题

首先是保密问题。争端解决机制作为 WTO 最重要的法律制度之一，它运作的基本特征是非公开性。根据 DSU 有关规定，争端解决机制的每一个阶段，都有明确的要求表示需要进行保密。例如 DSU 第四条第 6 款规定"协商是保密的，但并不妨害任何成员方在后续诉讼中的权力"，还有第十四条的规定"专家组审案是保密的"。自从世界贸易组织允许律师参与争端解决后，对于律师泄露商业秘密的担心就频频产生甚至导致了当事方在争端解决中的消极对待。因此，律师参与 WTO 争端解决最应该注意的问题是保密问题。参照相关国家法律及制度,世界贸易组织可以对律师加以约束,比如制定要求律师不得泄露与会议相关的任何内容的条款,如果违反则处以高额罚款并禁止该律师参与世界贸易组织任何争端解决。除此之外,世界贸易组织可以在秘书处设置一个执行监督机构,专门处理泄露商业秘密的律师,对违反保密制度的律师进行惩罚,记录在册并进行公示,以使当事方放心并达到对律师的警诫作用。律师也应该严格保密,遵守职业道德。

律师参与WTO争端解决还应该注意利益冲突的问题。利益冲突是指在个人或者组织涉及不同方面的利益时,向自己或者自己利益方作出的偏袒行为,表现为个人利益与委托人利益之间的矛盾。在世界贸易组织争端解决中,经常有不同国家律师代表某个成员或者是同一个律师代理不同成员国的现象,看起来似乎荒诞,但是律师的职业特点决定了律师代表不同利益方针对同一问题可能会作出不同解释的情况,而这种情况并不稀少。就现状来看,律师参与争端解决引起的利益冲突主要在以下几个方面:第一,一国律师代表他国与本国对抗,因世界贸易组织争端解决的结果影响重大,所以律师是坚持职业道德还是偏向本国存在很大不确定性;第二,律师在争端解决中会接触到许多商业秘密信息,尽管律师基于保密性不予泄露,但当律师又代表其他成员国时,会因为对对方信息的掌握而占据先机,从而对对方造成不公平的待遇;第三,专家组成员对争端解决起到了至关重要的作用,而成员国并没有选择专家组成员的权利,如果某一方聘请的律师被选为专家组成员,那么会使其他争端方在专家组的程序中处于不利地位。在这种情况下,律师应当遵守职业道德,保护代理方的利益,主动拒绝存在利益冲突的案件。

最后是律师费用的问题。随着世界贸易组织争端解决的流程越来越司法化,聘请律师势在必行。在世界贸易争端解决中,律师发挥着举足轻重的作用。因此各国为了胜诉,会花费大量的财政开支以选择更为优秀的律师。虽然对于大国而言聘请律师的成本无关紧要,但是对于许多发展中国家而言,维持本国代表团进行争端解决的费用和聘请律师的费用已然使他们捉襟见肘。因此这种法律资源上的不均衡也容易导致世界贸易组织争端解决结果的不公正。为解决这一问题,世界贸易组织可以建设一个基金会,对发展中国家进行财政支持,也可以安排有资历的优秀律师为其提供法律咨询与帮助。

第十章　模拟庭审训练

模拟庭审训练,是法律实践性教学的重要方式,包括模拟法庭审判活动和模拟仲裁庭仲裁,通过学习者分工扮演法官、检察官、案件的当事人、其他诉讼参与人或仲裁员、案件当事人及仲裁活动的其他参与人,以司法实践中的案例为脚本,参照实际的诉讼或仲裁活动进行模拟庭审的过程。在模拟庭审训练中,参加者通过案情分析、角色划分、法律文书准备、预演、正式开庭等环节模拟刑事、民事、行政审判及仲裁的过程,对法律文书、庭审表达等实用法律职业技能进行训练。因模拟庭审训练的优越性,法学院校除在学校内部会定期地举行模拟庭审比赛以外,还组织区域性和全国性模拟法庭竞赛,并派代表队参加国际性模拟法庭竞赛。通过了解与参加国内外知名的模拟庭审赛事,可以提高综合性的涉外律师实务技能。

第一节　知名模拟法庭介绍

一　杰赛普国际法模拟法庭

杰赛普国际法模拟法庭比赛(The Philip C. Jessup International Law Moot Court Competition,官方网站 https://www.ilsa.org/jessuphome),是由美国国际法学生联合会(International Law Students Association, ILSA)主办的专业性法律辩论赛。该辩论赛的宗旨为在全球范围内推动对于国际公法的学习与研究,并通过模拟国际法庭审判来提高学生运用法律进行专业辩论的能力。杰赛普国际法模拟法庭比赛是模拟在国际法院进行国家间虚拟的争议案件。这一赛事以国际法院知名法官杰赛普(Philip C. Jessup)命名,最早是在 1960 年在哈佛大学法学院两个学生队之间进行比赛,到 1968 年开始向美国之外的参赛者开放,是目前国际上规模最大、历史最悠久的专业性辩论赛,近年来该赛事吸引了世界上 90 多个国家和地区约 700 个法学院参加。国内选拔赛的优胜方于每年 3 月份齐聚美国华盛顿特区的联邦最高法院进行全球总决赛。

在比赛规则上,杰赛普比赛既不是以说服观众为目的的演讲(speech),也不是与对手针锋相对的对抗式的辩论(debate),它是一种与法官交流的对话式的说理(conversation)。采用的是海牙国际法院的开庭方式,由起诉方和应诉方分别向法官陈述并解释自己应当胜诉的事实依据和法律理由。比赛要求各参赛队伍充分研究案例事实（compromis），对所给案例中包含的相关国际法理论和规则进行分析与研究，以英文为工作语言，同时为原告与被告起草起诉状和答辩状，并就该案件代表双方进行口头辩论。为了帮助全球国际法专业学生更好地了解和参与到杰塞普国际法模拟法庭比赛中，美国 William S. Hein & Co., Inc. 公司推出了杰塞普国际法模拟法庭数据库（Philip C. Jessup Library），收录从1960年至今的杰塞普国际法模拟法庭辩论赛的相关资料，包括每一届辩论赛的题目、比赛规则、程序、法官的判决、最好的诉状文本等。

杰赛普模拟法庭比赛的基本模式参考了国际法院的诉讼程序，分为书面程序和口头程序两个部分，以考察参赛队的研究、写作和口头答辩能力。当然，与实际诉讼不同，每个队都必须同时写作诉状和答辩状，而且可能在不同场次的口头程序中代理不同国家，这就要求每个队（甚至每个队员）都必须从请求国和被请求国不同的立场出发理解案情，适用不同的法律规则或对其作出不同的解释，并在此基础上作出有理有力的口头辩护。比赛的基本案情（Compromis）由美国国际法学生联合会（ILSA）制作并于每年9月中旬发布。虽然它只是一个虚构的案情陈述，但包含一套经过精雕细琢的巧妙设计而形成的细致繁复的事实和或隐或显的法律争端，并且经常有机地糅合了国际法诸多领域的问题，同时，案情中的很多内容能使读者轻易地联想到国际现实中的法律问题[1]。

比赛的书面部分就是要求参赛队在仔细研究案件事实的基础上，分析、研究其中的法律问题，并以书状的形式（起诉状和答辩状）论证控辩双方的这些基本诉求。所以，在实体方面，书状即围绕双方的诉求完成。另外，比赛对书状的构成、格式与篇幅具有严格的要求。例如，任何一方的书状都要求具有典据索引、管辖权声明、事实陈述以及辩词等部分，而其中的某些部分，如事实陈述与辩词都须遵守篇幅方面的限制，此外，书状的字体、格式、引注以及版式也都须遵循明确的规范。所有这些要求集中规定在比赛的官方规则中，违反此类规则将导致对书状评分的罚减，而书状的得分会直接影响到口头辩论阶段的初赛排名。在赛事的官方网站上，提供了有关如何写作诉状（memorial）的建议[2]。参赛者要仔细阅读比赛规则中有关诉状写作部分的要求，认真研究每次比赛所给的争端材料及背后的法律资料，包括阅读与相关法律原则、国际条约/公约及相关法律法规材料有关的最新法律评论文章，以确保完全弄懂。在所制作的诉状中要做好参考文献的引证目录（Index of Authorities），并运用这些权威资料去展开法律分析从而推导出结论。在诉状的提出问题部分（Questions Presented），要紧紧围绕争端材料尾部的争议焦点展开，可以对争议问题做简要概括但不宜再提出额外

---

[1] 梁晓晖：《杰赛普国际法模拟法庭比赛及其在中国的推广》，《北大国际法与比较法评论》2006年第7期。
[2] 参见 https://www.ilsa.org/jessup/jessup15/Tips%20for%20Writing%20Memorials%20for%202015.pdf。

的问题。在事实陈述（Statement of Facts）部分，要认真对照规则要求，时刻牢记只引用争端材料已给出的事实，而不能为便于得出自己的法律结论而对事实材料做进一步演绎。在诉求摘要部分（Summary of Pleadings），要用不超过 700 个字针对每个争议焦点运用事实和法律提出实质的主张。在论述中的文献引用方面，要在引用这些宪法、法规、案例、条约及法学论文的同时阐明这些文献所表明的法律观点及对本案的适用性。通常判例会比著述更有说服力，应尽可能寻找国际法院或国内法院的判例。如果要证明一项规则是国际习惯法，需要同时对国家实践和法律确信进行举证。在搞不清所引证的资料与诉状主张的相关性的情况下，简单地将几个引文塞到脚注里是不当的。法官有权不考虑孤零零的一个引注。而如果发现引文与主张并不符，法官会予以扣分。因此，建议在引用之后加上一段注释，以进一步说明案件与论点的相关性。在诉状中通常采取问题、规则、分析及结论（Issue, Rule, Analysis, and Conclusion）的结构进行展开。要尽量使用简短的句子，做好缩写术语的界定，少用拉丁语或外来词。避免绝对或极端的立场。不要夸大其词，而用事实和法律来讲述你的故事来支持自己的观点，把想传达给法官和对方律师的东西写清楚。制作精良的诉状，论点应当合乎逻辑、清楚、有说服力，完整、清晰、简明、忠于事实、透彻地理解法律的含义。没有语法错误，具有原创性。

提交书状的期限过后，比赛就进入口头辩论的阶段。口头辩论则更倾向于表现队员的个人法律素养与表达魅力。杰赛普的法庭辩论并不在控辩双方的律师（队员）之间展开，而是双方律师各自与法官（裁判）之间的对诘。从这个意义上来说，所谓口头辩论似乎称口头答辩更为贴切。控辩双方应各委派两名律师出庭答辩，此外，各方认为必要，还可派出一名律师做答辩顾问，这位顾问只临场为两位答辩律师提供书面意见而不能作任何发言。虽然规则并没有限制各方答辩陈述的范围，但是各方一般都围绕书状的内容展开；法官的提问则可能补充、澄清律师的答辩观点，而更常见的情形则是法官的尖锐问题打乱了律师既定的答辩思路，或者暴露了其论点的软肋。

二 普莱斯传媒法国际模拟法庭

普莱斯杯传媒法国际模拟法庭比赛（赛事官网，http://pricemootcourt.socleg.ox.ac.uk）创始于 2008 年，由牛津大学社会法研究中心的"比较传媒法与政策项目"（Program in Comparative Media Law & Policy at the Center for Socio-Legal Studies）、牛津大学法律系（Faculty of Law Oxford university）、国际传媒律师协会（International Media Lawyers Association）共同举办，以美国宾夕法尼亚大学安娜伯格传播学院（Annenberg School for Communication at the University of Pennsylvania, USA）摩罗·意·普莱斯（Monroe E. Price）教授的名字命名。该比赛旨在增强学生对传媒法的兴趣，引领学生和法官对当代的媒体法、言论自由等问题进行充分的关注与探讨。

该比赛自创始以来，迅速由在牛津大学举办的单一模拟法庭发展成在欧、亚、非、北美各大洲拥有分赛区的国际赛事。2013 年，首次在中国创设中国赛区，2014 年变更为亚太赛区。亚太赛区比赛一般于 11 月底至 12 月初举行，产生的 4 支队伍于次年 3 月底至 4 月初赴英国牛津大学参加国际赛，主办方将为这 4 支队伍各提供资金支持。参与大赛评审的法官，来自欧美知名高校、欧洲人权法院、世界著名媒体、国际传媒及知识产权领域的律师协会等，均是在传媒法领域颇有建树的学者及实务界知名人士。普莱斯模拟法庭比赛分为书面答辩和口头答辩两个阶段，在书面答辩选拔通过的队伍方可进入口头答辩阶段，参加在牛津大学举办的国际赛区的比赛。

普莱斯杯模拟法庭比赛旨在增强学生对于传媒法的兴趣，提高学生用比较法视野进行法律文书的写作、法律辩论能力，促进不同法律制度背景下的学生之间的交流与学习，引领学生和法官对当代的媒体法、言论自由等问题进行充分的关注与探讨。比赛所用案例均为设计精巧的模拟案例，取材于现实，但经由加工增加其复杂性与可争讼性。案例均为十分具有现实意义和研究价值的问题。管辖机构方面，为了凸显专业性，比赛虚拟了一个"世界人权法院"分院作为受理法院。同时将准据法限制在以下几个方面：第一，人权方面的世界公约、条约等；第二，美国联邦最高法院判例；第三，欧洲、美洲、非洲人权法院判例等。

口头辩论部分占总成绩的 50%，只能使用英语，每支队伍派 2 名参赛队员。每支队伍需要准备两份原告起诉状和两份被告起诉状（因为各派两人上场），每支队伍有 45 分钟展示自己，包括回答辩驳方的问题。比赛顺序首先为原告 1 发言、原告 2 发言、被告 1 发言、被告 2 发言，然后是原告的反驳阶段，最后是被告的反驳阶段。比赛时，允许本队的一名队员坐在参赛队员的旁边，扮演"顾问"的角色。比赛的奖项包括最佳书状奖、最佳个人辩手、最佳辩手奖（决赛）。

三 红十字"国际人道法"模拟法庭竞赛

红十字"国际人道法"模拟法庭竞赛（Red Cross International Humanitarian Law Moot）是由红十字国际委员会（ICRC）、中国红十字会总会（Red Cross Society of China）等联合举办，中国国际人道法国家委员会协办的模拟法庭赛事。第一届红十字会国际人道法模拟法庭于 2007 年在中国人民大学法学院举行，当时只有八所高校参加。经过多年发展，中国大陆地区红十字国际人道法模拟法庭竞赛的参赛队伍的数量越来越多。

国际人道法比赛案例由红十字国际委员会（ICRC）的法律专家拟定，法官由来自不同国家和地区的国际法、国际人道法专家组成。比赛语言为英语，参赛队伍必须以给定案例为基础，运用国际人道法的原理进行分析。比赛分为初赛、半决赛和决赛，各队在初赛中分别以控方、辩方身份参赛，前六名以控方或辩方的身份晋级半决赛，半决赛前两名晋级决赛。半决赛的前三名将由红十字国际委员会资助参加在中国香港举行的亚太地区高校间红十字"国际人道法"模拟法庭竞赛,比赛一般于每年的 11 月、12 月进行。国际赛的官方网站为 http://www.redcross.org.hk/web/moot10/。该网站上提供了比赛规则、赛事日程、历年赛题、历年最佳书状。

进行参加国际人道法模拟法庭比赛的准备工作,可以从案例研读(case studying)、法律研究(legal research)、诉状写作(legal writing)、口头辩论(oral pleading)这四个方面进行。案例研读是模拟法庭准备的第一个环节,要牢记比赛给出案例的所有案件事实,以便在书状写作和口头辩论的阶段随时引用。在初步了解案件事实之后,就需要根据案件中涉及的法律问题研究相关的法律。要确定案例中涉及的法律问题有哪些。通常 compromis 或者 moot problem 里面都会告诉控辩双方的诉求。这些诉求可能很具体,可以直接转化为对一个法律问题的讨论,但也可能比较复杂和抽象,比如国际人道法模拟法庭常涉及的国际犯罪,每个罪名包括众多客观要件、主观要件和责任形式等内容。这就需要我们在确定法律问题时,不能太粗略也不能太细致。对于国际人道法来说,通常一个犯罪的要件是否满足、武装冲突是否成立、被告人的责任形式这些问题可以分别作为独立的法律问题。在确定法律问题之后,要找到相关的法律。可以按照如下的顺序逐渐深入:中英文的教科书—中英文的论文、专著—具体的条约、法律条文—案例的判决书及起诉书等相关文件。在诉状写作阶段,要注意给出较多的引注,显得论证较为有力。诉状结构要清晰,详略要得当,论证要有逻辑,语言要准确、简洁、有力、连贯。在口头辩论中,要事先充分了解自己的立场与观点,对自己之前做的法律研究要十分了解,还要对自己的口头辩论进行精心的策划,使法官尽可能把握所陈述的内容。为使自己的论证更为清晰有力,要尽量让自己对案件有一套完整的逻辑认识,从而形成鲜明的主旨,无论在陈述还是回答问题时都能够坚持自己的立场。

四 "贸仲杯"模拟法庭辩论赛

"贸仲杯"国际商事仲裁模拟仲裁庭辩论赛是中国国际经济贸易仲裁委员会(简称贸仲,英文简称 CIETAC)组织的、面向全国法学院校的仲裁法律专业年度竞赛。此项赛事的目的是进一步扩大仲裁法律制度的影响,加强我国法学院学生对国际商事立法和国际商事仲裁制度的了解,并促进我国高级仲裁法律人才的培养。"贸仲杯"是我国国际商事仲裁领域高级别的英文模拟辩论赛,同时也是国际权威的 Willem C. Vis 国际商事仲裁模拟仲裁庭辩论赛的中国大陆区选拔赛,更是后者认可的全球首场赛前赛。贸仲杯辩论赛语言为全英文,由贸仲委资深仲裁员、国内外知名律师等专业人士组成模拟仲裁庭,参赛选手模拟仲裁案件中申请人和被申请人的角色参与仲裁庭开庭审理的各环节。比赛中,双方根据模拟的案情进行陈述、答辩和辩论,并回答仲裁庭提出的问题。比赛采用模拟商事仲裁中提交书面文件与开庭审理的形式，突出理论与实务的结合，对参赛对手的英文表达能力、逻辑推理能力及临场反应能力提出了较高的要求，对于在校法学院学生提高法律实践水平、提升实战能力均有很大帮助。

五 Willem C. Vis 模拟国际商事仲裁庭辩论赛

Willem C. Vis 模拟国际商事仲裁庭辩论赛（官网，https：//vismoot.pace.edu/）在国际法领域影响深远。早在1992年，在国际商事仲裁法协会召开的由国际商法和国际商事仲裁法全体会员参加的大会上，专家们首次提出了建立国际商事仲裁模拟法庭的设想，其目的是提高各国法学院（或法律系）的学生们对联合国国际贸易商事仲裁委员会工作的兴趣和了解，特别是对联合国国际货物销售合同公约及国际商事仲裁的兴趣和了解，并定时为各国国际商法和国际商事仲裁教学交流提供场所。经过各方两年的积极努力筹备，第一届国际商事仲裁模拟法庭于1994年复活节（Easter）前一星期，在联合国国际贸易法委员会（UNCITRAL）的总部维也纳隆重举行，这可谓是国际商法和国际商事仲裁教学史上的一件大事。首届国际商事仲裁模拟法庭的举行。第一届国际商事仲裁模拟法庭召开后，人们为纪念美国纽约大学法学院国际商法研究所的资深教授、UNCITRAL 的前任秘书 Willem C. Vis 为国际商事仲裁模拟法庭作出的积极贡献，于是便以其名字来命名国际商事仲裁模拟法庭。

Willem C. Vis 国际商事仲裁模拟法庭由数百名来自不同国家的国际商法和国际商事仲裁法教授、律师和法律工作者参加庭审辩论、充当仲裁员，如此多的名家学者以及专业人士的出席给模拟法庭辩论赛带来了浓厚的专业学术气氛。通常用于模拟法庭比赛的法律论题（案例）会于每年的10月初通知到各个参赛队，这些案例通常是适用《1980 年联合国国际货物销售合同公约》（又称为联合国或维也纳销售公约、CISG）的国际货物交易问题，也包括一些仲裁程序问题。每个队在获悉了模拟法庭比赛的法律论题（案例）之后，就要开始着手准备起诉状。按照比赛规则，起诉状将于12月初提交给组委会。然后，组委会将在圣诞节前把各队递交的起诉状随机分配给另一个参赛队，以便让后者完成相应答辩状。各队的答辩状必须于来年2月初完成并递交给组委会。至此，各队已经做好收集事实和进行口头法庭辩论的准备。4月复活节前一星期，模拟法庭口头辩论将在 UNCITRAL 的总部维也纳举行。在 Willem C. Vis 国际商事仲裁模拟法庭的口头辩论中，最根本的是要抓住争议的焦点和问题的本质进行辩论。模拟法庭比赛采用的案例及证据资料，无论对原告还是被告均没有明显的偏向性——原被告胜诉的可能性各占一半，关键在于对垒的两个参赛队在辩论时是否能发现和抓住对方所没有发现的焦点问题（issue），并提供有力的证据支持自己对争议问题的立场和观点。综观历届比赛的获胜者，并非都出自英语为母语国家的参赛队，这说明良好的英语表述能力固然对赢得比赛非常重要，但它并不是帮助参赛队赢得比赛最后胜利的关键因素。

六 曼弗雷德·拉克斯空间法模拟法庭竞赛

曼弗雷德·拉克斯空间法模拟法庭竞赛就是为了纪念曼弗雷德·拉克斯（Manfred Lachs）博士，由国际空间法学会（IISL）于1992年创办的每年一度的全球性高水平的空间法模拟法庭赛事，因其每年的全球总决赛由国际法院三位现任大法官亲自出庭审理而成为当今世界最高级别的模拟法庭大赛，也成为宣传和普及国际空间法、培育专业法学人才的重要平台。

竞赛分三个步骤依次展开：国内选拔赛、区域选拔赛和国际决赛。国内选拔赛在各国国内进行，国内冠军将取得参加区域竞赛的机会，并由国际空间法学会提供资助。就区域竞赛而言，国际空间法学会将全球分为亚太区、欧洲区、北美区三大区。中国属于亚太区。区域竞赛中产生的三个地区冠军将晋级国际决赛，争夺世界冠军。具体而言，以亚太区为例，首先要进行各校代表队的书状审查和选拔，从而获得参赛资格，比赛分为两轮，依照参赛队伍的书状和初赛庭辩总分排序，排名前四的队伍进入半决赛。半决赛淘汰一支队伍，剩下三支队伍进入总决赛，分别决出冠亚季军的得主。中国空间法学会自2003年开始通过举办全国选拔赛的方式组织国内高校学生参加国际空间法模拟法庭竞赛。比赛采用模拟商事仲裁中提交书面文件与开庭审理的形式，突出理论与实务的结合，对于在校法学院学生提高法律实践水平、提升实战能力均有很大帮助。参赛选手模拟仲裁案件中申请人和被申请人的角色参与仲裁庭开庭审理的各环节，比赛中，双方根据模拟的案情进行陈述、答辩和辩论，并回答仲裁庭提出的问题。

七 其他影响较大的模拟法庭比赛

第一，"史丹森"国际环境法模拟法庭竞赛（International Environmental Moot Court Competition，IEMCC）创始于1996年，由美国史丹森大学法学院（Stetson University College of Law）主办，是世界上最负盛名的国际模拟法庭赛事之一，参赛队员来自世界各地大学的法学院。每年的比赛内容都是热点的国际环境法问题，以模拟国际法院诉讼为形式。每个参赛队的队员均须分别代表原被告双方提交诉状，并在法庭上展开辩论，全程以英语进行。竞赛分为地区预选赛和国际决赛两个环节。地区选拔赛分为北美太平洋赛区、北美大西洋赛区、拉丁美洲赛区、东亚赛区等8个赛区。

第二，纳尔逊·曼德拉世界人权模拟法庭大赛（Nelson Mandela World Human Rights Moot Court Competition）是全球最为著名的人权法模拟法庭。为向人权斗士曼德拉致敬，2009年，比勒陀利亚大学法学院（University of Pretoria）人权事务中心与联合国人权事务高级专员办事处合作，组织了首届世界人权模拟法庭比赛，面向全世界范围内的大学的学生开放。该比赛定期于每年夏季（大约在7月18日，即纳尔逊·曼德拉的生日）在瑞士日内瓦万国宫（Palais des Nations, Geneva, Switzerland）举行。该赛事是针对全球所有大学生的高水平专业性国际赛事，所以，大赛的参赛对象为本科生和研究生，大赛官方语言为英语，所有参赛队员必须以高校为单位组成代表队。

举办该模拟法庭比赛的目的是为学生、学者和来自不同法律背景和人权制度的专家在跨领域人权问题上建立一个辩论、交流和合作的平台，使年轻的律师和国际专家了解国家和跨国人权问题，并帮助他们掌握联合国条约机构和区域人权机构的判例，通过概述人权保护制度，加深学员对联合国条约机构的了解，构建一个充满活力的律师、法律从业人员、学生、专家和法官，专门从事人权领域的世界各地的网络，使在世界各地的大学之间进行有关人权问题的交流，巩固和促进联合国条约机构的中心作用，使一些人权机制不完善的国家与地区开始重视人权保护，让世界人权迈向更高的领域。曼德拉世界人权模拟法庭大赛赛程较短，比赛总体包括一个书面阶段和一个口试阶段，在书面阶段通过之后，小组将会被选入口试阶段。根据大赛组委会的官方规则，大赛分为地区资格赛和全球预决赛两个部分：在地区资格赛阶段，比赛在联合国范围内的五个大区进行，联合国五大地区为非洲区（African Group）、亚太区（Asia-Pacific Group）、东欧区（Eastern European Group）、南美洲和加勒比区（Latin American and Caribbean Group）、西欧和其他区（Western European and Others Group），各参赛队需要以大赛组委会发布的假想案例（A Hypothetical Case）为背景撰写答辩状，由人权法领域的权威专家进行审阅；在全球预决赛阶段，各个地区出现的前五强共计25个优胜队将受邀前往联合国人权事务高级专员办事处总部日内瓦参加预决赛的竞争。比赛共分为半决赛和决赛两个环节，半决赛环节共分为四轮，在第一阶段出线的前五名队伍分别代表联合国五个大区，每支参赛队伍分别以被告和原告的立场展开激烈的基于诉状和口头答辩（口头辩论队员须为两名队员代表，其中一名最好为女性）的两轮比赛，最终积分最高的两支队伍将直接脱颖而出，参加最终决赛环节的冠军角逐，半决赛期间，评阅法官由国际人权领域的专家组成。在决赛中争夺冠、亚军的队伍，不能来自同一个联合国地区，他们的表现将由来自国际法院和国际特别法庭的法官进行评判。

第三，"理律杯"全国高校模拟法庭竞赛由清华大学法学院和台湾理律文教基金会共同主办，基于法学素养"向上发展、向下扎根"的理念，希望通过模拟法庭比赛的形式，吸引社会各界对法学教育、法律问题的关注，并为即将踏入社会的青年学子，在学校的课堂与课本学习之外，提供熟悉实务工作的经历与机会。通过各法学院校之间的交流，鼓励学子们从不同方面深入学习，加强工作能力，积累经验，进而促进其对法律问题的思辨。

理律杯共有书状与言辞辩论的两个程序。书状程序部分：参赛队伍应于最后一次赛务会议时上交以中文撰写的书状，经抽签决定比赛顺序后，由在比赛中互为对手的两队交换该场比赛各自持方之书状。书状的提交期限,份数与交换,书状格式,原、被告方书状的内容,书状的修改都遵循严格的程序。言辞辩论程序部分:比赛双方在辩题所确定之事实基础上进行法律辩论,并依一定的诉讼程序进行模拟辩论。言辞辩论的内容包括原告陈述、被告陈述、原告方提问和被告方答辩、被告方提问和原告方答辩、原告总结陈述和被告总结陈述五道程序。

另外,为培养相关职业技能,还可参加模拟联合国大会活动。以中国联合国协会直属的中国模拟联合国会议为例,自 2004 年创办以来每年由不同高校轮流举办,已成功举办十四届。通过参加模拟联合国活动,学生不仅能够学习和讨论国际事务,还能够通过实践来锻炼自己组织、策划、管理的能力,研究和写作的能力,演讲和辩论的能力,解决冲突、求同存异的能力,与他人沟通交往等多方面能力。

第二节 模拟法庭诉状范例

大多数知名的国际模拟法庭赛事都会公布往年比赛的一些诉状,提供给后来的参赛者学习和参考。例如,Willem C. Vis 国际商事仲裁模拟法庭的官网上,就可以看到几乎所有此前历次比赛的排名比较靠前的队伍的诉状材料[①]。为了进一步学习,现提供一些模拟法庭诉状材料。

一 关于杰赛普模拟国际法庭诉状写作的对照分析范例

在前文提到的杰赛普模拟国际法庭赛事的官网给出的诉状写作指南中,提及了为 2014 年的比赛所制作的诉状范例。其中一种写法是比较差的,内容如下。

"Ritania's conduct with respect to Excelsior Island Project complied in all respect (sic) with its obligation under international law and the terms of the Malachi Gap Treaty (A) and the landslide is force majeure therefore Ritania has no obligation to compensate Amalea (B).

"Ritania fulfilled its obligations under international law. According to Article 56 of the United Nations Convention on the Law of the Sea, Ritania has the right to establish artificial island. And the construction process fully complied with the terms of the Malachi Gap Treaty. Moreover, Ritania fulfilled the cautiousness duty before established the island. Ritania prepared an E. I. A. for the Excelsior Island project. From the report of E. I. A., it showed no

---

① 例如在 https://vismoot.pace.edu/site/previous-moots/24th-vis-moot 中,可以下载第 24 届 Willem C. Vis 模拟国际商事仲裁庭比赛中不同赛程的正反方共 6 份完整的最佳诉状;在 https://www.ilsa.org/jessuphome/2014-08-15-09-28-30/jessup-archives 可以看到杰赛普国际模拟法庭比赛历年比赛材料及最佳诉状。

potential impacts for the dredging program on the waters of the Malachi Gap or the fish species living there. According to Art. 12 (b) of the Malachi Gap Treaty, Ritania has a right to explore the natural resources of the seabed and subsoil. "

其大意为:"Ritania（被告）对怡东岛项目的行为在所有方面遵守了国际法和玛拉基海沟条约的义务，滑坡是不可抗力，因此 Ritania 没有义务赔偿 Amalea（原告）。

"Ritania 履行了国际法义务。根据联合国海洋公约第 56 条的规定，Ritania 有权建立人工岛。建设过程完全符合玛拉基海沟条约的条款。此外，Ritania 建岛之前履行了谨慎义务。Ritania 为怡东岛项目准备了环境影响评估报告。从该报告看，报告没有显示对玛拉基海沟的海水及生活在那里的鱼类的疏浚机制产生影响。按照玛拉基海沟条约的第 12（b）条，Ritania 有权探索海床和底土的自然资源。"

另一份诉状对同一问题做了较好的辩论:

"Under international custom, the obligation of due diligence requires an environmental impact assessment ('E. I. A.') to be conducted when there are reasonable grounds to believe that activities under a State's control may cause significant transboundary harm. A State must take a precautionary approach to the assessment, establishing that the activities are safe before it can approve them. Certain activities require an E. I. A. because they are presumed to be harmful. Dredging is one such activity under the United National Convention for the Law of the Sea ('U. N. C. L. O. S.'). Excelsior Island Gas & Power Limited's ('E. I. G. P') dredging required an E. I. A. not only because it was presumptively harmful, but also because the International League for Sustainable Aquaculture ('I. L. S. A.') report provided reasonable grounds to believe that dredging would be environmentally harmful. The report, prepared by an international nongovernmental organization with expertise in marine science, indicated that some harm from dredging was likely and catastrophic consequences were possible.

"Although international law does not specify fixed content for an E. I. A., an adequate E. I. A. must consider the nature and magnitude of the proposed development and its likely adverse impacts, to ensure that it is environmentally sound. Comparable regional and international standards are relevant. At minimum, an E. I. A. must evaluate the possible impact of the proposed activities on the persons, property, and environment of other States, and identify practical alternatives and risk-mitigating measures. This allows a State to determine the extent and nature of the risk involved in an activity, and preventive measures it should take."

其大意为:"按照国际惯例，当有充分的理由相信一个国家在其控制下所实施的活动可能会造成重大跨界损害时，尽职调查的义务要求对该活动进行环境影响评估（简称 E. I. A.）。一个国家必须对评估采取审慎的预防措施，确定这些活动在批准之前是安全的。某些活动的确需要进行环境影响评估，因为他们被假定为是有害的。联合国海洋法公约（简称 U. N. C. L. O. S.）中，疏浚就是这样一个被假定为有害的活动。怡东岛天然气和电力有限公司的疏浚工程需要进行环境影响评估，这不仅因为它被假定为有害，还因为可持续养殖的国际联盟（简称 I. L. S. A.）的报告提供了合理理由使人相信疏浚会对环境有害。这份由一个具有海洋科学专门知识的国际非政府组织编写的报告表明，疏浚可能带来一些危害，甚至可能造成灾难性后果。

"虽然国际法没有对一份环境影响评估报告的内容作出具体的规定，但一份充实的环境影响评估报告必须考虑所拟进行的开发活动的性质、规模及其可能的负面影响，以确保它对环境是无害的。可供比较分析的区域标准和国际标准都是相关的。至少，一份环境影响评估报告必须评估该活动可能对其他国家的人员、财产和环境的影响，并找出切实可行的方案和风险缓解措施，从而使一国能够确定一项活动所涉及的风险的程度和性质，以及应采取的预防措施。"

从上面举例的诉状内容来看，后面一份诉状能够结合争端案件所适用的国际条约的内容进行更为具体深入的分析和展开，对于被告为何须进行环境影响评估以及环境影响评估报告所应包含的内容进行了分析论证，从而为形成自己的结论做了较好的铺垫。

二 普莱斯传媒法模拟法庭的诉状范例

以下为天津外国语大学学生参加 2017—2018 年度普莱斯传媒法模拟法庭比赛所提交的一份起诉方诉状。因篇幅所限，仅提供部分内容。

The 2017 – 2018 Price Media Law Moot Court Competition
Niam Peaps & Scoops（Applicants）V. Turtonia（Respondent）
Memorial for Respondent
Table of Contents（略）
List of Abbreviations（略）
List of Authorities（略）
Statement of Relevant Facts

Background of ethnic tensions in Turtonia

A. Turtonia is a small country with a democratic elected government and an ethnically homogeneous population. In the past three years, Turtonia has seen a significant influx of immigrants from neighboring country Aquaria, of which the most citizens share the same ethnicity and religion as the Turtonians.

B. True Religion, which is widely regarded as a terrorist organization in Turtonia, has gained popularity with some people in Aquaria since 2015. The wave of Aquarian immigrants has caused a furor among some Turtonians, who claim that the immigrants have disrupted the economy and diluted the culture.

C. Beginning in late 2015, a particularly vocal group of nationalist Turtonians, calling themselves Turton Power, began publicly denouncing the Turtonian Minister of Immigration, Wani Kola for allowing Aquarians to enter the country. They've called for her resignation and have occasionally protested outside her office. Kola has been subject to harassment and abuse online, and one person- a member of Turton Power-has been convicted of attempting to assault her in a public office.

Turtonia's efforts to protect online dignity

D. The ODPA was enacted in response to a growing problem of Non Consensual Sharing of Intimate Images (commonly known as "revenge porn").

E. Section 1 of the ODPA prohibits the knowingly distribution of intimate parts without consent. Section 2 defines the scope of distribution, image and intimate parts. Section3 (a) and Section3 (b) represent exceptions of the Act, in which voluntary exposure and disclosures made in public interest are excluded. Section3 (b) imposes fines and prison sentences on any 'person' guilty of an offence under the Act.

Turtonia's efforts to curb false information

F. The IA was enacted after the distribution of fake documents ahead of the 2005 Turtonia General Elections (the famous "Micron leaks"), which aimed at preserving the integrity of the democratic process and avoiding the hijacking of elections as well as to safeguard the peace.

G. Section 1 of the IA prohibits the communication of false information with the intent to incite civil unrest, hatred, or damage the national unity. The Section 1 (a) also limits the scope of banned communication. Section 2 imposes fines and prison sentences on any 'person' guilty of an offence under the Act. Section 3 provides the exceptions for an online service provider and the application conditions for the exclusive clauses.

Scoops and XYZ News in Turtonia

H. Scoops is the most popular social media platform. Through the app, users build a profile that consists of (1) a screen name, (2) topics of interest, and (3) friends. The content of their posts will appear on the screens of the devices of friends of the poster and up to 20 other users who have listed a matching topic of interest and elected by an algorithm. Additionally, users can pay to have their posts "boosted", and each user has a publicity-visible "influencer score" based on how many people have seen content of the posts. Furthermore, Scoops use human review to assist the algorithm in reaching the right users who may interest in the content.

I. XYZ News is a popular TV news network in Turtonia. XYZ is well-respected in Turtonia and neighboring countries for being a reliable and objective news source. XYZ maintains a Scoops account called "XYZ News."

Peaps posts and the XYZ News 12

J. Niam Peaps is a Turton Power member who, on May 1, created a Scoops account with the screen name "XYZ News 12." At noon on May 2, Peaps used the "XYZ News12" account to post an image that appeared to show Kola standing naked in a hotel room and dating with the leader of the True Religion, Parkta. The post went viral on Scoops, reaching more than 10,000 on Scoops within the first hour of appearing, and spreading to other websites and social media.

K. By 5:00 p.m., the XYZ News made a declaration to clear the relationship between the posts and itself and the Kola's office released a statement to deny the posts and the facticity of the image.

L. At 7:00 p.m. on May 2, Kola' staff tried to request the removal of the posts through the service of Scoops but failed to finish due to the limitation of given options. On May 3, at 11:00 a.m., Kola's legal counsel submitted a letter to Scoops, threatening a civil action for defamation and violation of privacy. Scoops removed the post and all shares of the post at 1:00 p.m. on May 5, 50 hours after the submission of the complaint. At that point, it had 21,000 shares and 145,000 views.

M. After the posts, the political party that opposes Kola's party took advantage of the posts and impeached Kola. Protesters gathered outside Kola's office. Two Aquarians immigrants were beaten to death by an angry mob of at least 10 people that were yelling anti-Aquarian epithets. Kola resigned from office on May 10 without public statement.

Prosecution of Peaps and Scoops

N. After the posts and violence followed, the Turtonia's government charged Peaps with violations of the ODPA and the IA. The Turtonia's Court found him guilty on all charges and sentenced him to two years' imprisonment under the ODPA and issued $100,000 fine under the IA.

O. The government of Turtonia charged Scoops with violations of the ODPA and the IA. The Turtonia's Court found it guilty on all charges and issued $200,000 fine under the ODPA and $100,000 under the IA.

Statement of Jurisdiction

Peaps, Scoops and Turtonia has submitted their differences to the Universal Court of Free

Expression ("this court"), and hereby submit to this Court their dispute concerning Article 19 of the ICCPR.

On the basis of this foregoing, this court is requested to adjudge this dispute in accordance with the rules and principles of international law, including any applicable declarations and treaties.

Questions Presented

1. Whether Turtonia violated Peaps' right to freedom of expression by prosecuting Peaps, for distributing private pictures, which is photoshopped, on yhe most popular social media platform Scoops.

2. Whether Turtonia violated Scoops' right to freedom of expression by prosecuting Scoops, for distributing private pictures and failing to regulate the content of its users, despite the wide spreading of the post.

3. Whether Turtonia violated Peaps' right to freedom of expression by prosecuting Peaps, for inciting violence, or being reckless as to whether violence was incited, through false information through posting fake news and pictures of Kola.

4. Whether Turtonia violated Scoops' right to freedom of expression by prosecuting Scoops, for knowingly communicating fake pictures and fake news fabricated by Peaps.

Summary of Arguments (略)

Arguments

Ⅰ. Turtonia's Prosecution of Peaps under the ODPA does not Violate Article 19 of the ICCPR

1. A person's right to freedom of expression[①] is not absolute[②] and does carry with its special duties and responsibilities[③]. As stated in ICCPR, the right to freedom of expression *may be subject to certain restrictions while those restrictions are provided by law and are*

[①] UDHR (adopted 10 December 1948) UNGA Res 217A (Ⅲ) Art 19; ECHR (adopted 4 November 1950, entered into force 3 September 1953) 213 UNTS 1932 Art 10; ICCPR (adopted 16 December 1966, entered into force 23 March1976) 999 UNTS 171 Art 19 (2); ACHR (adopted 22 November 1969, entered into force 18 July 1978) Art 13; CHPR (adopted 27 June 1981, entered into force 21 October 1986) (1982) 21 ILM 58 Art 9.

[②] UDHR Art 29 (2); ECHR (adopted 4 November 1950, entered into force 3 September 1953) 213 UNTS 1932 Arts 8 (2) and 10 (2); ICCPR Arts 17 (1) and 19 (3); ACHR (adopted 22 November 1969, entered into force 18 July 1978) Arts 11 (2) and 13 (2); ACHPR (adopted 27 June 1981, entered into force 21 October 1986) (1982) 21 ILM 58 Art 9 (2); HRC, 'General Comment 34' (12 September 2011) UN Doc CCPR/C/GC/34 ('General Comment 34') para 21; Recommendation CM/Rec (2014) 6 of the Committee of Ministers to Member States on a Guide to Human Rights for Internet Users (adopted 16 April 2014) para 2.

[③] International Covenant on Civil and Political Rights (adopted 16 December 1966, entered into force 23 March 1976) 999 UNTS 171 (ICCPR) Art 19 (3); *Rios et al v Venezuela* IACtHR (2009) Series C No 194, para 346.

necessary. ① Therefore, Peaps' right to freedom of expression was interfered in a proper way. Peaps' post of a nude image caused protests and the humiliation to Kola, therefore, the interference on his post is reasonable.

2. The prosecution of Peaps under the ODPA is proper and justified because it is prescribed by law, pursues a legitimate aim, and is necessary and proportionate to the aim pursued. ②

A. The prosecution of Peaps under the ODPA meets the requirement of "prescribed by law"

3. A statute is prescribed by law if: (1) it is sufficiently precise; (2) it contains adequate safeguards; and (3) any prosecution under it had a legal basis. ③

<u>(1) The ODPA is sufficiently precise as Peaps could foresee liability for distributing private images onto the Internet</u>

4. The ECtHR stated in *Delfi AS v. Estonia* that, a norm *"cannot be regarded as a 'law'" unless it is formulated with sufficient precision"* and *"he must be able-if need be with appropriate advice-to foresee... action may entail"* ④ The ODPA is sufficiently precise since Peaps could foresee liability. In section 2 of the ODPA, the specific definition of "Distribute", "Image" and "intimate parts" clearly and precisely. ⑤ The image posted by Peaps met the criterion of section 2 of the ODPA. In the present facts, the ODPA indicated the possible legal consequences of distributing such image. Therefore, Peaps had visibility of the consequences that actions of posting may entail.

5. There's no doubt that terms in section 2 of the ODPA are not broad. The ECtHR stated in *Müller v Switzerland* that *Laws need not be absolutely precise to "keep pace with*

---

① International Covenant on Civil and Political Rights (adopted 16 December 1966, entered into force 23 March 1976) 999 UNTS 171 (ICCPR) Art 19 (3).

② *Handyside v the United Kingdom*, App no 5493/72 (ECtHR, 7 December 1976); *Lingens v Austria*, App no 9815/82 (ECtHR, 8 July 1986); *Jersild v Denmark*, App no 15890/89 (ECtHR, 1994); *Zana v Turkey*, App no 18954/91 (ECtHR, 25 November 1997).

③ *Silver v UK* App nos 5947/72, 6205/73, 7052/75, 7061/75, 7107/75, 7113/75, 7136/75 (ECtHR, 25 March 1983) ("Silver") paras 85 – 90; *Malone v UK* App no 8691/79 (ECtHR, 2 August 1984) ("Malone") paras 67 – 68; *Weber and Saravia v Germany* App no 54934/00 (ECtHR, 29 June 2006) ("Weber") para 23; *Editorial Board of Pravoye Delo and Shtekel v Ukraine* App no 33014/05 (ECtHR, 5 August 2011) ("Editorial Board") para 51; *Ahmet Yıldırım v Turkey* App no 3111/10 (ECtHR, 18 December 2012) ("Ahmet") paras 57 – 59; UNHRC April 2013 Report (n 10) para 29; International Covenant on Civil and Political Rights (adopted 16 December 1966, entered into force 23 March 1976) 999 UNTS 171 (ICCPR), "Concluding Observations on the Fourth Periodic Report of the United States of America" (23 April 2014) CCPR/C/USA/CO/4 para 22; UNHRC, "The Right to Privacy in the Digital Age, Report of the Office of the United Nations High Commissioner for Human Rights" (30 June 2014) UN Doc A/HRC/27/37 ("UNHRC June 2014 Report") para 28.

④ *Delfi AS v Estonia* App no 64569/09 (ECtHR, 10 October 2013) ("Delfi October 2013") para 121.

⑤ Para 10. 2 of the facts.

changing circumstances". ① Firstly, terms in section 2 of the ODPA can easily be recognized while related to specific behaviors since terms were explained strictly. The preciseness of terms in ODPA has been stated before. ②

6. Secondly, the ODPA was enacted in response to a growing problem of Non Consensual Sharing of Intimate Image (commonly known as "revenge porn")③. This problem reached a peak in the years before the passing of the ODPA. ④ Therefore, it is necessary to draft the terms relatively boarder considering current situation in Turtonia.

(2) The ODPA has adequate safeguards as it presented specific element of "distribute" and decisions can be appealed

7. The ODPA has adequate safeguards. The ECtHR stated in *Liu v. Russia* that, *the law must indicate the scope of any such discretion conferred on the competent authorities and the manner of its exercise with sufficient clarity.* ⑤ In terms of the scope of discretion, in section 3 (c) of the ODPA, a clearly maximum sentence and fine were presented⑥ so that the abuse of discretion can be avoided. In terms of the manner of its exercise, as mentioned above, behaviors were defined seriously in section 2 of the ODPA. Additionally, exceptional circumstances including circumstances when image involving voluntary exposure in public or commercial settings or disclosures made in the public interest were pointed out in section 3.

8. Absolutely, the image posted by Peaps does not fit the above exceptional cases since the court has found the fact that the picture was photoshopped by an unknown member of Turton Power. ⑦ That unknown person put the fake picture on the Turton Power website in a discussion thread saying, "If Kola had a boyfriend it would be this guy! Ha!"⑧ A person of full age and capacity can understand that the above sentence was a joke on Kola's open policy of immigration but not a disclosure of the truth.

---

① *Müller v Switzerland* App no 10737/84 (ECtHR, 24 May 1988) ("Müller") para 29; *Kokkinakis v Greece* App no 14307/88 (ECtHR, 25 May 1993) ("Kokkinakis") para 40; *Lindon, Tchakovsky-Laurens and July v France* App no 21275/02 (ECtHR, 22 October 2007) ("Lindon") para 41; *Delfi AS v Estonia* App no 64569/09 (ECtHR, 10 October 2013) ("Delfi October 2013") paras 71, 75.
② See para 4 of this memorial.
③ Para 10.1 of the facts.
④ Ibid.
⑤ *Liu v Russia* (no 2) App no 29157/09 (ECtHR, 26 July 2011) ("Liu") para 88 (see also in *Lupsa v Romania*, no 10337/04, §§ 32 and 34, ECtHR 2006; *Al-Nashif v Bulgaria*, no 50963/99, § 119, 20 June 2002; and *Malone v the United Kingdom*, judgment of 2 August 1984, Series A no 82, §§ 67 and 68).
⑥ Para 10.3 (c) of the facts.
⑦ Para 12.3 of the facts.
⑧ Ibid.

9. Peaps' behavior for posting such image onto the Internet obviously has his subjective malice. Besides, with the image, he also posted a short passage including descriptions on sex trade① between Kola and the leader of the terrorism organization without any evidence but a fake picture.

10. This harmed Kola's basic right of reputation and honor.② Kola, as a female minister, also does have the right of reputation and honor. Basic on the existed facts, Kola has been subject to harassment and abuse online. ③ No one shall be subject to arbitrary or unlawful interference with his privacy, family, home or correspondence, or to unlawful attacks on his honor and reputation. Everyone has the right to the protection of the law against such interference or attacks. ④ Here, the persecution of Peaps is also a protection against such humiliations and harassments.

11. Additionally, the right to an appeal is an adequate safeguard. ⑤ It is highlighted by the UNHRC that *the judiciary is an appropriate check against the executive.* ⑥ Since Peaps' conviction exhausted domestic remedies and have applied to the Universal Court of Free Expression,⑦ apparently the ODPA provided for the right to appeal, which constitutes an important safeguard. ⑧

(3) There is a legal basis to prosecute Peaps

12. There was a legal basis to prosecute Peaps: (a) as Peaps was justified in posting private images onto the Scoops; and (b) the prosecution for Peaps was not retroactive.

　　a. The prosecution under the ODPA was justified as the image was identifiable from the image itself or information displayed in connection with the image and intimate parts are exposed

13. By publishing the image on Scoops, Peaps knowingly distributed an image of Kola ap-

---

① Para 8.3 of the facts.
② International Covenant on Civil and Political Rights (adopted 16 December 1966, entered into force 23 March 1976,) 999 UNTS 171 (ICCPR) Art 19 (3), http://www.ohchr.org/en/professionalinterest/pages/ccpr.aspx.
③ Para 4.1 of the facts.
④ International Covenant on Civil and Political Rights (adopted 16 December 1966, entered into force 23 March 1976) 999 UNTS 171 (ICCPR) Art 19 (3).
⑤ *Klass v Germany* App no 5029/71 (ECtHR, 6 September 1978) ("Klass") para 56; Malcolm Ross (n 10) para 11.4; *Uzun v Germany* App no 35623/05 (ECtHR, 2 September 2010) ("Uzun") para 72; *Gurtekin v Cyprus* App nos 60441/13, 68206/13, 68667/13 (ECtHR, 11 March 2014) ("Gurtekin") para 28.
⑥ Malcolm Ross (n 10) para 11.5, See also Klass (n 25) para 56.
⑦ Para 14.2 &14.3 of the facts.
⑧ *Malcolm Ross v Canada*, Communication no 736/1997, UN Doc CCPR/C/70/D/736/1997 (2000) para 11.4; *Uzun v Germany* App no 35623/05 (ECtHR, 2 September 2010) para 72; *Gurtekin v Cyprus* App nos 60441/13, 68667/13 (ECtHR, 11 March 2014) para 28.

pearing to show her intimate parts.① Since intimate parts are not recognizable and faces is usually the first and only way for others to recognize, Peaps' post obviously harmed Kola's right of reputation and honor regardless of the photoshop.

b. Peaps' distribution of the image was after the enactment of the ODPA

14. The IACtHR stated in *Kimmel v. Argentina* that *the principle of non-retroactivity of law regulates that there is no legal basis for a prosecution where it is retroactive.*② The ODPA was enacted in 2015 in response to growing problems of revenge porn③ and the fake picture was released in March 2016④. Therefore, there's no doubt that Peaps' distribution was after the enactment of the ODPA.

B. The prosecution of Peaps under the ODPA peruses a legitimate aim

(1) The related rules in ODPA aim at protecting public order

15. The persecution of Peaps pursues the legitimate aims of protecting public order.⑤ On the one hand, nude pictures violated rules online and gave bad influence to Internet since user ranges from children to elders. On the other hand, the spreading of nude picture of a female minister of immigration⑥ may aggregate the existed contradiction on immigration problems.

(2) The prosecution under ODPA aims at preserving the rights and reputations of others as nude image may affect the order of online platform

16. Kola suffered a lot after the post and resigned from the office on May10, a week after the post⑦. The prosecution of Peaps is a protection of her basic right and the respondent has explained the harm of Kola's right above.⑧

C. The prosecution of Peaps under the ODPA is necessary in a democratic society

Interference is necessary in a democratic society if it: (1) corresponds to a pressing social need; and (2) is proportionate to the legitimate aims pursued.⑨

---

① Para 12.3 (5) of the facts.
② *Kimmel v Argentina* (IACtHR, 2 May 2008) paras 66 – 68.
③ Para 10.2 of the facts.
④ Para 12.3 of the facts.
⑤ UNHRC, "Report of the Special Rapporteur on the Protection of the Right to Freedom of Opinion and expression" (7 September 2012) Kola suffered a lot after the posting of the image. The prosecution of Peaps is a protection of her basic right. UN Doc A/67/357 ("UNHRC September 2012 Report") paras 36 – 40; UNHRC April 2013 Report (n 10) para 28, see also Malcolm Ross (n 10) para 11.5.
⑥ Para 4.1 of the facts.
⑦ Para 9.6 of the facts.
⑧ See para 10 of this memorial.
⑨ General Comment 34 (n 3) paras 22, 33 – 34; UNHRC April 2013 Report (n 10) para 29; Delfi June 2015 (n 17) para 131; Perincek (n 9) paras 196, 228

(1) There was a pressing social need to prosecute Peaps as he posted an image of naked body and spreaded widely

17. As highlighted in ICCPR, *a person's right to freedom of expression carries with special duties and responsibilities.* ① A state has the right to interfere with a person's right to freedom of expression when it contains fake statement about country's policy and may mislead the public.

18. Over the few years, conflicts and protest caused several incidents②. Considering the special situation of Turtonia and people's complaints on immigrants, Peaps' post stimulated the breaking of the stability of the society.

(2) The prosecution was proportionate as it was in line with the punishments imposed by other states and it was necessary due to current situation in Turtonia

19. As stated in HRC, General Comment, *Proportionality requires that states go no further than necessary to achieve the relevant legitimate aim,*③ so as to balance the community's and the individual's interests. ④

20. The two years' imprisonment is proportionate for Peaps. On the one hand, Peaps' post had caused in really bad consequences. People not only spread the picture online but also connect the picture to the policy. On the other hand, in other states like USA⑤ and UK⑥, the maximum jail for posting nude picture and causing in serious consequences are ranging from 1 year to 5 years.

II. Turtonia's Prosecution of Scoops under the ODPA does not Violate Article 19 of the ICCPR

21. Social media, which provide a platform for the public to discuss and share information

---

① International Covenant on Civil and Political Rights (adopted 16 December 1966, entered into force 23 March 1976) 999 UNTS 171 (ICCPR) Art 19.

② Para4. 1 of the facts.

③ UN Economic and Social Council, UN Sub-Commission on Prevention of Discrimination and Protection of Minorities, "Siracusa Principles on the Limitation and Derogation of Provisions in the ICCPR" (1984) Annex, UN Doc E/CN /1984/4 principle 11; HRC, "General Comment 22" (30 July 1993) UN Doc CCPR/C/21/Rev 1/Add 4 para 8; General Comment 34 (n 3) para 34.

④ *Cossey v UK* App no 10843/84 (ECtHR, 27 September 1990) para 37; Rolv Ryssdal, "Opinion: The Coming Age of the European Convention on Human Rights" (1996) 1 European Human Rights Law Review 18, 26; Ozgur Gundem Turkey App no 23144/92 (ECtHR, 16 March 2000) ("Ozgur") para 43; *Christine Goodwin v UK* App no 28957/95 (ECtHR, 11 July 2002) para 72.

⑤ Noe Iniguez was sentenced one year imprisonment for posting his ex-girlfriend's nude picture online for revenge. (http://world.huanqiu.com/exclusive/2014-12/5229245.html).

⑥ UK has added amendment that an individual who post other's nude picture for revenge may be sentenced up to two years' imprisonment. (http://www.chinanews.com/gj/2014/10-14/6675835.shtml).

and news, is making information sharing more interactive, correlative and convenient. In the meantime, the spreading of rumors through social media are more common and easy. Scoops, as the most popular social media platform,① need to shoulder its responsibility in providing a healthy environment for users.

22. The Respondent hold the statement that in the case at hand, Scoops' prosecution under the ODPA is proper and justified because it is prescribed by law, pursues a legitimate aim, and is necessary and proportionate to the aim pursued.

A. The prosecution was prescribed by law as Scoops could foresee liability for distributing images of naked body

23. A statute is prescribed by law if: (1) it is sufficiently precise; (2) it contains adequate safeguards; and (3) any prosecution under it had a legal basis.②

24. The Respondent has explained the preciseness of rules in the ODPA.③ The ODPA is sufficiently precise since Scoops could foresee liability for distributing nude pictures on its app. A statute is sufficiently precise even if an entity has to take appropriate legal advice to assess the consequences of a given action.④ There is a risk that posts on Scoops can go beyond the boundaries of acceptable and the facticity of posts, it should have sought legal advice on the scope of section 1 and section 2 of the ODPA.

25. The post went viral on Scoops, reaching more than 10,000 within the first hour, and spreading to other websites and social media.⑤ Obviously, this picture caused a great sensation online.

26. In section 2 of the ODPA, it is clearly presented that "Distribute" includes transferring, publishing and reproducing.⑥ Scoops, as the initial platform where Peaps sub-

---

① Para 5.1 of the facts.

② *Silver v UK* App nos 5947/72, 6205/73, 7052/75, 7061/75, 7107/75, 7113/75, 7136/75 (ECtHR, 25 March 1983) ('Silver') paras 85 – 90; *Malone v UK* App no 8691/79 (ECtHR, 2 August 1984) ('Malone') paras 67 – 68; *Weber and Saravia v Germany* App no 54934/00 (ECtHR, 29 June 2006) ('Weber') para 23; *Editorial Board of Pravoye Delo and Shtekel v Ukraine* App no 33014/05 (ECtHR, 5 August 2011) ('Editorial Board') para 51; *Ahmet Yıldırım v Turkey* App no 3111/10 (ECtHR, 18 December 2012) ('Ahmet') paras 57 – 59; UNHRC April 2013 Report (n 10) para 29; IC-CPR, 'Concluding Observations on the Fourth Periodic Report of the United States of America' (23 April 2014) CCPR/C/USA/CO/4 para 22; UNHRC, 'The Right to Privacy in the Digital Age, Report of the Office of the United Nations High Commissioner for Human Rights' (30 June 2014) UN Doc A/HRC/27/37 ('UNHRC June 2014 Report') para 28.

③ See para 3 & 4 of this memorial.

④ Sunday Times (n 12) para 49; Editorial Board (n 14) para 51; Centro Europa (n 18) para 141; Delfi June 2015 (n17) 121

⑤ Para 8.4 of the facts.

⑥ Section 2 (a) of the ODPA; see para 10.2 of the facts.

mitted the post, knowingly ignored this topic even when it has a human review system①.

27. As mentioned above,② the ODPA has adequate safeguards since it presented specific element of "distribute". Additionally, the ODPA provide for right to appeal.

B. The prosecution pursued the legitimate aims of protecting public order and preserving the rights and reputations of others as the information displayed in the image is in connection with Kola and intimate parts are exposed

28. Scoops, as a platform for information sharing and message posting, is liable for hosting fake news and pictures to ensure the protection of the reputations of others or national security or of public order. As stated before, the related rules in the ODPA aim at protecting public order. For the perspective of the perseverance of rights and reputation of others, both Kola and the public users were victims of this case. （以下内容省略）

Prayer

For the foregoing reasons, the Respondent respectfully requests this Honorable Court to adjudge and declare that:

1. Turtonia's Prosecution of Peaps under the ODPA does not Violate Article 19 of the ICCPR.

2. Turtonia's Prosecution of Scoops under the ODPA does not Violate Article 19 of the ICCPR.

3. Turtonia's Prosecution of Peaps under the IA does not Violate Article 19 of the ICCPR.

4. Turtonia's Prosecution of Scoops under the IA does not Violate Article 19 of the ICCPR.

Respectfully submitted on 2nd, November 2017,

DENG Zu-chen, CHEN Si-lu, ZHANG Ming-jing,

ZHANG Zi-wei, HUO Yu-dong, CAO Sheng-ting

Dr, HUANG Ying as the Coach

Agent for the Respondent

三 模拟联合国大会立场文件范例

以下为天津外国语大学参加2017年第十四届中国（杭州）模拟联合国大会的一份获得最佳立场文件奖的立场文件。

---

① Para 5.1 of the facts.
② See para 7&8 of this memorial.

Delegates: Zhang Mingjing & Li Jiajia
School: Tianjin Foreign Studies University
Country: Turkmenistan
Committee: General Assembly-Social, Humanitarian & Cultural Committee
Topic: Countering terrorism & protection of human rights

Terrorism clearly has a very real and direct impact on human rights, with devastating consequences for the enjoyment of the right to life, liberty and physical integrity of victims. Turkmenistan has resolutely opposed all forms of terrorism and will continue to stand firm and participate in international cooperation against terrorism.

Since the terrorist attacks on 11 September 2001 in New York and Washington made the fight against terrorism a top political priority for the international community, It's been sixteen years and the human cost of terrorism has been still felt in virtually every corner of the globe. Looking 2016 alone, more than 13,400 terrorist attacks took place around the world, resulting in more than 34,000 total deaths, including more than 11,600 perpetrator deaths. The vast majority of attacks (87%) and deaths (97%) occurred in the Middle East & North Africa, South Asia, and Sub-Saharan Africa.

Encouragingly, the international world never stops taking actions to human rights protection in the context of the threat of terrorism and had made some achievements. Since UN was founded, human rights protection has become one of the three underlying tenets. UN has passed more than 70 treaties and documents for the protection and promotion of human rights. Some famous and far-reaching declarations and treaties like the Universal Declaration of Human Rights (UDHR) and International Covenant on Civil and Political Rights (ICCPR) are becoming standard principles in international or regional courts of human rights.

Turkmenistan has been closely collaborating with international organizations aside from the UN, including the Organization for Security and Cooperation in Europe (OSCE) and the Eurasian Group on Combating Money Laundering and Financing of Terrorism, in order to enhance its counter-terrorism efforts and border security. And increased its participation in regional efforts to counter terrorism, and took steps to strengthen its capacity to counter money laundering and terrorist financing. No terrorist incidents were reported in Turkmenistan last year. On 28 May 2009 Turkmenistan adopted the Law "On Combating the Legalization of Criminal Income and Terrorist Financing" (ver. 2015) as well as a number of amendments to existing laws. Since then, the country has taken steps to harmonize its laws with international standards. In 2015, Turkmenistan's government announced a large-scale mobilization of its reserve military forces, aimed at hedging any threat by IS forces gathering in Afghanistan.

To protect and promote human rights in the context of the threat of terrorism, each country should shoulder its responsibility. Turkmenistan, as a permanent neutral country, member state of the United Nations and friend to the world, will spare no effort on making contributions. Considering functions and power of our committee, Turkmenistan would like to divide the general issue into three specific parts—right of life, right of liberty and right of dignity. Here, to deal with the global serious situation, Turkmenistan would like to give the following suggestions.

1. Right of life

Turkmenistan suggests each country completing immigration managements and safeguard. Besides, measures existed should be taken appropriately to the situation. On the one hand, developed countries are strongly suggested enhance their supervision system for the prevent of attacks by terrorists. On the other hand, while waiting for the help from the international community, countries who existed conflict areas or basis of terrorism groups should take domestic measures and build the authority of local governments firstly.

2. Liberty

Turkmenistan suggests focusing on freedom on religious belief since the respect on religious faith is the basic of a person's right. Meanwhile, freedom of expression and freedom of thoughts can never be challenged as long as it is prescribed by law. Article 19 of the ICCPR and Article 22 of the UDHR both ruled it clearly.

3. Right of dignity

Since right to education is the essential part of right of dignity, Turkmenistan highly calls for special protection on schools and academic institutions in every country. What's more, awareness of education should be raised through generations.

Turkmenistan looks forward to different countries' suggestions and opinions. And we firmly believe, issues on human rights protection in the context of the threat of terrorism may find efficient solutions with the contributions of all the countries.

BIBLIOGRAPHY

i. "Turkmenistan Terrorism Index 2002 – 2017", https://tradingeconomics.com/turkmenistan/terrorism-index, last access in October, 2017.

ii. "Protecting human Rights While Countering Terrorism", http://www.un.org/en/sc/ctc/rights.html, last access on September 10, 2015.

iii. "The Global Terrorism Index", http://www.worldatlas.com/articles/the-global-terrorism-index-countries-most-affected-by-terrorist-attacks.html, last access on April 25, 2017.

ⅳ. "Overview: Terrorism in 2016", http: //www. start. umd. edu/pubs/START_ GTD_ OverviewTerrorism2016_ August2017. pdf, last access in August, 2017.

ⅴ. "Protect Human Rights", http: //www. un. org/en/sections/what-we-do/protect-human-rights/index. html, last access in September, 2017.

ⅵ. "Turkmenistan: Profiles, foreign relations, and human rights.", http: //trove. nla. gov. au/ work/178155335? q&versionId = 193955599, last access in September, 2017.

参考文献

段祺华、龚晓航：《涉外法律实务操作及深度剖析》，法律出版社2013年版。

范文祥、吴怡：《英文合同草拟技巧》，法律出版社2008年版。

高尔森：《英美合同法纲要》，南开大学出版社1984年版。

高玉美、王刚：《涉外法律文书范本》，世界知识出版社2015年版。

何主宇：《涉外法律函电英文写作范例》，法律出版社2005年版。

何主宇：《英美法案例研读全程指南》，法律出版社2007年版。

何主宇：《最新法律专业英语读写全程点拨》，机械工业出版社2003年版。

君合律师事务所：《律师之道（二）：资深律师的11堂业务课》，北京大学出版社2011年版。

林克敏：《中国律师实训经典：中英商务合同精选与解读》，中国人民大学出版社2012年版。

罗国强：《涉外法律实训教程》，武汉大学出版社2009年版。

陶博、龚柏华：《法律英语：中英双语法律文书制作（第2版）》，复旦大学出版社2012年版。

徐家力、王文书：《律师实务（第四版）》，法律出版社2009年版。

张宏乐、张伟、盛钢：《涉外法律实务》，清华大学出版社2014年版。

赵泽君、高峰：《律师实务英语：涉外律师执业必备》，中国法制出版社2012年版。

中国涉外律师领军人才：《涉外律师在行动：中国涉外律师领军人才典型涉外案例汇编》，法律出版社2015年版。

中华全国律师协会编：《中华全国律师协会律师业务操作指引①》，北京大学出版社2009年版。

中华全国律师协会编：《中华全国律师协会律师业务操作指引②》，北京大学出版社2013年版。

中华全国律师协会编：《中华全国律师协会律师业务操作指引③》，北京大学出版社2016年版。